# TOIL & TROUBLE

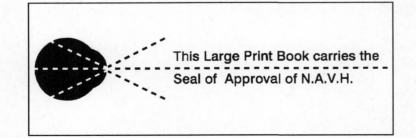

# TOIL & TROUBLE

# AUGUSTEN BURROUGHS

**THORNDIKE PRESS**

A part of Gale, a Cengage Company

**GALE**
A Cengage Company

Farmington Hills, Mich • San Francisco • New York • Waterville, Maine
Meriden, Conn • Mason, Ohio • Chicago

**LIBRARY OF CONGRESS CIP DATA ON FILE.
CATALOGUING IN PUBLICATION FOR THIS BOOK
IS AVAILABLE FROM THE LIBRARY OF CONGRESS**

ISBN-13: 978-1-4328-7053-9 (hardcover alk. paper)

Published in 2019 by arrangement with Macmillan Publishing Group,
LLC/St. Martin's Publishing Group

Printed in Mexico
1 2 3 4 5 6 7 23 22 21 20 19

*For Vince Gerardis,*
*who fixed a broken thing in me*

# ACKNOWLEDGMENTS

My publisher just blew me away with the creativity, enthusiasm, brilliance, and care put forth in the creation of this book and I am deeply grateful to these people: Paul Hochman, Danielle Prielipp, Olga Grlic, Jeff Dodes, Laura Clark, Tom Thompson, Michael Criscitelli, Tracey Guest, Jessica Zimmerman, Dori Weintraub, Kim Ludlam, Rachel Diebel, and Matie Argiropoulos. Janet Byrne is simply the finest copy editor any writer could be fortunate enough to work with. I made mistakes I didn't even know it was possible to make and she caught them. I would also like to thank Dr. Phil who had me on his show for *This Is How* and before we went on air quipped, "You sure use a lot of adverbs." I realized that he was right. This marks the first time a therapist has actually been *helpful* to me. Jennifer Enderlin has been my editor for twenty years and we have shared an incredible journey together. Thank you, Christopher. Without you, there simply wouldn't be any such thing as *Toil & Trouble,* there would be only toil and trouble separately and entirely off the page.

As far as the laws of mathematics refer to reality, they are not certain; and as far as they are certain, they do not refer to reality.

— ALBERT EINSTEIN

Eye of newt and toe of frog,
Wool of bat and tongue of dog,
Adder's fork and blind-worm's sting,
Lizard's leg and howlet's wing —
For a charm of powerful trouble,
Like a hell-broth boil and bubble.

— WILLIAM SHAKESPEARE,
*MACBETH*

# ADDER'S TONGUE

There are three things you should know about witches.

Number one: as long as there have been human beings there have been witch beings.

Number two: witches have *always* been misunderstood. For most of recorded history they have been persecuted and killed, and this continues today in many parts of the world. Since the majority of those accused and convicted have been female, the hunt for witches is yet another vehicle for the persecution of women of every color by (of course) white men.

When the hateful Puritans landed at Plymouth Rock, the men wasted no time launching their bigotry grenades against any women who didn't fit their image of what a woman should be and how she should behave. This began with — surprise! — a woman of color, a slave named Tituba, but any woman who wasn't subservient or who exhibited a modicum of individuality and independence was likely to be accused. Several men were also put to death in colonial Salem, so one can only speculate that they, too, failed to behave in a manner expected of the White Puritan Male, America's first frat guy.

It is no longer a crime in this country to be a witch, but that's mainly because Americans consider the notion patently absurd. Scientifically minded people look back on the witch trials and cringe at the primitive stupidity, not so much because alleged witches were killed but because the accusers actually believed that witches *existed.*

Which brings me to number three: witches are real. And witchcraft — the work they do, their craft — is also real.

So what is a witch?

I define a witch as someone — female, male, neither, other, both — who has the innate ability to focus on a desired outcome with such perfect clarity, intensity, and singularity that the desired outcome can materialize, provided it does not violate the natural laws of the universe. This is why a witch cannot turn a man into a goat, but a witch may very well know if a man five thousand miles away is about to be trampled by a goat. Witches may experience what we

12

call "time" and "distance" in such ways that "time" and "distance" collapse or are circumvented. Frequently, they possess information that it does not seem possible one could have, such as knowledge of events that will occur further down the time line.

Witchcraft is not a religion. Wicca is a religion, started by Englishman and occultist Gerald Gardner in the early 1950s. Many Wiccans are witches, too, practicing some form of craft as part of their faith. Druidism is another pagan religion that incorporates witchcraft.

There are many different "styles" or "schools," from the extremely formalized and ritualized to the improvised and spontaneous. There are those who engage in highly structured rituals, and while these are interesting and kind of cool, they aren't necessary.

Different witches have different abilities. Some are excellent at creating shields: protecting loved ones from harm, hiding in plain sight, traveling through life without a scratch. Others are adept at causing things to happen or not happen. Which is to say, they are sculptors of matter, exerting influence — and change — over the energy we observe as matter. Still others have amazing powers of perception and reception. They might feel a devastating storm coming long before it arrives, or perhaps they know of events occurring many miles away. Witches can possess any of or all these traits in greater or lesser degrees.

Here's a partial list of things I don't believe in:

God
the Devil
heaven
hell
Bigfoot
ancient aliens
past lives
life after death
vampires
zombies
Reiki
homeopathy
Rolfing
reflexology

Note that "witches" and "witchcraft" are absent from this list. The thing is, I *wouldn't* believe in them, and I would privately ridicule any idiot who did, except for one thing: I *am* a witch.

This is a fact I've kept to myself. Even my husband didn't know for years. Yet witchcraft has been an almost daily part of my life since I was a little boy. It was the strongest bond my mother and I had when I was young: our common power, our shared secret. She was a witch from a long line of witches and I was her second-born son — an accident — and, as she would discover eight years after my birth, also a witch. She schooled me, day after day, story after story, passing her knowledge and wisdom along to me, until her mind was quite abruptly shattered by mental illness just as I entered adolescence.

From that point, I was on my own.

I had no idea I was a witch until the day I knew something that was simply impossible for me to know — or at least impossible according to mankind's empirical understanding of the fundamental laws of the universe. I was staring out the school bus window on my way home, the trees a blur. My seat was over the left rear wheel, the one with the hump on the floor. I concentrated on the flow of liquid leaves without a single thought in my mind. At eight, I was already accomplished at gazing into the distance while thinking nothing at all.

The bus bounced as it went over the first wooden bridge, then again as it crossed the

15

second one, and at that moment I saw my grandmother's forehead and her thinning hairline, and my being was suddenly occupied by the spirit of *certainty*. Certainty was all that I contained. This was followed by feelings of fear and anxiety.

The bus came to a stop at my house, the second house after the second bridge. I ran up our steep gravel driveway as fast as I could and rang the doorbell once, then again, then again and again until my mother opened the door, the phone pressed tight against her ear, the cord stretched taut from the kitchen wall.

"What happened to Amah?" I asked desperately. "Something very bad happened to Amah!"

My mother's eyes widened and she lowered the phone from her ear, pressed it against her heart. She bent down. "Why do you say that? How do you know?"

"I was on the bus," I told her, still out of breath from running. "And after we bumped over the bridges, I just knew. What happened to her?" I was frantic and on the verge of tears.

"I'm on the phone with your uncle Mercer right now. He just this minute, not thirty seconds ago, called to tell me that your grandmother has had a car accident. She's in the hospital."

She brought the phone back up to her ear. "Mercer, I had to open the door, I missed whatever you were saying."

She held her index finger up to me and listened. She nodded and chewed at her thumbnail. "Okay," she said. "Okay, then. I will. Call me as soon as you know more."

I followed her into the kitchen, where she hung up the phone and turned around.

"She was in a car accident and her forehead was cut and she broke a rib and has a punctured lung, but they say she's going to be okay."

Now I was even more frightened than before. Hesitantly I asked, "Mom? How did I know?"

My mother lowered herself to one knee, wrapped her arms around me, and held me tight. Then she released me and looked into my eyes, tears glittering in the corners of hers. "You are *my* son. *That's* how you knew."

"I don't understand."

"I didn't, either," she said, her voice trembling with emotion. "Until today. I had no idea. I just —" Her voice cracked and she dabbed the underside of her wrist beneath each eye to blot the tears. "I watched and waited, but when I never saw

17

anything out of the ordinary, I suppose I assumed you were like your brother. Well, not like your brother, because he's very odd and distant. What I mean is, normal. Mortal."

"I still don't understand," I said.

She stood and led me into the living room, and then she leaned against the arm of the sofa and patted the spot beside her for me to sit. A True Blue cigarette slid from the pack in her hand and she lit it, waving the flame out before dropping the match into the green glass ashtray on the teak side table. She inhaled and held the smoke in her lungs for a long time before letting it stream out her nose.

"Remember the witch in *The Wizard of Oz*?"

"The good one or the bad one?"

"Either one of them," she replied with a dismissive wave of her hand, which caused ash to tumble from her cigarette onto the carpet.

"I like the bad one better," I said. "She had flying monkeys, and the good one was tacky and seemed kind of dumb."

My mother said, "Well, that's entirely beside the point, but yes, the bad witch was actually the interesting witch and the good witch was vain and tedious, but in any case, neither one of those characters represents

18

what witches *actually* look like or how they behave. A witch doesn't wear a pointy black hat and have green skin and a long nose with a wart on it. A witch doesn't fly through the air on a broom. She also doesn't wear a sparkly polyester gown and float away inside a soap bubble. But that's what people think witches are, and" — her voice lowered to almost a whisper — "they don't think witches are real."

"Are they real?" I asked, my voice quiet, too, like we were suddenly in a library.

My mother nodded. "Yes, they most certainly are."

"So what *do* they look like?"

She took a long, deep drag from her cigarette and then blew the smoke through her pursed lips. "They look like your grandmother Amah. They look like me. They look like your uncle Mercer, though he would beg to differ. And they look like you." She raised her eyebrows like, *Get it?*

I said, "I'm a witch?"

"You are."

"Okay." This was simultaneously the most confusing and most comforting thing anyone had ever said to me.

"And that's how you knew something that was impossible for you to know."

"If I'm a witch and you're a witch and so

19

are Amah and Mercer, where did it come from?"

My mother mashed her cigarette out into the ashtray and immediately lit another. "So, your grandmother Amah's father — that would be your great-grandfather — was named Mercer Lafayette Ledford. Many of the Ledfords were witches, going all the way back to Lancaster, England. Lancaster was very famous for their witch trials in the early sixteen-hundreds, even earlier than ours in Salem. Of course, none of our relatives were suspected of being witches, naturally, because they *were* witches and could elude detection. I believe the Ledfords didn't come to America for almost a century after the witch trials."

Maybe if my mother were my teacher, chain-smoking her way through lectures, I wouldn't hate history so much, I thought.

"This Gift has been passed on and on and on throughout the years," she continued. "Of course, not everybody on that side of the family had the Gift. There's really no telling why one sister might inherit it but her brother might not, or the only son in a family with four daughters. I imagine some did have it but didn't even know it. Your grandmother Amah has the Gift, though she has always been somewhat troubled by it.

Amah could sometimes see things that were hidden to other people or hadn't even occurred yet. When I was a little girl, she would become so upset because of something she knew was about to happen. I think it was not *what* it was that upset her so much as her knowing in advance. Amah's father had the Gift. And so did *his* father. Uncle Mercer is like us but it frightens him, so he pushes it away. He tries very hard not to believe something he knows perfectly well is true."

She balanced her cigarette on the lip of the ashtray. "I knew your brother didn't have it. There *is* something very different about your brother, but it's not this. It's not like what you have and I have, which is spread throughout my mother's side of the family, the Ledfords. Mother always believed the Richter side had it as well. Those are my daddy's people, and Mother always said Daddy's daddy was a witch. But you know, even in this day and age it's still all very hush-hush," she said, reaching for her cigarette. "Amah's sister, your great-aunt Curtis, is a witch, too. And she's always been much more comfortable with who she is, and more open to talking about the history of it running through the family. Even so, it's impossible to know for sure who was

21

a witch and who wasn't."

"Is it a bad thing to be a witch?"

"Oh, no, absolutely not," she said, blowing smoke above my head. "It's a wondrous thing. But it's a *private* thing. Sometimes when you have a special talent, you put it on display — like that girl Ji-hoon from school, and how she is such a talented violin player that she plays for people? Or if you're a painter, maybe a gallery hangs your work up on their walls. But there are other kinds of *gifts* that confuse people because they are uncommon. It's very strange and disconcerting to be able to see things that happened miles and miles away. So if you were to tell your teachers at school or a friend that you knew something happened to your grandmother before anybody told you, they would ask you how you knew."

"And if I said 'because I'm a witch,' they'd think I was crazy."

"That's exactly right," she confirmed.

"Because everybody knows witches aren't real."

She nodded. "Yes."

"Except they really *are* real."

She continued nodding. "Mm-hmm."

"But you also told me Santa and the tooth fairy were real."

"Those were lies," she said. "But they're

lies every parent tells their children. So they're not really lies so much as a script."

"I slept with teeth under my pillow, so it seems like a lie to me."

"I'm telling you the truest thing there is to tell you in the world right now."

"Okay, I believe you."

My mother's tutoring set me free. Every new thing I learned seemed like I'd already known it but didn't know I knew. Like, *Oh, of course I don't need a phone to call Charlie.* My mother did this with her friends all the time, but now I understood how. I could simply visualize him standing at the wall phone in his green-and-red-plaid wall-papered kitchen, reaching his hand up, placing his index finger in the rotary dial and turning it, and then the phone on our own kitchen wall would actually ring and it would be Charlie. It happened with my friend Colleen, too, but it never worked with Bryan. My mother explained: "Nothing works on everyone one hundred percent of the time. Magick itself never works one hundred percent of the time, and some people are highly resistant to outside influence. Either they are so fully preoccupied with the ongoing static of their own thoughts and worries and to-do lists that there's no entry point, or they're dim-witted and their neurological system simply isn't equipped to receive our high-energy signals and instructions."

My mother always thought Bryan was an idiot. He kind of was, but I liked him anyway because he was brave. If I wanted to loop a rope over a thick tree branch so we could swing like apes, he was all for it, never mind the possibility of breaking our necks.

It was good to know that witchcraft wasn't something that could ever be perfect. When a spell didn't work, it might not be because I messed up but because the spell just didn't work that time. Maybe it would next time or maybe it wouldn't.

Sometimes my mother would be in the middle of something, vacuuming or painting, when she'd suddenly stop and use her toe to shut off the vacuum cleaner, or dunk her brush into the jelly glass of turpentine and wipe it on her cotton rag. "I need to get the phone," she'd say, an instant before it rang.

"Hearing the phone ring *before* it actually rings is a different skill than causing it to ring," she explained. "To trigger somebody to call you, you must visualize them so thoroughly that the visualization quite literally becomes them, or rather they move through physical time and space until they occupy your visualized image, almost like you were projecting a photograph of them against the wall and they step into position so that they line up with it perfectly. But to hear a phone ring that hasn't yet physically rung requires the opposite of visualization: complete openness. It is a state of mind lacking any and all desire for control or even thought. A perfectly clear mind. I expect this is what you experienced when you were on the school bus and saw what happened to your grandmother. That clear, white, blank state of mind is the receptive mind. Meaning we are able to *receive* information — the ringing of a phone, for example — perhaps a bit earlier than an ordinary person. Having this ability to completely vacate the mind is what allows for divination, or seeing what's just ahead. Your grandmother was particularly gifted in this area, and I expect you are as well. There isn't only one future, you see. There are many. But as that future point in time gets closer, it's like it begins to solidify. We try to see things while it is still possible to change them, but sometimes that's not possible and we see things in time only to sound a warning. Not every witch is gifted in this particular area. Most people, even most witches, have a stream of thoughts running through their mind all the time. It's very rare to possess a silent mind."

In that moment I understood that something I had been bullied over (*Hey, zombie, anybody home in there?*) was in fact an essential part of me. It was not a flaw but a unique ability. It was part of the Gift.

I loved my uncle Mercer. He had loopy blonde hair and green eyes, like me, except his face was round and full, like my mother's, while mine was pointy, like my father's. Mercer was gentle and quiet, but something about him always made me sad, too. I guess it was a deep loneliness that I sensed and could relate to.

My bond with Uncle Mercer was special, and not solely because he sent me a folded-up twenty-dollar bill each year on my birthday. My mother told me, "He was the first person to hold you after you were born, even before I did. In fact, it was your uncle Mercer who placed you in my arms."

Mercer lived down south in Cairo, Georgia, with Amah, in the same bedroom he had when he was a kid. He was old now, at least thirty, and he didn't have any kind of job, though he had been in the navy, living aboard a submarine. Then something happened, and he left the navy. My mother said he had a "nervous breakdown," so they sent him home, but they still gave him money, because he always drove a brand-new Corvette.

One year when I was little he came up for Christmas. My parents had briefly separated, and I was living in Amherst, Massachusetts, with my mother in a small apartment on the third floor of an old white multifamily house. I figured Mercer decided to visit us because he felt bad that we were on our own.

He brought me a present, and I sat on the living room rug to unwrap it. When I tore away the last piece of wrapping paper and saw the box, I was thrilled and also astonished to the bone. My mother glanced down from her position on the sofa at the photo on the box, then looked at me like, *See?* Finally she fixed her gaze on her brother.

I asked her, "Did *you* tell him?"

My mother shook her head. "I most certainly did not. He came up with this gift entirely on his own."

"Well, that's interesting, don't you think?" I said to my mother.

She smiled. "Oh, very interesting indeed."

Mercer was looking back and forth between me and my mother. He was smiling, but he looked a little worried, too, the way his eyes became kind of squinty and his pale eyebrows inched together into one. Also, he quickly bit his thumbnail, something my mother did and I also did when I was nervous. "So is it okay? Do you like it?" he asked. He plucked a cigarette from a crumpled pack and lit it.

"I love it," I told him.

He looked relieved. "Well, good, good, I'm so happy. I didn't know what to get you, and then all of a sudden I saw this at the store and thought, Well, now, there it is."

"It's *exactly* the thing I wanted," I said.

Something in the way I emphasized that word, *exactly,* seemed to trigger a mild internal alarm within Uncle Mercer, and his voice became somewhat detached, almost robotic. "I'm so glad," he said. "I'll help you put it together."

The large, shallow box contained a cardboard rocket that looked just like a real one, with plastic for the windows and a cockpit loaded with printed controls.

"Mom, it's so much better!" I said excitedly.

"Well, yours has a great deal of character," she said, "but, yes, this looks much more like the real thing."

Now Mercer looked openly worried. "What are all y'all goin' on about? Better than what?"

"Little brother, why don't you come into the kitchen."

He rested his cigarette in the ashtray and followed her.

I stayed behind to open the lid of the box, but I could hear them. "Well, what the — ?" Mercer cried out.

No doubt he was looking at the crude cardboard rocket I had assembled myself out of three boxes my mother got from the trash bin behind the liquor store.

"It really is exactly what he wanted," my mother said.

"Sister, this . . . it's not normal. It's gotta be some kind of coincidence."

"Oh, for heaven's sake, Mercer, you know damn well it's not." Her voice dropped to a deep whisper that I could hear perfectly. "He's connected to things, too. He's like me and Mama — and like you, if you'd only stop trying to run away from it."

"Sister, that's plain nonsense. You're stirring things up the same way you always have because real, ordinary life is just too damn boring for you."

"That may be true about ordinary life," I heard my mother say, "which is probably why I became an artist. But that has nothing whatsoever to do with the fact that strokes, madness, genius, and witchcraft have all run through our bloodline for generations. Insisting that the earth is flat does not make it flat."

When they returned to the living room, I already had all the cardboard pieces taken out of the box and placed on the floor. "It has a real door, Uncle Mercer. I had to lift my whole rocket up and climb in from the bottom. Plus, my rocket is square, and this one is rocket-shaped. It's so much better, like a real one."

Uncle Mercer grabbed his pack and lit a cigarette, ignoring the one burning down to the filter in the ashtray. "Hand me those there directions," he said, pointing to the sheet of paper on the floor. His index and middle fingers were stained yellow from the nicotine.

I didn't really have to do anything; Uncle Mercer set the rocket up all on his own, and fast, too. He stayed overnight but left abruptly early the next morning, the day before Christmas. "I really just wanted to pop up real quick and wish y'all a happy holiday; I best get back home." He never came north again.

I would see him only a few more times in

my childhood, when I flew to Georgia to visit both sets of grandparents for the summer. Even then, it seemed like Mercer was always out somewhere, driving around, not returning home until after I was already in bed.

A month after I turned twenty-one and could finally legally drink, my grandmother died. Mercer continued to live in the house they had shared, remaining in his childhood room and leaving my grandmother's bedroom exactly as it was the day she died.

That's when we became close.

I would drunk-dial Mercer when I got home from the bars and we would spend hours on the phone. "You know there are people who would call you insane for keeping the house like that?" I said. "I mean, have you even washed Amah's sheets?"

"Hell, no," he replied. "You can still see an indentation on the bed where she sat to put on her stockings."

Mercer never spoke of ladies — or men, for that matter. I asked him where he went at night, and he replied, "Just around. Always have had trouble sleeping, so I drive until I finally get tired, and then I come home."

"Why'd you get discharged from the navy?"

31

"My head wasn't right."

I loved that I could ask him anything and he would always give me some kind of answer.

"Do you miss it?"

"Hell, no, it was being inside that tiny, sealed-up sardine can underwater that drove me half out of my mind in the first place. I much preferred being on the ships. I miss a couple of the fellas, and I miss seeing the sky at night. You have no idea how filled with stars the sky really is until you are out at sea far, far away from any land. The word *universe* doesn't really mean anything until you can see it with your own eyes."

Mercer had a sixth sense about my life's daily events. In 1990 I was a writer for an ad agency in New York. I was on a big shoot for American Express, one that took me from the Grand Canyon to the Redwoods to the Caribbean to Hawaii, where, at the end of a long day, I decided to wade into the water. Instead of sand under my feet, though, there were rocks, or that's what I thought at first. I looked closely and saw it was coral, which is when my foot slipped into a crevice and got stuck.

I was waist-high in the water. At first I thought, *Well, this is ridiculous.* Very quickly the surf got increasingly aggressive as the tide came in, and I started to panic. I could actually die here, I realized, with my foot caught in coral.

On a fucking commercial shoot.

No.

In one swift motion, I yanked my foot free, losing the skin along the top in the process. That night, back in my luxurious beach-front suite, bleeding from room to room and completely over Hawaii and missing New York, I called my answering machine. Mercer had left me a message.

"Hey, there, I was sitting around watching the tube when I drifted off and had a dream about you, that you were stuck somewhere and needed help. I woke up and you know how dreams are, I couldn't remember if you were out of gas or if you were in a car that got stuck in the mud or what it was. Give me a holler when you can so I know all is well."

When I called him and told him about getting my foot trapped in the coral, Mercer was unaccountably distraught. "It's okay, Uncle Mercer, I'm fine. I just have to make sure the scrape doesn't get infected, that's all."

"I'm glad you're safe but I don't like this business," he said. "I know your mama is all gung-ho for it and says it's a special gift, but I think there's something not right about it."

Several years later, I decided I needed a pickup truck because *of course I did,* living in Manhattan and never leaving the island. I absolutely *required* a pickup truck to park in the garage next door to my apartment. I was at the Chevrolet dealer on Eleventh Avenue, sitting in a midnight-blue Silverado, when my snazzy Motorola flip phone trilled in my pocket. I took it out and saw that the call was from Uncle Mercer.

"Hey," I said, my hand caressing the steering wheel.

"Hey," he replied. "You must be at work, and I don't want to take up any of your time, but I just wanted you to know something: if I were to die, I want you to have my pickup truck."

When there was no reply from me, he said, "Are you there? Can you hear me?"

"I didn't know you had a pickup," I said.

"I just got it. It's a Chevy Silverado, but I had a Corvette engine put in it."

I knew if I told him where I was at that exact moment, Mercer would be beside himself with anxiety. "Well, don't die," I told him, "because what would I do with a pickup truck in Manhattan?"

"I'd still want you to have it," he said.

When Mercer died a few years later, he was only fifty-four. My mother said he had a lung infection, but I suspect he killed himself. Mental illness, as well as witchcraft, ran rampant in the family. His early nervous breakdown, his Norman Bates existence, the fear of his own ability, the endless driving — that never sounded like a lung infection to me, no matter how much he smoked. After he died, the house and everything in it, along with the pickup truck, was absorbed by Mercer's older brother, my other uncle, Wynman. I'd met Wynman only a few times, when I was very young. My mother was estranged from Wynman, so I was estranged from him, too.

My mother sat on a tall metal stool that was splattered with every imaginable color of paint. Her easel was before her, positioned at a right angle to the sliding glass door that led to the black wooden deck. Late afternoon sunlight, filtered through the pine trees that surrounded the house, cast the room in a soft, greenish glow. She was painting a portrait of her grandmother.

I sat to the side of and slightly behind the easel.

At school we were learning about the Salem witch trials of 1692.

My mother's eyes traveled between the palette she had hooked through her left thumb and the canvas, but she didn't look at me. "So what are they teaching you?"

"Well, we learned that the whole thing basically started because of two horrible little girls who started acting all crazy and saying weird things and told everyone they were possessed by the Devil, and then they accused a slave plus a bunch of women of being witches. And then it all spread from there and eventually one-third of the whole town was accused of witchcraft and twenty witches were executed."

My mother scratched at the canvas with her brush. "Is that what they taught you, that the twenty people put to death were, in fact, witches?"

"Well." I thought about it. "They didn't exactly say they were witches, but they were *convicted* of being witches."

"I would imagine," my mother said, tilting her head from side to side, inspecting her work, "that not a single person executed was, in fact, a witch."

I watched her load her brush with blue pigment, then tip it into the white. She smeared the paints together on her palette. "A witch knows how to deflect attention. A witch knows how to hide in plain sight."

What did that even mean? "How can you hide in plain sight?"

"Well," she said, brushing quick, light strokes against the canvas, "if you were funny, for example. Being very funny can be very distracting. Or you could silence your mind and listen. What does somebody else need to hear or see to believe you are *not* a witch? And then you can give that to them. It could be everyday small talk or a quote from the Bible.

"Witches terrify people. We anger people because they don't understand what we really are. Most people believe that a witch makes a pact or a deal with the Devil. But we don't believe in the Devil; that's a Christian invention. Witchcraft was a threat to early Christianity, so they had to crush it. That's the reason why there aren't ancient texts on magick; so much of our written early culture was destroyed. So it has always been the Way for one witch to verbally pass the knowledge on to another. As my mother did with me. As I am doing with you, as you will do someday."

I told her something was troubling me. "I had a dream where I was able to rise up above everybody in the room and I could float and glide along. I tried to do it when I was awake, but it didn't work."

"And why do you think that is?" my mother asked, cocking an eyebrow and staring at the corner of her canvas.

"My intent for it must be too weak."

"No," she said. "It didn't work because hovering above a roomful of people and then gliding along over their heads is not something we can do when we are awake. Just as, no matter how much I might like to, I can't turn that irritating Lucy Halburton into a fruit fly."

Lucy Halburton was one of my mother's on-again, off-again poet friends. My mother held weekly poetry workshops in the living room, and Lucy was so cloyingly upbeat that you wanted something bad to happen to her, but not something terrible. Like you wanted a seagull to shit on her sandwich next time she went to the beach, and maybe you also wanted her cat to claw her favorite silk top. The worst was if a single word of her poetry was questioned, you could see the Herculean effort it required for her to maintain her smile as she said, "Thank you, that's very helpful," while her eyes were all box cutters and vats of boiling oil. Nobody likes a repressed emotional cripple, but my mother loathed such people even more than an ordinary person. Her poetry workshops were fascinating to me, and I eavesdropped on every one of them outside the door.

My mother dipped her brush into a deep blue and used one hand to support the other as she painted the canvas with surgical precision. "A witch can't turn a person into an owl. Or fly on a broom. Or defy the laws of physics. We can't do anything that's impossible. But we *can* do many things that people *believe* are impossible.

"When something is hanging in the balance, as they say, we can add more . . . sort of *molecular* weight on the side of the outcome we desire. There are certain things we can prevent, other things we cannot. We are deeply connected to nature and have a great deal of influence here. Nobody grows better tomatoes than a witch, for example. But we can't vanish in a cloud of blue smoke."

"So I couldn't rise up off the floor and hover over everybody, because that's not a thing that can be done."

"Exactly," she said, and now she looked at me.

"Someday will you paint me?" I asked.

"I would love to paint you."

(She never did.)

"You know what coincidence is, right?" my mother asked.

"Yeah, that's like when you find a skeleton

39

key on the ground so you pick it up and put it in your pocket and then at school, there's a brand-new skeleton for science class and then when you get home, it turns out the skeleton key opens the lock to the treasure chest in your bedroom."

My mother said, "That's a better example of what Carl Jung, the Swiss psychoanalyst, calls 'synchronicity,' because the skeleton key opens the treasure chest and is therefore deeply meaningful. *Coincidence* is a set of unrelated events that we perceive as having meaning but which are, in fact, to be mathematically expected. Synchronicity says there *is* meaning in coincidence."

I was flunking out of elementary school, but this I got. "Okay, so then coincidence would be when there are three red cars waiting for the traffic light. But *synchronicity,* that's like the other week when *I Love Lucy* was on and you said it made you think of Lucille, the black lady who worked for your mother but who really raised you. And you talked about how it had been more than ten years since you spoke to her and you missed her and then she called after dinner and said you had been on her mind."

"That wasn't synchronicity," my mother said with a sly smile. "*That* was witchcraft."

# LION'S TOOTH

I've always had insomnia. My husband, Christopher, is snoring within thirty seconds of turning off the light. He has one mood (upbeat, funny, fun-loving) and he falls asleep at the flip of a switch, so it's possible I married a robot.

I am the opposite — wildly moody and wide awake, swinging like an ape from paranoia to anxiety, and this doesn't drive him crazy at all because he's entirely easygoing. Or sleeping.

Our corgi-shepherd mix, Radar, is a rescue, but Wiley, the Italian greyhound, is an Untouchable: a pet store dog. He was a trembling mess to begin with, and living with me has not improved his mental health. Housebreaking was a Sisyphean nightmare.

He has finally learned to pee outside. This has taken three years. And there are caveats. He does not do it outdoors 100 percent of the time. And his preferred time is 3:00 a.m.

41

Of course, that is one of my prime wide-awake hours, so I get dressed and take him to the only spot (besides the apartment floor) where he lets loose: right next to a new playground in glittering, freshly de-terrorized, and renovated Battery Park City. The playground is quite spiffy, catering to the children of the Uber generation. No weedy asphalt or tetanus-festering rusty monkey bars here.

It has flooring: colorful, thick, interlocking rubber puzzle pieces. While there isn't a jungle gym per se, there is a post-modern *structure* that kids can climb, a beautiful, Instagram-friendly dodecahedron for the whole family. It is safe and ergonomic and it feels like it was vetted by several high-powered attorneys who scrutinized every corner and surface in advance of monstrous, litigious parents.

They'd be lawyering up for a different reason, though, if they knew about the playground after dark, which hosts a nocturnal rat fest.

I'm not talking about a stray rat or two skittering from one sand island to another. This is a conglomeration — a rally, really, of rats that have traveled to get here. Not the relatively small "maybe-it-was-a-big-mouse" creatures that scuttle across the subway tracks; the hipster playground rodents are massive, overstimulated from munching on the Adderall tablets that tumble out of smock-dress and jeans pockets during the day. These are meaty, fleshy, muscular rats on stimulants, dragging their weighty genitals over all the bright yellow, sky blue, and fire-engine red child-friendly surfaces.

What if parents knew that the very same playground equipment their expensive and gifted children scrambled across each sunny day was, by night, a rave for beagle-sized rats? That the padded rim of the merry-go-round moonlights as a superhighway for Gambian pouched rats stuffed with *monkeypox*? Rodent scholars have identified that the monkeypox virus, which began in monkeys, like everything horrible seems to, has spread to rats, and that these sharp-toothed toxic nightmares can pass it along to people. In 2003 there was an outbreak in America that spanned several states, including New Jersey, which is an easy commute for a rat. Monkeypox is a pustulating, ulcerating rash that spreads across the body like smallpox and has no treatment or cure.

In other words, it's the rat's greasy middle finger to mankind.

This is further evidence (as if I need it) of

how I love and loathe New York in near-equal measure. Sadly, the rats might be winning, because I no longer find it energizing. It's draining. Maybe it is a result of growing older, but I have wanted to leave New York City for years and return to the New England countryside where I lived when I was very young.

When I bring up the possibility with Christopher, he dismisses it with a curl of his lip. "There *is* nowhere else."

I have to accept that the City That Never Sleeps is also the City of My Final Sleep.

New York is both the past and the future. The present is slippery, because when change and progress and technology and innovation and tomorrow blast in your face like a constant wind, it's hard to look away and stare at your feet, at the now, at the moment, at the present. For people like me, who vacillate between being swallowed whole by their past and longing to escape their lives and run screaming into the future, there's only New York. Since the day I moved here, in 1989, I figured I would also die here, my body discovered by police officers called to my apartment building by a neighbor who was bothered by an increasingly foul odor.

For so many years I had felt like, *I am New*

*York, New York* is *me. I could never live anywhere else.* Later this became, *I am in prison, I can't breathe.*

Then Christopher and I fused our lives, and he, who has occupied the same sprawling Upper West Side apartment for more than half his life, from which he now runs his literary agency, has no trouble catching his breath in the city. He does not long for the trees and woodlands of his childhood, because he was raised in an Ohio suburb. He has friends here that he's known for decades, a "Breakfast Club" of the same five people who have met every Thursday at the same diner for more than twenty years. His roots run deep beneath these skyscrapers and brownstones, and they are exactly what is keeping him tethered to the island of Manhattan.

# SNAKE'S BLOOD

One night we are in bed, the TV across the room playing Turner Classic Movies on mute, both of us on our laptops. Christopher is visiting his usual music websites, exploring new releases, when I ask, "Hey, where is Baby Jessica?"

He turns and looks at me with his fingers poised above his keyboard, mid-type. "Wait. Was she the one who got the baboon heart?"

"No, that was Baby Fae. She died. Baby Jessica is the one that fell down the well in her aunt's backyard in Texas, remember? Everybody thought she was going to die, and it took, like, two days, but then they pulled her out?"

"That's right," he says, slapping his thigh. "Of course. Yeah, what did happen to her?"

"I wonder," I say.

Then my attention drifts back to the 1920s Australian black opal ring I have been looking at for the past ten minutes.

A minute or two passes, and Christopher reaches over and in one swift motion closes the lid of my laptop.

This has the intended effect of startling me into giving him my undivided attention. "What'd you do that for?"

"You need to hear this. Do you know what today's date is?"

"I don't even know what month it is."

"Of course you don't. Today is March 26th, 2011."

"Okay."

"I'm going to read you something from an old news story I googled. Here it is: 'On March 26, 2011, Baby Jessica will turn twenty-five and receive a trust fund of donations worth up to eight hundred thousand dollars.' "

"No way," I say.

"What made you ask about her?"

"I have no idea. I haven't thought of her for years. I was looking at something, this black opal ring that has so much red in it; red is the most valuable color in a black opal — it's the rarest — so I was kind of staring at it in a daze, really, when all of a sudden I saw that old media image of the girl being pulled out of the well and kind of held up, and I wondered, What ever happened to Baby Jessica?"

"Mm-hmm," Christopher says. "I love that movie, too."

There have been periods in my life when I have watched no news and removed myself from society because I am consumed with a project. Sometimes these can be stretches of years. When Ronald Reagan was elected president, I couldn't have told you whether he was a Democrat or a Republican.

In 2012 I enter such a void.

I am writing and I am hoarding antique jewelry, always hunting for an overlooked treasure. Normally I wake up after Christopher leaves for the day. I hop out of bed, take a shower, make the bed, and then climb back on top of it. Today I unexpectedly depart from my routine.

I climb out of bed and shower as usual, put TCM on mute. I make the bed, grab my first Red Bull of the day, climb back on top of the bed, lean back against a dozen pillows, and go to one of the websites I visit each morning to look at jewelry, starting with the most recently added items. I scroll through hundreds of images, instantly assessing each brooch, ring, necklace, or bracelet: nice, pretty, pretty, hideous, maybe, pretty, wow, horrible.

A thought occurs to me with no context,

for no reason whatsoever. Certainly it can't have been sparked by something I'd seen: an art deco bracelet of coral and onyx set in platinum? A natural (uncultured) pearl necklace with a clasp of single-cut diamonds surrounding an unheated sapphire?

No, this is what has suddenly consumed me: if something were to happen on the island of Manhattan, the fact that we are, indeed, on an island would suddenly become a deep and terrible problem. I am wholly unequipped for a disaster. Vulnerable. The safety in numbers I had always felt in the city was an illusion. All those numbers could turn against each other under the right circumstances.

Next to the bed stands a tall glass display case from the 1940s. It has a tacky, faux-Chinese design, but it is also cool because it's so gaudy. The display case is nearly seven and a half feet tall and contains glass shelves from top to bottom. The shelves themselves are fully covered with pieces of jewelry I have collected over many obsessive years: platinum rings set with rare emeralds from the Muzo mines in South America, a chrysoberyl cat's-eye ring finer than any I have ever seen, several impossibly rare jade rings and pendants. Dozens of rings, hundreds of pieces.

If the power grid goes down and banks close, this is money.

The first two things I need: a good shoulder bag, something tough that fits close to the body. And several thousand dollars in cash.

I leave the apartment and head up to a sporting goods store in SoHo. As I pass a bike shop on the way, I see in the window what appears to be the perfect bag. It is orange, which is fine, I suppose. It is made of a very tough nylon fabric with several exterior pockets, each fitted with a high-quality metal zipper. The design is such that once it is over the shoulders, it vanishes beneath the arms, resting against the edge of the back.

This is ideal. I buy it.

Then I go to the bank, deplete my account, and walk away with it in cash.

I return to my apartment and, as a test, empty everything from the cabinet and place it into the bag. It is shocking how well it fits, down to the last gold necklace. The money is easily stashed in one of the exterior pockets.

For the next several hours I visit websites that sell survival items. Although I have nowhere to store it, a Zodiac boat would be a smart thing to own — that and an electric pump or, better yet, a hybrid electric/ manual pump.

Amazon sells everything, really. I begin to Add to Cart. Tactical flashlight, Navy SEAL knife, a Kevlar vest with pockets everywhere, Kevlar cord, water purification tablets, steel-toe boots.

When Christopher comes home that evening, on the floor beside my leather doctor's bag–style carry-on suitcase that I take on book tours is a pretty hideous orange bag he's never seen. (I have mastered the art of packing. The secret is to roll everything and use those plastic sleeves with a one-way valve, so that when you place your item inside and then roll it in the bag the air is pushed out, significantly reducing the volume. You can pack enough clothes for weeks in a carry-on if you do it right.)

Christopher eyes the bags, the display case now empty of my treasures, me on the bed with both dogs, who are barking and wagging their tails. "Wow, you're already ready."

I smile at him. "Well, not quite yet. But soon I will be ready for anything."

He smiles back at me. But he doesn't start emptying his pockets and taking his jacket off like usual. "So, is it just these two bags? What about the dogs? We should bring their toys, yeah?"

I have no idea what he is talking about. "What?"

"*What* what?" he says back. "Let's grab another bag and pack their toys."

He is annoying me. "Why? Pack their toys for what?"

As he leans forward and stares at me, he says, "Because we're taking them uptown for a few days because of Sandy?"

"Who the hell is Sandy?"

Now his entire posture changes and it isn't a smile but a strange kind of expression I don't know how to describe. He asks, "Have you not seen the news?"

I shrug off the question. "No, I'm not watching any right now."

He crosses his arms, and the dogs watch in the funniest way, like they are trying to follow what we are saying. "All your jewelry is in one of these bags?"

"Yeah," I say enthusiastically. "The orange one, and clothes in the other."

"And why did you pack today?"

"I don't know. It suddenly hit me that if something horrible were to happen here, it'd be a nightmare. So I packed and —"

"Augusten" — he pauses — "its name is Hurricane Sandy, and they're calling it the storm of the century. It's headed straight for Manhattan. They're probably going to evacuate Battery Park City tomorrow."

"Oh my God," I say, my mind reeling.

"Yeah," he says. "How did you know? Without knowing?"

I close my eyes. Then I scrub my hands up and down my face. When I open my eyes, he is still waiting for an answer. I shrug, both palms up like I'm catching rain. "You know me, sometimes I just know things."

"I'm going to start keeping a list of all the weird shit that happens around you. I really am."

*It's gonna be a* long *list,* I think but don't say, and instead I smile.

# SPARROW'S TONGUE

At my elementary school I had the distinction of being a third-grader for two consecutive years. I'm not certain my parents even *realized* I repeated the third grade. If they did, it certainly didn't trouble them, which is odd considering my father was an Ivy-educated doctor of philosophy and my mother held a master of fine arts degree.

The town of Shutesbury was located in the untamed wilds of western Massachusetts, where there was barely enough electricity to go around and everything smelled vaguely like rotting mushrooms, pine, and dirt because, of course, there was no pavement. I'm not sure Shutesbury qualified as a small *town.* It didn't even have a traffic light.

I was the least popular kid in school — bullied, teased, tormented, and generally loathed more than anyone else. The teachers knew this, but I think I disturbed them as well, so they let nature take its course. At the time, I was mystified by my unpopularity. In retrospect, I see it perhaps too clearly.

No other boy was obsessed with jewelry. No girl, for that matter, cared as much about jewelry as I did, and I wore more of it than all the girls combined. I'm talking about gold electro-plated necklaces from Zales that I bought with my allowance, tiger's-eye rings, foreign coins with holes in the center through which I ran a white elastic cord so I could hang them around my neck en masse. I pilfered my mother's meager jewelry box for silver rings that I wore on every finger, including my thumbs. I wore my mother's Indian corn necklace. *It was purple. It was corn.*

All my clothing came from one of two stores: Chess King, at the Mountain Farms Mall, which sold fashionable polyester disco shirts and bell-bottom polyester pants and even carried platform shoes in my size, or Faces of Earth, in Amherst. Faces was located behind the Exxon station, where one of the pumps was permanently leaking, so you had to walk through puddles of leaded gas to reach it. They sold more *ethnic* clothing — handwoven ponchos from Peru, fringed pigskin vests that smelled sickeningly sweet, but I wore them anyway. It was impossible to get the frankincense odor out of their bell-bottom jeans no matter how many times you washed them. The store was filled with an opaque cloud of incense, and the aroma bonded to the fabric on a molecular level. They had silver rings set with small geodes, which were cool, and feather earrings, which were gross, not cool. *Feather* was not an acceptable gem.

All the other boys at school wore exactly the same outfit: Lee jeans and football jerseys with three-quarter-length sleeves. The exception was a boy whose parents were from India. He wore turtlenecks and corduroys, and even though his dark complexion bothered the other boys (*it won't wash off, even if you scrub really hard?*), he was popular, because he loved and excelled at all sports. Plus he had met Leonard Nimoy in person and had the Polaroid to prove it.

I was also the only boy who didn't watch *Star Trek.* Why would I? There was not a single cute guy on it.

I watched *Soul Train.*

The boys at school listened to Electric Light Orchestra and Pink Floyd, and the girls were all obsessed with Joni Mitchell. I not only loved the African American folk-

56

singer Odetta, but I could do a brief though nearly convincing imitation of her. I liked disco and R&B. There were no other children of color at my school; in fact, I had never met anybody who wasn't as pink as me. But the African American culture that I saw on TV and in movies was inspiring to me. Even though I had naturally curly blonde hair, I had it permed for a much tighter curl, a sort of frizz. And I alternated between wearing a red and a black Afro pick in my hair. Decades before there was Rachel Dolezal (or Nkechi Amare Diallo, as she calls herself now), there was me, Chris Robison (or Augusten Burroughs, as I have called myself since legally changing my name in 1984). I look back now and think, Thank God there weren't any black children at my elementary school to loathe me for my vile acts of ignorant cultural appropriation.

Also, I was gay, and although not everybody knew the word for it, everybody knew I was different, I was other, I was a *them,* not an *us.* Five boys did know the word for it — "faggot" — and would pounce on me with their bodies and fists while calling me *freak, girl, faggot.* Basically, they assaulted me with the whole kitchen sink.

I was hit a lot in elementary school. I

never cried. I didn't hit back. While it was happening, I pretended it wasn't. I was icy and stoic, above it all. Inside, I was tormented and filled with rage. On the outside, I was my mother's nonstick skillet, the one she used to sauté her tofu squares.

Of the five boys, one was meaner than the others. His punches went deeper; they hurt more. His name was Brandon Rhodes and he was relentless. He was a stocky boy with a blocky head and thicker bones than the other kids. His little sister was also a bully, but only to the girls. Her name was Misty ("Misty Rhodes," poor thing), and she looked like she was made out of sausage and gravel, mixed with your hands, and shaped into the crude form of a Neolithic girl. Both were ugly creatures on the inside, with exteriors that perfectly matched. They lived in a beat-up old ranch house that had indoor furniture outside: a sofa on the front porch, an old metal kitchen table under the dying elm in the front yard. A German Shepherd was chained to the patchy, weedy lawn, and whenever the school bus pulled up in front of their house, the dog strained at the chain and barked until lather started foaming out its mouth. There were several rusty old cars on the property, including a blue Chevy pickup with yellowed white trim.

Weirdly, Misty kind of liked me. "Can you make Brandon leave me alone?" I asked her once.

"No, he'll beat the crap out of me," she said, "if I ever say one word to him."

"So, if you know how mean he is, why are you so mean to the girls?"

Misty smirked. "Because the girls here are such prissy little dips. They deserve to have their bony asses kicked."

God, what a pair of apes, I thought. Then I realized, that was really it, wasn't it? Brandon looked like he hadn't finished evolving into an actual human, like he was one or two links further back. With his shallow forehead, missing neck, the way his nose and forehead kind of fused together, he really looked like some kind of ape creature.

In addition to all my apparent faggotry, I had to contend with being a little witch. A little *boy* witch. Nobody, of course, knew this. But it was yet another form of isolation, another way in which I was different.

While I was generally disliked by everyone, there was an exception to their mistreatment of me. Every once in a while I would be inspired to write, produce, and direct a play. I would approach one of the teachers and explain that I had come up with an idea, and that was it for the day.

Classes ended, and casting and rehearsals began.

My plays were not about princesses being rescued from ruffians or astronauts flying to Mars. They were about husbands who beat their wives while the children hid under beds and begged imaginary friends to "make it stop." I wrote one about a mother who ran away from home — she just vanished — leaving Dad to raise the kids alone. In other words, I wrote plays based on the lives of every kid in school. For reasons that to this day puzzle and astonish me, the teachers not only allowed me this strange freedom, but they seemed thrilled by my theatrical presentations. Even the horrible boys who beat me up daily would ask for roles. Except Brandon. Brandon never wanted to be in one of my plays, and he never wanted to watch them, either.

As soon as my theatrical event was over, life returned to the brutal mundane. The catcalls resumed, the punches came, once again I was shoved from behind right above the kidneys so I would lose my balance and fall, the wind knocked out of me. It was after one of these ordinary, incessant attacks that I decided: *Enough.*

Just like that. It was going to end. I was not going to be tormented anymore. Someone else was. My mother had told me I was never to use witchcraft *against* somebody else. "It's not a weapon," she said.

*Screw that,* I thought, and after school I went outside and gathered several thick sticks. I bound them together with thin branches of wild grape vine so that I had a crude human-ish figure.

A voodoo doll.

When I looked at my wooden figure, I didn't see peeling bark with bits of moss clinging to it. I saw Brandon's smudged features, his thuggish, unilluminated eyes, a specific color combination of brown and green that when normally encountered was wiped up with a rag. Never had I seen *eyes* this putrid color.

I let my mind go blank. Everything stopped for a moment. Unbidden, an image slid into my mind of Brandon, older. Thicker, larger. Hairier. A coarse mustache filled the limited space between his nose and upper lip. I saw hair not only on his chest but up his neck, around and down his back, blanketing both shoulders. His eyebrows fused into one.

Instead of taller, my Brandon was wider. Slower-moving.

I laid the stick figure atop a large flat rock in the woods behind our house, and with the matches I'd lifted from the kitchen table, I lit it on fire. It took half the pack, but I eventually got it to burn. I said these words as I stared at the smoking figure.

Over many years does a boy become a
    man
except for one Brandon, and I have a
    plan.
In the time of a blink, Brandon Rhodes
Shall turn from pollywog into toad.

Nothing happened.

At school the next day, Brandon was still Brandon, as mean and full of punches as always. Nothing happened the following week or the week after that, and as the weeks turned to months and we finally reached the summer, it was a blessed relief to be gone.

I hated fall, because it meant a return to school. But when class started, it was not the same. A new kid had arrived. *If* you could even call him a kid. And he wasn't new at all. It was Brandon. But something had . . . happened to him.

"The doctor calls it 'precocious puberty.' Isn't that funny?" Misty said, laughing and clapping her hands as we sat on the stinking railroad-tie flower planter at recess. "He has to shave *twice* a day and you should see his back, it's so disgusting. Even Mom can't look at him."

Brandon at ten now looked thirty.

"Hey, Ape-face," kids shouted at him. "Sasquatch!"

Oh, they were merciless. And Brandon shrank. I mean, he was twice the size he had been the previous year, but he was so unprepared for what had happened to him that he withdrew into an enormous ball of meat and hair and he became the punching bag for the other boys — even though he was a giant. Brandon had experienced devolution and become a true Neanderthal. Though I remained a friendless freak and I was still bullied and teased, with Brandon now hobbled by a man-suit, the worst of it was over. Fourth grade passed suspiciously quickly.

In fifth grade I had a substitute teacher named Miss Grady, who wore her frizzy red hair pulled back into a bush of a ponytail. Her style ran toward batik blouses and flowy cotton skirts in colors like violet and saffron, along with lace-up leather boots. She also wore a distracting number of cheap bangles on her right arm. Our regular math teacher, Mrs. Sharpton, was on leave because she'd had a baby, so Miss Grady was my new tormenter. She sensed something in me she did not like from the very first day she was introduced to the class. I saw it on her face, in her eyes. I also saw a meanness that started deep inside her and radiated out.

Math was the subject in which I was the only student left entirely behind. I didn't grasp *any* of the concepts. I had some sort of block — not so much the numbers but the symbols — so I got Ds or Fs on every test, while the other students rarely had questions and seemed to understand everything perfectly.

Miss Grady frequently called on me in class, a subtle smirk on her face. She knew I wouldn't have the answer, which of course I never did. I hadn't even understood the question. She teased me in front of the other kids, so they knew it was okay to tease me, too. "Einstein," she called me. I just tried to make it through each hideous day.

Though Brandon may not have bullied me anymore, other kids stepped forward to take his place. Lunch was the worst part of the day. "You're not sitting with us, go somewhere else." It was humiliating to stand in the cafeteria holding my plastic tray, scanning the room for a table that was at least partially empty and seeing that there was nowhere for me to sit, nowhere at all. So I started skipping lunch. (To this day, I don't eat lunch. And I've never eaten breakfast.)

One ordinary (terrible) afternoon math class, Miss Grady decided to post a new challenge on the blackboard. She began writing numbers: fractions, with symbols in between them requiring one fraction to be multiplied by another, divided by a third, subtracted from a fourth, and so on. An *x* and a *y* appeared on the board. I remember looking at the problem scrawled in pale blue chalk and feeling afresh the depth of how lost I was. Nothing she'd written looked even vaguely familiar.

When she finished, she placed the chalk on the tray below the board and said, "Anybody want to give this a try? Does anybody know what those letters might mean?" When there was only silence, she pointed to me. "I know, how about *you* solve this equation and give the class the answer, since you're our resident math genius."

A look of hateful confrontation twisted her face. Kids snickered. *Genius, right, as if.*

I met her nasty gaze and thought, What did I ever do to you? Why are you so nasty to me? Then I looked away from her and back at the board. But everything had changed. The indecipherable scrawl had been transformed and it all suddenly made perfect sense.

*Certainty* entered my being. And certainty is the primary feeling of witchcraft.

I knew the answer. It was right in front of me.

Floating in three-dimensional space in front of the chalkboard there appeared several geometric shapes, the names of which I did not know. Each shape rotated slowly in midair. And each shape was a different pale color.

What I did was count all the sides of all the shapes and add them together. The triangle was a *four* because it had three sides and a bottom; the square was a six. I counted the surfaces of the more complex shapes and added this to my tally.

"Thirty-four," I announced.

I felt good, because verbalizing a number, any number, was better than saying nothing. This was the first time I had ever spoken in math class. Throwing out a wrong answer was the next best thing to throwing out the right one.

Except I wasn't wrong. I was right.

The sarcastic smirk vanished from Miss Grady's face, and her eyebrows pinched together. "How did you solve that so fast in your head without paper? You haven't been able to solve *simple* problems." She placed her hands on her hips and stared at me. "Tell me, how did you do this? I haven't taught the class how to solve this yet." Her tone was accusatory.

My mother sometimes told me I used an *imperious* tone of voice. "What does that mean?" I had asked her.

"It means haughty, arrogant, superior. Imperious. It means exactly how it sounds."

I used that tone now. "No, you *didn't* teach me how to solve the equation. Because you are *not a teacher.* You are the *substitution* for a teacher. You are what stands in front of the chalkboard *instead* of a teacher."

Her mouth opened into an O. She was *furious.*

There was not one sound, not so much as the squeak from a plastic chair.

She wanted to hit me. Her cheeks flushed bright red.

Something gathered inside of me, like a twister of red and orange fall leaves spinning on the ground, and when I said it, it came out sounding like both a promise and a fact: "You have the soul of a cashier."

She reacted physically, pulling back as if I had blown in her face or startled her. After I said it, I realized how odd it was. *Where did* that *come from*?

For the first time, Miss Grady looked at me without that hateful condescension. She looked at me like she was almost a little afraid of me.

She never called on me again or made fun of me or even looked at me, even though I never took my eyes off her. Then, a few weeks before school ended for the year, I left and never finished the fifth grade, which means the fourth grade is the last grade I completed without incident.

I would go on to junior high, briefly attending sixth grade, and then after a very bad month I was moved into the eighth grade. The bullying was even worse and I'd had enough. I stopped going to school, started focusing on what I wanted to do with my life.

In my twenties, when I was living in Manhattan and working in advertising, I returned to western Massachusetts, to Northampton, the town where I spent my adolescent years. I parked my truck at a meter and walked to Wally's Tobacco & Sundries, below the railroad bridge. It was still there — I couldn't believe it. It was still yellow and still had the same green awnings.

I went inside to buy cigarettes, and who should be standing behind the counter, ready to ring up my purchase, but Miss Grady herself.

*A cashier.*

I have spent a great deal of time researching satisfying explanations for these events and the many similar ones I have experienced.

A coincidence, as defined by the *Oxford Learner's Dictionary,* is "the fact of two things happening at the same time by chance, in a surprising way."

". . . by chance." What does that mean?

Influential statisticians Persi Diaconis and Frederick Mosteller wrote a significant and widely cited paper on coincidence in the late 1980s, in which they describe what they call the law of truly large numbers: "with a large enough sample, any outrageous thing is likely to happen." They go on: "Truly rare events, say events that occur only once in a million . . . are bound to be plentiful in a population of 250 million people."

Here's the statement I found particularly telling: "What we perceive as coincidences and what we neglect as not notable depends on what we are sensitive to." Thus it is rational to attribute no significance to the coincidences I have experienced in my life. And I understand that the *truly* shocking thing would be for me to experience no coincidence, ever.

In contemporary cosmology, many scientists believe we occupy what is called a "multiverse." Numerous theories describe this concept in different ways. One popular idea is that there exists within infinite space an infinite number of universes where every possible event will occur, and occur an infinite number of times.

Coincidence only *feels* significant to us because we are ignorant of mathematics and statistics, which together all but guarantee we will experience events that "seem" related but in fact are not.

If my name was Jill and I was born on March 3, 1989, and I had red hair and a scar on my right knee, and at the gym one day when I was thirty-two I met another redhead with a scar on her right knee whose name was also Jill and who shared my birthday, and nothing like this had ever happened to me and my mind was blown? Yes, I can see how the law of truly large numbers could explain it. Sooner or later, I was bound to experience some kind of freaky coincidence.

But what if this sort of thing were to happen to me on Monday, and then again on Thursday, and again the following week and the week after that, and so frequently that it confounded those closest to me? The law can account for a striking coincidence happening. It cannot account for a continuous string of them starting in childhood and continuing on and on and on throughout one's life.

But witchcraft can.

The name John Cheever was familiar because I knew the orange book of collected stories with the large *C* on the cover. It was usually downstairs on the bookshelf in my parents' bedroom, but it moved around. Sometimes it would be upstairs on the table beside the sofa. Occasionally I'd see it on my mother's antique writing desk, tucked into the corner against the redwood paneling.

There were several books like this, volumes that seemingly wandered around the house on their own. Emily Dickinson's collected poems, Tillie Olsen's *Tell Me a Riddle,* and of course John Cheever. I hadn't yet changed my name to Augusten, so I was still little Chris, as my parents had named me, which was probably why I liked the Cheever book: the big *C* on the cover was like the backdrop to my own variety show, except of course my *C* would be encircled with lights.

One afternoon in the spring of 2015, I encounter the string of words "John Cheever's Ossining house for sale; exclusive tour" on a website, and I feel an odd little kick in my chest. I don't know how else to describe it other than to say that it felt like the first time I had tried NyQuil, which my grandfather sold and sent to us up north by the case. I took my first gulp and thought, *Not quite, but it's in the right direction.* NyQuil — with 10 percent alcohol, nearly as much as wine — was my gateway drug to . . . well, alcohol.

I look at the virtual tour online and can tell that the house — which was built in the eighteenth century by "a sea captain," which I assume means a rich guy with a dinghy — is beautiful, but I can also see that it has issues. It is hard to be sure from just the careful, professional photographs, but there is a possibility the house is ready to fall over.

And this is precisely why I have a hunch Christopher might love it.

Obviously, we are never leaving the city to which Christopher is inextricably bound.

I conjure the image of the giant rats dragging their monkeypox-laden dicks across the playground teeter-totters that evening and casually say, "I know we would never

73

move out of Manhattan, but if we did? Imagine living here, in John Cheever's house. How perfect would that be? I mean, you being a literary agent and me being a drunk memoirist who doesn't drink anymore? And look at it."

We are sitting on my four-poster iron bed, which is draped with Indian sari fabric. The dogs are asleep at one end on the Eileen Fisher silk comforter. We are both on our laptops and I turn mine around toward him so he can see the pictures.

He waves me away without a glance up from his screen. "Yeah, I really don't need to look at it. You made one boyfriend move out of New York before, and look how well that turned out."

He is referring to the unfortunate period in my not-too-distant past when I selected exactly the wrong person for me, lock-and-key wrong, and then persuaded him to move back to my hometown, where I had such a horrible childhood that the book I wrote about it became a sort of benchmark for dysfunctional childhood. So he does have a point.

"No, this is completely different," I say.

"Is it, now?" he mutters sarcastically, scrolling through the new music on some Canadian indie rock site.

I stare at him so hard that I know he feels the heat on his cheek, because he turns and looks at me like I've hit him in the face with a hair dryer. I start, "The thing is . . ."

"Tell me," he says, rolling his eyes. "What's *the thing*?"

"It's that I know you. I mean, *I know you*. And I know for a fact that despite your believing the opposite, you would be happier and healthier living in the country." Then I raise my hands, palms up, and add with utter insincerity, "But, hey, I also totally get that we're never leaving New York, so that's fine." I make a show of turning the laptop around so that it no longer faces him.

When we first started dating and I asked him, "Do you frequently experience coincidence?" he replied, "No. I'm not even really sure what frequent coincidence means." He thought for another second and said, "Well, there is the 111 thing."

"What's that?" I asked.

"It's a number that kind of follows me through life. My friends and I used to see it on digital clocks a lot in college. We all smoked, and a pack of cigarettes cost $1.11. It was the address of one of my offices. Like that?"

"Not . . . quite. But that's a really good start."

"I wrecked the same car on the same date two years in a row," he offered.

He's got untapped potential.

It's after he is with me for several months that his worldview changes. He sees the shit that happens around me — or because of me — so now he is only 99.99 percent certain I can't turn him into a frog.

"Let me see that house. His kids don't live in it?"

I display it for him once more. "It doesn't look like anybody has been in it for years. Plus, I read his daughter's great memoir about him, and I wouldn't be surprised if she wished it would burn to the ground."

I've never shown him a picture of the kind of house I've wanted to live in for my whole life. An old house, as old as America itself, built with trees and hatchets and stones and made to last for centuries. The Cheever house is that kind, though it has been modernized in places . . . if the 1970s can be considered "modern." It has been ne-glected, which I fear has ruined it, but once it was magnificent. And that kind of beauty still cuts clean through ruination.

"Wow," he says. "It's stunning."

If he hadn't liked it, nothing I said could

have convinced him of how beautiful it was. He is stubborn that way. When he likes something it is immediate and powerful, and he likes this house. He takes my laptop and clicks through all the pictures. "It's amazing."

"Right?" I say.

"It's true that I never want to move, but somehow this is different. This would be really cool." There is a sharp intake of breath. "The article says they're selling it furnished, including these books and papers on Cheever's desk."

I spin the laptop back and expand the photo. "And look at that shelf with a bottle of scotch on it. How great would it be to write a book about relapsing on John Cheever's actual liquor?"

He says, "Is there a number for a real estate agent? We should make an appointment and go see it, for sure."

The Realtor's name is Corky. "How perfect is that," he says. He calls her and asks about the house. I hear only his end of the conversation. "Like what kind of work?" he asks. He nods. "*Fully* rotted, like all the way through, or just part of it?" He nods some more. "Oh, that's a great thing!" he says. "Well, we kind of like wrecks."

I think, *We do?*

He makes an appointment to see the house the following day at noon.

Once we pull into the driveway, I know right away: this house is a vampire. It will want all our neck blood and then the blood of our unborn parallel universe children. The neglect is rampant. A neon sign may as well be flashing above with an arrow pointing below: OWNED BY ALCOHOLIC!

But if you squint and sort of look sideways, it is stunning.

Corky the Realtor arrives several moments later in her gold Mercedes station wagon. She is dressed exactly how a white woman from Westchester County ought to be dressed: vintage Chanel with a double strand of silvery South Sea pearls, the clasp of which features a significant Colombian emerald cabochon. I estimate the value of the necklace to be fifty-five thousand dollars, mostly because of that emerald clasp. She is probably in her early sixties, though she could pass for forty-something, and looks like she has done Pilates all her life. She probably has a gin and tonic every day at four o'clock and will live to be 102.

Yet today Corky seems fatigued, like the house itself. She is quite warm and friendly, but there is a curious air of hopelessness about her, as if on the way home she might suddenly change her mind about it all: pull a Kennedy and stomp on the gas, plow straight through the guardrail down the cliffs and into the Hudson River.

She removes a set of keys — the brass key ring is attached to a white cotton rope monkey's fist knot and I think, *How sailboat* — and she sets about attacking the lockbox on the door. "I must have shown this house to every English major on the Eastern Seaboard last summer," she kind of murmurs, and I suddenly understand her fatigue. We are the billionth people to see it, and the hundreds of millions before us were all gawkers.

A vintage home in Westchester, priced super-low, with five acres of seriously landscaped, terraced yard with stone walls and specimen trees. I can feel it. The house is a trap; the price is the bait.

I remind myself of my first NyQuil experience: *Not quite, but it's in the right direction.* I think about how it's not about *this* house, it's about getting Christopher open to receiving his destiny — which is to move out of the city. I feel confident that the correct house will find us, and I also feel confident that this once-beautiful but ruined-by-an-egomaniac-alcoholic-who-never-lifted-a-finger house isn't it. But it's essential that Christopher believe this might be the house, probably is the house, so that he mentally steps off the subway and looks up at the sky, realizes it's even there.

My mother always told me that what belongs to you will find you.

"We love the pictures in the listing," Christopher says, maybe to let poor Corky know *we're serious.*

She pauses before opening the door and looks at us, her expression both apologetic and annoyed. "Those were very, very good pictures," she says, her hand poised on the doorknob. "All the furniture you saw in the pictures is gone. The house is completely empty. Which means you see more of the actual house and . . . well, nothing is hidden now, is what I'm trying to say."

"Warts and all," Christopher says cheerfully.

"Warts," she says as she unlocks and tries to open the door, but it sticks, so she cleverly kicks it with the bottom of her shoe, not scuffing the creamy leather on top.

We enter what was once the dining room, where there is a lovely fireplace set into a wood-paneled wall. It is a classy, large room — except that the floors are shot, warped from water damage and badly patched with the wrong kind of wood. Most of the planks appear to be chestnut, and the patches look like cheap pine. I step into the room, and the top of my head grazes the peeling plaster ceiling. Christopher steps in ahead of me. "Wow, this is amazing." He turns around and sees me literally pinned in place. "Oh," he says, slightly alarmed. "That's not good."

"No, not really," I say. Then to Corky: "Do you suppose we could have these floors lowered?"

Corky looks at me as if I have asked her for the atomic symbol for bismuth. "I, I, I really wouldn't know" — she frowns — "what's under there. You'd have to bring in a structural engineer. I suppose anything is possible if you throw enough money at it." *That's the WASPy spirit!* I want to say.

That's not going to happen, so the first floor is gone, poof. I am hunched over as we pass a row of windows, and I see that all the beautiful old trim is rotting, so not only would we need to re-trim the windows, but there would be water damage in the walls.

The '70s kitchen renovation has its sad orange brittle laminate countertops still in place. The ceiling in this room is inexplicably high — twelve feet, fifteen? — but the floor feels spongy, like it might give way at any moment and plunge us into a John Wayne Gacy crawl space.

Around the corner from the kitchen is a lovely little bathroom — or what *could* be lovely, with a year's worth of skilled work — and beyond this is a guest room with splotchy black walls. Had they been sponged in the 1980s? Had this ever been a "look"?

"That's black mold," Corky says, pointing to the walls and covering her mouth. "We shouldn't go in there."

Wow. The walls down here are literally *made* of mold. I am doing the renovation math in my mind as we walk, and we are now at around four hundred thousand dollars.

So far, I kind of hate it.

"I love it," Christopher tells Corky.

Christopher has always loved a good wreck. He married me, after all. When we first started dating, he asked, "Have you seen *Grey Gardens*?" I told him I hadn't. He said, "Oh, you have to watch it. It's a crazy, great documentary." He'd already seen it a few times, he loved it so much. But I told him to shut it off after the first five minutes. "I'm sure it's amazing, but this reminds me *way* too much of my childhood. People living in squalor and eating cat food is a horrible memory, not entertainment, even if they are related to Jacqueline Kennedy."

There's a (large) part of him that could live in this disaster of a house as is. I love that about him, but I am quite the opposite. I like an old, old house, but one in which every inch of wood is waxed and polished to a gemlike finish.

Corky leads us through the rest of the house and it is just plain sad: what once was a stunning, handcrafted, perfectly proportioned structure had been neglected for decades by an alcoholic. Nothing fixed, nothing maintained. The gutters were so packed with dirt and established plants that when it rained, water simply streamed down the sides of the house, rotting everything — walls, floors, joists, window frames.

Cheever had lived exactly as I had when I was drinking, except I was in a rental apartment.

Once we are outside and looking at the two decks — verandas, really, that span the length of the house on both the first and second floors (and would need to be completely rebuilt) — Corky mentions the buried oil tank.

"Oh," I say. That means the soil has to be tested, and if there is any evidence of leakage, the Environmental Protection Agency must be notified. Lawyers, naturally, get involved. A buried oil tank alone could end up costing six figures. The absurdity is even larger considering what town we are in.

Ossining is the location of Sing Sing prison, once home of the legendary "Old Sparky" electric chair. Surely there was some parolee living in the faceless, charmless town who would dig the leaky old tank up in the middle of the night with a backhoe, drop it in the bed of his pickup, and then dump it in the Hudson. One leaky old oil tank would make exactly zero difference to the Hudson River. I mean, what's one more turd in the diaper?

I love what the house *could* be and surely once was, but I don't love it the way it is. Christopher, however, is enamored of it, flaws and all, which says everything about him.

I know with certainty that we will never live there. When I try to visualize us at any point in the future in that house, all I see is static. This is how I know when something that's scheduled or is expected is not going to happen. Countless times throughout my life I have experienced this buzzing light. Often it occurs around something I myself have planned.

I was enrolled in a computer programming school in the '80s, a technical school that gave you a certificate and not a degree.

All the time I was there and imagining where I might end up working as a coder, all I saw was static, like when your TV is on but the cable isn't plugged in. But that didn't make sense, because I was entering an industry in dire need of what I was being trained to do: write programs to control automated teller machines at banks, even though I might have to start out as a computer operator first and work my way up to programmer, then systems analyst. Control Data Institute was the best place to learn this stuff. *Of course* I would get a job. So why was I seeing this static instead of my future in the computer industry? Why couldn't I form even a hazy image of myself sitting at a computer terminal writing some Fortran subroutine?

Right before graduation I saw a TV commercial for the school, and it was cheesy and awful. *Somebody got paid to think of that,* I realized. I would have made a much better commercial. I sat down and rewrote all the ads in the nearest magazine as a makeshift portfolio, and several months later I got my first job in advertising. I did have to move out of the Boston area to San Francisco, but I never worked a single day as a programmer.

When I encounter the static wall, I pay attention to it now.

We will not be living in John Cheever's wreck of a house. I don't tell Christopher, because the messenger is frequently shot, one of many clichés that is true. Instead, I fan his enthusiasm. Enough wind from the fan could blow him out of the city and into the *right* place.

The house is about to go into foreclosure, and our offer would have to be cash; the bank would not give us a mortgage on a house with a buried oil tank and no certificate of occupancy, and that's before we get to the black mold and the spongy balcony. I finally tell him, "It's not meant to be."

He reluctantly agrees. He is kind of heartbroken, though, and this makes me sad. But more than it makes me sad, his heartbreak *thrills me.* Using Cheever's disaster as the NyQuil gateway drug worked. Now I need the right house to find me. Then I can make the required course correction for our lives.

Christopher is a gifted and successful literary agent with an impressive roster of clients. Maybe in Olde Times (the '80s and '90s), it was essential that you lived in Manhattan. But it doesn't matter anymore, because everything is done through texts and emails. Even the phone, formerly an agent's best friend, is a thing of the past.

Christopher can drive into the city when he has a meeting. I just don't want him living in it anymore. I want him away from the noise, the pollution, the eighty-dollar grilled salmon, the stench of summer and the icy sidewalks of winter, the bomb threats, the entitled brats moving into the multimillion-dollar apartments their parents buy for them. I want him to engage with the Natural World, not the only worlds he's ever known: man-made suburbia and man-made Manhattan.

I want him to be as physically healthy as possible and happier than he is now. Even though he is healthy, even though he is happy, I want the "-er" for him.

He will love pulling weeds. I can see him in the dirt, the wires from his earbuds dangling down his shirt and into his pocket. You could call it a "vision" or a "premonition," because I can see it, I can see him. I can watch him yank one clump of weeds out of the ground and toss it in a wheelbarrow beside him, then go back and yank out another clump.

But where are these weeds?

I wish I knew how to call out for the house to find me. I wish I had more wisdom. What magick do I use to draw a home to us? I feel like a second-year med student working

87

the ER alone, but, hey, two years of med school is better than none.

"Everything you need to know, you already know. It's all inside of you. Centuries of knowledge reside within your cells. Never forget that."

Those were some of the last lucid words my mother spoke to me before psychosis completely ravaged her mind. I was fourteen. Her maniac of a psychiatrist had become my legal guardian, and I was living in his squalid house and being molested by one of his patients.

Even witchcraft can't protect you against everything.

But a witch can survive this shit, that's the thing. Witches have skin made of stone and we are fueled by the moon.

I regret *nothing* that happened to me.

I am grateful for the horrors I experienced.

I am deeper because of them.

I am wiser having lived through them.

Beauty and youth drain away as time progresses. But a witch's magick grows stronger, her instincts louder, his ability to move distant molecules more effortless and more successful.

My youth is gone, but something far better has taken its place.

Everything I need to know is inside me. I tell the house, *Find me. Find me now.*

# SEVEN BARKS

It was the summer of 1976 and I was eleven. My parents had dumped me on an Eastern Air Lines jet to Tallahassee, Florida. First, my maternal grandmother, Amah, would pick me up at the airport and drive me to her house in Cairo, Georgia. After I spent two weeks with her, she would take me back to Tallahassee, where Jack and Carolyn, my father's parents, would put me in their silver Cadillac Fleetwood and we'd head to their Lawrenceville, Georgia, estate, Stagwood.

In a way, I thought of my visit with Amah as being like the greasy canned salmon patties my father fried on Saturday nights and served with canned black-eyed peas: a necessary awfulness that I was required to endure before I could eat the chocolate sheet cake with vanilla frosting.

My grandmother Carolyn was fun and rich: she took me shopping and never made me choose between anything. She wore heaps of jewelry and a mink even in the sweltering Georgia summer. While I was terrified of my gruff grandfather Jack, I almost never saw him, because he was always away. It was usually just me and Carolyn alone in that big, beautiful plantation house with black-and-white marble floors and ice-cold jade statues.

Amah, on the other hand, had been a Latin scholar and spent all her time reading and wished "not to be disturbed," so visiting her was like a school detention, sitting silently while the teacher reads the papers and gives everybody a D. We had tuna sandwiches for dinner almost every night, the one time during the day when she wasn't reading. Instead, she would ask me questions: "Are you enjoying school?" To which I would reply, "I hate it, everybody is mean and dumb." She would dab the corners of her mouth and say, "First of all, *hate* is a very powerful word and I'm sure you don't mean it. Second, dumb means *mute,* either lacking the ability or willingness to speak. Certainly that is not the word you intended. I believe the word you meant to say was *stupid,* and if that's the case, that's extremely rude and dismissive. It sounds to me like you need to apply yourself to your studies instead of standing in judgment."

I was afraid Amah could read my mind, so I smiled neutrally and repeated the Pledge of Allegiance to myself over and over until I was excused from the table. Only then would I dare think: *Why didn't you die in that car accident? You are awful.*

Though Uncle Mercer lived with Amah, he was rarely home when I visited, which I didn't understand. "Your uncle certainly does love to go for his drives," Amah would say, as if this explained why I never saw him. Maybe once during my two-week stay he would finally be home, the day before I left.

So it was me and my grandmother alone. It was as if I somehow displeased her. I was polite and tried to stay out of her way, and she was never unkind to me, but she was also never warm or even remotely personal. I was like Somebody Else's child, not her own daughter's. The truth was, I didn't even really think of her as my grandmother. My *real* grandmother, I decided, was Amah's sister Curtis, who lived right next door.

Curtis had been a computer programmer for AT&T's Bell Laboratories and had helped program the first communications satellite that America launched. Better still, her husband had dumped his girlfriend — a pilot named Amelia Earhart — so he could date Curtis. Curtis's husband died before I was born, but Curtis did have in her possession a compass that once belonged to Amelia. She gave it to me one summer. At first I felt like it was too important for me to have, Amelia Earhart's compass. "It's not like it did her any good," my great-aunt said.

I could talk to Aunt Curtis in a way I never could talk to my grandmother. I could also talk *about* her. "She doesn't like me. It's like I've done something awful to offend her, only I don't know what."

"Oh, goodness gracious, no! Louisa was born a disappointed old woman and she'll die a disappointed old woman. She has always had a chip on her shoulder, and I never could figure out why. Of course, it may have something to do with the Gift."

It was so funny to hear my grandmother's name spoken out loud: Louisa. I never really thought of her as even having an actual name. "How could that upset her? Did she feel like you got more of it than she did?"

Aunt Curtis laughed. "Oh, I think it's quite the opposite. You see, I've always called it the Gift, and that's how I've always thought of it, too. But Louisa has always called it the Curse."

"I didn't know that!"

"Yes. Even as children, when we were

93

discovering ourselves and who we were and what that meant, she was always so bitter about it. But you see, the Gift is very different for us, even as girls. I could always conjure a future for myself. I could visualize myself winning the spelling bee in third grade, for example, and then I would win it. But your grandmother was not as adept at manifesting; she was gifted at seeing, at knowing something long before it happened. And to be fair, a lot of what your grandmother saw was frightening. Her father's death the week before he died, her own husband — your grandfather, whom you would have adored — losing his business and financial security. Back when they owned the pecan orchards, your grandmother knew months and months and months in advance the yield that season would be low."

"And Harriet? Did she know about Harriet?"

My aunt Curtis let out a sigh. "Yes. And I think that, more than anything else, changed how your grandmother views the Gift. When your mother, Margaret, was twelve, your grandmother became pregnant. I remember, I was beside myself with the news. I couldn't wait to have another nephew or niece, although I felt certain the baby would be a girl, just as soon as she told me she was pregnant." The smile drained away from Curtis's face. "But sister — your grandmother Amah — she had a terrible time with that pregnancy. She would sit at the kitchen table and just cry and cry, and I would stand at the stove and fry eggs, which is the extent of my culinary ability, and I would try and comfort her, put my arms around her, and she would say, 'Oh, sister, something is going to be terribly wrong with this baby.'

"I tried to tell her, 'Now you hush with that nonsense, that's not true! She's going to be a perfect baby!'

"Your grandmother couldn't have been more than one or two months along. I will never forget her eyes, the terror in them. 'No, sister,' she said, 'something is very, very wrong.' "

My mother had told me stories about my aunt Harriet before, but not this one. "And when she was born, her arms were stuck?"

"Yes," my aunt Curtis said. "Her arms were locked up like this," and she made two fists and brought them up below her chin. "She had cerebral palsy and she could never speak, but she loved being read to and having her hair brushed. And oh, how your mother adored that little girl. But when

95

Harriet was a baby, your grandmother would only take her out in the carriage for a walk at night, never during the day. She didn't want anybody to see that child. I think she was ashamed of her disability. That makes me feel ashamed to even say, but it was very difficult on your grandmother. And I believe that with the birth of Harriet, the Gift became the Curse.

"Now, she has also seen many positive, wonderful things happen before they've happened. I remind her of this fact continuously. But, well, she chooses to focus on the negative. And I suspect this is one reason why your uncle Mercer struggles with accepting his own Gift. He's seen his mama torn apart inside, and I think he blames the Gift. So he tries to pretend it away."

"Wow. I guess I can understand why she calls it the Curse," I said.

"No, honey, no," Curtis said, laying her hands on my shoulders. "It is *never* a curse. Information, knowledge, is *always* only a gift. Even if it's upsetting. One must never be a victim, even if one is victimized. One must never focus on the dark, even when all the lights are out. Heavens to Betsy, do you think the men working at Bell Labs in New Jersey were delighted when a *woman* mathematician joined their ranks? I mean to tell you, I cannot even repeat in polite company some of the things that were said to me. But I have a thick skin and a sharp mind, and I am a witch, and none of those men was a match for me! I had them all trained like monkeys within a week." Her smile was so big it spread all the way over onto my face.

Curtis went to the cupboard and pulled down two tall glasses, filled them with lemonade. "Yes, that old woman next door drives me crazy, yet here I am, living not even thirty feet away."

"With only a patch of rattlesnake-infested bamboo between you," I added.

Curtis cackled. "Yes. Some people are frightened by the rattle, but I myself think it's very thoughtful of the snakes."

We both laughed.

I wondered if my aunt knew I had the Gift, too. "Did my mom tell you I knew something had happened to Amah when I was on the school bus?"

"Oh why heavens, yes, of course she told me. It made me so very happy." She smiled.

She must have registered the confusion on my face, because she clarified herself. "I mean, I was happy that you knew, not happy about the accident, of course." Then she said, "As a matter of fact, there's a lady I would like you to meet. Have you ever heard of a rootworker?"

"Is that somebody who works in a garden?"

Curtis shook her head, took a sip of her lemonade. "A rootworker is somebody who practices African folk magick. The woman I'd like you to meet has been a dear friend of mine for many, many years. Her name is Regina. Maybe tomorrow we'll pay her a visit."

The next afternoon, I went next door to Curtis's house, followed her outside to the carport behind her kitchen, and climbed into the passenger seat of her huge yellow Mercury Marquis ("but with a Lincoln engine"). She drove us out of Cairo, which itself was a tiny town. "Blink and you'll miss it," Mercer always said, and I thought he'd made that phrase up himself.

She took me deep into the country until we reached a dumpy dirt road, which reminded me of the one I lived on back in Massachusetts. Finally, we arrived at a rundown shack that seemed to be made out of wood scraps, cardboard, and prayers. I could not believe such a house still existed. It sat by itself in a field edged with woods. It wasn't a plowed, neat field but a wild one, overflowing with tall grass and wildflowers.

Curtis parked the car and climbed out, smoothing the front of her skirt. She reached for her pocketbook, which had been on the bench seat between us, but then changed her mind and left it, closing the door.

She knocked on the peeling wood frame of the screen door. "Regina, honey, it's Curtis. I've brought somebody special to meet you." She opened up the door and stepped inside, but I hesitated, because we hadn't even seen Regina, let alone been invited. Just then she appeared from a room in the back, a sewing needle sticking out from her lips. Miss Regina must have been the same age as my aunt, but there was not one line on her face. Her skin was dark, the color of coffee with the smallest splash of cream, and she had the brightest, bluest eyes I'd ever seen. She had full lips, with perfectly applied deep coppery lipstick, and her silver hair was pulled back from her face, which emphasized her fine bones.

I was hypnotized by Miss Regina. And oddly, I wanted to weep. Her eyes radiated intelligence, but also such knowledge that I felt safe merely standing in her doorway. When she smiled, revealing perfectly white teeth that were definitely her own and not dentures, her warmth was overwhelming.

She looked at Curtis, standing in the kitchen, and then back at me, outside on the porch, the screen door closed. "You figurin' on stayin' out there, or you gonna come in and say hey?"

Now I was extra-mortified. I opened the door. "I'm sorry, I didn't mean to be weird, I was just —"

Regina cut me off, her face and voice as warm as the sun. "You were just being polite, young man, and good manners are nothing to apologize for."

"Yes, ma'am," I said. "My aunt Curtis knows you and everything, but I felt funny following her in."

"Well, of course it would have been perfectly okay, but I am delighted by your sense of propriety. It's such a fine and welcome quality, especially in one so young."

I was embarrassed but also happy that she was happy. "Well, thank you, ma'am," I said.

"Regina, this is my nephew Chris. You know, Margaret's son."

"Oh," she said, recognition illuminating her face. She studied me closer, the smile on her face opening into an expression of amazement. "How can that be? My Lord, has it been so long? Margaret married that preacher boy, did she not?"

Curtis nodded. "Mmmm-hmmm, but he

100

became an atheist and a professor of philosophy. They've got two boys, there's an older one. But only Chris was born with it."

Miss Regina put her hands on her hips. "Now, I wonder why that is," she said. "So often, it's the firstborn who inherits it. Funny the way it works." She motioned toward the small kitchen table, around which were four painted white wooden chairs. "Y'all have a seat," she said. As we pulled out the chairs and sat, Miss Regina said to my aunt, "Did I ever tell you I knew a set of identical twins, young ladies from over in Attapulgus — and you know Attapulgus is the birthplace of Hosea Williams." She raised her eyebrows to register the significance of this fact.

"Oh, I did not know that," Aunt Curtis said.

"In any case," Miss Regina continued, "these twins, as identical as can be, one had it and one did not. How that is even possible, I could not say."

I looked around the beautiful kitchen. It had a stove and refrigerator from the olden days, except they looked brand-new, and the sink was one of those long ones that's more like a shallow bathtub. It smelled like lemons and beeswax, also like pie, and there was a small cut-glass decanter in the center of the table between the salt and pepper shakers that I knew was filled with vinegar, because we had almost exactly the same one at home for when my father cooked collard greens.

Miss Regina carried a large glass pitcher filled with ice and tea from the refrigerator and set it on the table. From the cabinet above the sink she removed four tall, fluted glasses and arranged these around the table as well. The fourth glass was placed before the empty chair. Miss Regina noticed that I noticed this, and as she filled our glasses, including the extra one, she said, "I always set a place for Ruth, just in case she decides to pay me a visit."

"Who's Ruth?" I asked.

Miss Regina looked at Curtis, who smiled and shrugged one of her shoulders in what was clearly a reply to an unspoken question.

"Ruth was my very best friend, and we shared this home together for forty-three years. She passed almost eleven years ago, and I still miss her every moment of the day." Then she closed her eyes and smiled. "Mmmm," she said, like she'd taken a bite of something wonderful. "I was lucky to have had her for as long as I did." Then Miss Regina looked right at me. "Whenever you lose something of great value, it's important to focus on its value to you and not on the loss of it. Someday you'll understand what I mean."

Except I thought maybe I did understand what she meant. It frightened me. It comforted me.

Miss Regina took a long pull from her glass of tea. "Your aunt Curtis and I, we go way, way back," she said. "We were probably about your age when we first became friends. We recognized something we shared, isn't that right?"

"Oh, yes. Best of friends from the first moment our eyes met."

"Wow," I said.

"Wow, indeed," Miss Regina agreed. "Little white girls and little black girls were not supposed to mingle back in those days. I mean, things were very different then. It was a dark, shameful time, but it was also a time of glorious hope and light. And of course your aunt would never allow anybody to tell her whom she could or could not be friends with. And anybody who dared to cross her, oh my, how they paid a price for it."

"Oh, hush," said Aunt Curtis. "You make me sound like a terror."

"Well, I'm just telling it the way it was.

You *were* a little terror when the situation warranted it."

"We did have some fun, didn't we?" Aunt Curtis said, grinning.

"Oh, yes, we did," replied Miss Regina. "So tell me why you have given me the privilege of meeting this nice young man today."

Curtis said, "He's just learning about himself. He's at the very beginning of his journey. But I wanted him to meet you, Regina, because, well, just because. Some things aren't right for him at home. I worry about what's ahead. His Gift is a large one, I believe."

"I know that," Regina said, looking at me. "I can see it." She reached her hand over and touched me lightly on my left cheek. Her fingertips were cool, electric. She nodded. "Mmmm-hmmm," she said. "He sees. He sees inside of people and he sees ahead. He is a healer. He can create. There hasn't been anyone like this boy in your family for over a century."

Curtis nodded. "I did suspect that was the case."

Miss Regina shook her head, sucked in her bottom lip. "Somethin' is wrong with his daddy. A drinker? Maybe something else, something darker. And Margaret, bless

104

her heart. She is like a glass in midair, about to shatter." Her gaze was slightly off to the side of my head, like she was seeing something in the distance.

Miss Regina looked back to me suddenly. "Young man, why don't you have another sip of your tea."

I reached for my glass, and as I did, Miss Regina removed a white candle from the pocket of her apron. I took a long swallow of tea and set the glass back down.

Miss Regina lit her candle with a silver Zippo and rolled it gently from side to side to burn the top edge and allow wax to pool in the center around the wick. Then quickly she tipped the candle over my iced tea and let the wax drip down into the glass, where it was seized by the cold liquid, frozen into shapes. She held the candle upside down, letting the last of the pooled wax drizzle into the tea. I was fascinated to see the shapes gathering around the edges. Miss Regina then plunged the tip of the candle under the surface and it hissed out.

She picked up the glass and brought it close to her face, turning it slowly, examining the forms, scrutinizing them.

Curtis watched, mesmerized.

I watched, too.

I did the same thing at home in my bedroom, only I used a bowl of water. I liked that sometimes I could see real things in the shapes, sometimes things that I'd been thinking about but hadn't told anyone. Miss Regina was so focused and silent, but I wanted to tell her — I wanted her to know. "I do that," I said. "In my room with a bowl of water."

She looked up at me. "You learn from your mama?"

"No. She's always burning candles, but, I don't know, because they're pretty, I guess."

Miss Regina said, "But she doesn't read the candles? She doesn't see anything in them?"

I shook my head. "I don't think so. My mother and me, we're different."

"I," Miss Regina said, correcting me. "My mother and *I*, not me."

"My mother and *I* are different."

"How so?" Regina asked, setting the glass down onto the table, letting the melted figures swirl unwatched.

"Well, a lot of times, she'll wake up with something on her mind, like a yellow umbrella, and then she'll go to a café and they'll have yellow umbrellas, and then one of her friends will show up wearing a skirt printed with yellow umbrellas, and then there will be a movie on TV and somebody will be carrying a yellow umbrella. But I don't think my mother sees things that haven't yet happened. And I don't think she can change things, like make them happen or not happen."

"And you can?"

"I can. But not always. But sometimes. A lot of the time."

"So when you drip candle wax into a bowl, what do you see?"

It felt so good to talk about this with somebody. "It depends. Sometimes I see blobs and nothing else. And then sometimes I will see . . . like, an answer to something. Or a shape of something that's about to happen. Like, there's this teacher at school and he was everybody's favorite but not mine. I didn't like him. I thought about how I didn't like him, and I did a candle thing into the water and it swirled around and around and it looked exactly like those stripes on the uniforms prisoners wear in cartoons? So that's when I knew: he's going to jail. Because he was doing things with some of the boys, and I knew what he was doing, and he knew I knew, so he stayed far away from me."

"Did he go to jail?"

"He's in jail now. It happened about half a year after I saw it in the wax."

"Do you know the name for what this is?"

"It has a name?"

"It most certainly does. We rootworkers call it ceromancy." She spelled it for me. "That's when you read the wax from a candle. There are several ways. You can drip it into the water or the tea like we've done here just now. Or you can simply allow the candle to burn and see what shapes occur."

"Or you could hold it up high and let it splatter down onto the ground."

Miss Regina smiled. "That you could do, I imagine. Same hoodoo."

"Voodoo?"

"No, hoodoo. Not the same, so don't get 'em mixed up. Hoodoo is old, old magick that the slaves brought over with 'em from different parts of Africa. Rootworkers use hoodoo. That's what I do, I work the roots of life, the roots of truth."

She turned back to my tea. "There's more," she said, looking up from the glass and meeting my eyes. "There are some things I can see which may or may not happen, it's up to you. These are choices you will have to make much later in your life. You see all these loops and twists and split-aparts?" She pointed to a large section that hadn't formed into blobs but was more of a tangled wax string. "That's struggle. I'm

108

afraid things might not be easy for you, but more will be possible because of what you were given, because of what you are."

I swallowed. I tried to focus on "more" and not "split-apart."

"I see something else far, far down the road, long into your journey. I'm trying to think of how I can put what I see into words that will make sense. I suppose it's like this: there may come a day in your life when you find you need to move a tree. Say, transplant it from one part of the yard to another, maybe it's not getting enough sunshine. Always wait until the early spring or the late fall, when the roots are dormant. Not when it's blooming, not when the ground is frozen." Then she sat back in her chair, satisfied. "That might not make much sense to you sitting here today, but one day it will."

"Thank you, Miss Regina, ma'am, I will try to remember that."

She waved my remark away. "Oh, young man, you don't need to *try*. It'll be there when you need it. Those words, they are a part of you now."

"You make me feel better." I blurted this out.

"Feel better about what, sugar?" She took my wrist gently.

"About everything. Just knowing you're

you and you're real and you're here and I don't feel so alone."

"Oh, bless your heart, but if there's one thing you are not, it is alone. Believe me, most folks are not like us. But enough folks *are* like us, and somehow, sooner or later, we find each other without even trying or looking. We find each other."

Miss Regina wouldn't let us leave without serving us each a huge slice of her home-made fourteen-layer cake, each layer as thin as a pencil. How was such a cake even possible?

Curtis thanked Miss Regina for her hospitality and time. They hugged good-bye. And then I thanked her for everything she'd said and done for me.

We were silent in the car on the way home for a while. Finally I said, "Miss Regina misses Ruth so much."

Curtis glanced at me and then quickly looked back at the road. "Yes, she does. Ruth was a wonderful, absolutely brilliant woman. She was a physician back when not many women were doctors, especially not down here in the South. Ruth was from Boston. She had blonde hair and was quite beautiful."

"What did Miss Regina do?"

"Oh, she's never held a traditional job.

Miss Regina has always owned a great deal of land, and that's how she met Ruth; Ruth rented one of Miss Regina's houses."

"So is Miss Regina rich?"

"That's not polite to ask," Curtis said.

Silence again filled the air until Curtis said, "I'm so glad you had the chance to meet her. She was enormously fond of you, I could tell."

This made me happy. I had noticed the bowl of rattlesnake rattles next to the sugar on the counter. Something told me that if Regina didn't like you or you crossed her, you'd be in serious trouble. Terrible, unexplained things happened to people all the time. I saw on TV the other day that a set of teeth was found inside somebody's head. The explanation was that a twin hadn't fully formed and had been reconsumed. I felt positive that Regina could stick a set of teeth inside your head if you did her wrong. But I also felt positive that she could shine a light into the shadows for you so that you could see your way.

"It's weird, Aunt Curtis, but I feel like I've known Miss Regina my whole life," I said.

Curtis stepped on the gas even though we were already in the passing lane going at least eighty. "Oh, but you *have* known her your whole life. The first time your mother brought you down to Cairo when you were a baby and you met your grandfather, who held you in his arms, you also met Miss Regina, who had come to my house for tea. And you will always know her," she said, looking at me, a smile on her face, her eyebrows raised.

I smiled as we sailed along the highway passing every car in Curtis's souped-up yellow Mercury Marquis. How strange, I thought, to be part of this Southern family of witches. I wasn't even sure what it meant to *be* a witch. I knew that sometimes, like when I was sitting in Miss Regina's kitchen, I felt unaccountably powerful — me, powerful. But other times, back at home or in school, I felt an uneasiness, like bad things were going to happen and I had no control over anything at all and no power, and it didn't matter what I was or wasn't.

I wondered about something. "Aunt Curtis, does all magick come from black people?"

Curtis smiled, reached down, and patted my knee. "Honey, of course it does. And so do we. Everyone in the world is a descendant of one single African person of color who lived many tens of thousands of years ago."

I was quiet again. Then: "How can there be so much wonderful and so much terrible at the same time?"

"It is easier to bear as you grow older," Curtis said.

"What is?" I asked.

"Everything," Curtis said. I thought her chin trembled ever so slightly, as if she might cry, but she did not; she drove steady and fast, and I thought about Ruth and the glass of iced tea Miss Regina had set out on the table for her. I wondered if the ice had melted. I wondered when Miss Regina would decide to pick up the glass and pour the tea into the sink. I wondered if I would ever be loved that much by anyone.

# PRIEST'S CROWN

Yellow has never been my favorite color. As I was nearing my teen years and my mother was descending into a deeper state of mental illness, she developed a fondness for yellow. After my parents divorced, my mother rented a yellow house across the street from the Emily Dickinson homestead. "I need to be near Emily," she told me. "She's very helpful to me in my writing."

She took to wearing yellow caftans in the same shade as Plochman's Mild Mustard, which came in a yellow plastic squeeze barrel with a bright red nipple tip and was her favorite, the only mustard she would have in the house. My mother consumed an extraordinary amount of mustard — on Wheat Thins, celery sticks, spiraled in loop after loop onto pumpernickel bread that was then layered with pickle slices and bologna. Unshowered and wild-eyed, she repainted the white kitchen entirely yellow. Cabinets, walls, molding, trim, switch plates, all the same. Perhaps my distaste for yellow began back then, but it still runs so deep that I don't even care much for most yellow gemstones, like citrine, heliodor, and Mali garnet — and I *really* care about gemstones.

After several weeks of searching real estate online and finding an abundance of beautiful antique homes within two hours of Manhattan, I haven't found "the" house. I am certain it will make itself known to me, its very correctness somehow transcending the website slurry of properties.

My mother used to say, "Our belongings find us, we don't find them." Even though she was in a straitjacket at a Vermont psychiatric hospital when she said this, it still rang true to me. So when I see the slightly blurry picture taken from an odd angle of a house that is not merely *yellow* but actually *three different shades of yellow,* a ménage à trois of my least favorite color, I stun myself by announcing out loud in my apartment at four o'clock in the afternoon, "There you are!"

In the first photograph, the house is in the background because there is a small river in the foreground with a stone dam, and on the bank is a tiny cottage, also yellow. Up the sloping lawn is the old and dramatic house.

I continue clicking through the pictures. The kitchen is galley style, with upper and lower wood cabinets painted a crisp white. The countertops are also white. Shelves run along the far wall, above a window over the sink and on top of the doorways, and two pendant barn lights hang from the barrel-vaulted ceiling. The floor is clay tile.

By modern standards, it is a primitive kitchen. Where are the double ovens? The glass-front Sub-Zero? But I love it. This kitchen was last "renovated" when Franklin D. Roosevelt was in office. This is a kitchen where you used a hand mixer, not a KitchenAid. Once I go back and read the description more carefully, I see that the kitchen is actually a repurposed one-room schoolhouse from 1710 that was moved and attached to the house in the early twentieth century. The school bell over the door still works.

The dining room off the kitchen is the perfect size for a table to seat six, with room for a large cabinet against one wall. I don't like the faux-old iron candelabra that hangs above the dining table, but that's fine, because I already own a brass candelabra from the early 1700s that I've never used anywhere.

Obviously, I purchased it many years ago for this very room.

The living room has wide-plank chestnut floors and a huge fireplace, with a beehive oven on the side. Around the corner is a tiny second fireplace, and above it a deacon's cabinet, common to many homes from this period. You kept your brandy in there so that when the preacher paid a visit, you could offer him a nice warm snifter.

The windows are twelve-over-twelve double-hung with their original wavy glass. There are three bedrooms, plus a "craft room" above the dining room. As I click through the pictures, I grow more manic and excited.

Every detail makes me swoon, from the old blacksmith-made iron door latches to the sliding lock on the front door. The house has completely escaped modernization. No overhead lights, no central air-conditioning. I see radiators. I love radiators. Wiley would love radiators.

Two more fireplaces upstairs in two of the bedrooms. A finished attic, lined with cedar. I cannot wait for Christopher to come home so I can show him. When I finally read the description, I nearly swallow my tongue. The house was built in the early 1800s by the founders of the town, the Curtiss family.

It's no relation, of course, but the name immediately conjures my aunt Curtis. Who wore yellow and drove a yellow car and grew yellow roses in her garden.

Two hours later, Christopher walks in the door. As soon as the dogs hear the key they start barking and gleefully jumping around on the bed, waiting for him to come over so they can both jump up on his chest. "Look how tall!" he cries, as he does every single time. They stand on their hind legs and stretch against him.

He tosses his soft leather briefcase on the midcentury black iron garden chair I've never really known what to do with but it looks cool, so. "And how was your day?" he asks, as he changes out of his work clothes and into shorts and a T-shirt.

"Fantastic," I tell him.

"Really?" he says, turning now to look at me, because I usually say "fine."

"Yes. I found our house."

"Uh-oh," he says.

I already have it pulled up in my browser, so I hand my laptop to him.

He begins clicking through the pictures. "Yeah," he says in that perfectly dismissive way he has where that single word —

stretched out — can be a tsunami, wiping everything away. "I'm not really a fan of yellow."

"No, I'm not, either. Look past the yellow. That can be changed. Look at the house."

"I'm looking," he says. "And painting the exterior of a big house is not cheap or easy."

*Oh, and how would you know, Mr. Same Apartment Since 1985?* I want to say, but I need to lead him further in.

"Bunny wallpaper in the kitchen!" he blurts. "Oh my God, that is the worst!"

Wait, there's bunny wallpaper? "Let me see," I say, angling the screen back toward me. "Oh, that's just the backsplash, one strip of wallpaper. Honestly, that will take all of one hour to change. And cost like twenty bucks."

He clicks to the next picture. "God, what a hideous sofa."

"But look at the fireplace behind the sofa. Look at the floorboards upon which the ugly grandma sofa is sitting."

"Yeah, it's a fireplace. And those are floors. I don't get why this house is so special."

He is using Dick Voice. It is rare, but it does happen that Christopher can be a dick. It seems to me that it happens when he is resisting something unfamiliar. (It also hap-

119

pens the entire time he is working, but I write that off as his "agent personality." He's *paid* to be a dick.)

He clicks on an unfortunate picture of a guest room.

"Dolls!" he cries. "Of course there are dolls. Where there are bunnies there are *always* dolls."

I loathe dolls every bit as much as he does, but they don't come with the house. Saying this out loud, however, will not help.

He continues looking at the pictures and says finally, "Well, the barn or garage, that's very beautiful. And the cottage is pretty amazing down by the edge of the river like that. But it's centuries old and people were tiny then — like, shorter than me, so we might have a Cheever-ceiling issue. I mean, it's a *nice* house? But I don't see why you think it's *the* house."

In advertising, it was sometimes helpful to have what we referred to as a "straw dog," which was an ad campaign that was specifically created for the client to hate and kill. It was executed with the utmost care, to include features and elements known in advance to displease them. In the 1990s, building a commercial around a gay couple was a fantastic straw dog, because the client would be incredibly complimentary and polite, always finding numerous points to praise — wanting very much to seem hip and progressive — but there was absolutely no way they were going to run a commercial with a couple of faggots. This campaign was always killed, and the one you wanted to sell them in the first place was the one they bought.

I need a straw dog.

I show him a house I found that is not in Connecticut but upstate New York. It is wildly eccentric, a sort of ski lodge gone mad, perched on a cliff. It is beautifully designed and brilliantly executed, with massive old timbers for joists and a substantial slate roof. It was built in the 1930s and then updated by somebody with good taste and money more recently, because the kitchen is new and very nice.

He loves it. I knew he would. So do I.

How unfortunate that I now must kick him in the kidneys. "The one *point of discussion* with this house is the tax situation." I click on the tax history, and if you were to graph it, it would be a single vertical line. And over the past two years, the annual property taxes have doubled. "If they're twenty-five grand now, what will they be next year? Fifty? Sixty? It's completely out of control."

121

"No New York," he says. "Don't look at anything else in the entire state."

Oh, he doesn't have to worry about that. I'm not looking at anything else in any state, because I've found our home. He just can't quite see it yet.

But he will.

I'll make sure of that.

# CALF'S SNOUT

When I was young and before her psychological decline, my mother made an effort to teach me what she knew about magick in its numerous forms and disciplines. But before this she taught me that the early modern English spelling was preferred to the more common *magic,* to differentiate it from the illusions created for the stage by magicians.

I learned of Enochian magick, which originated in the late 1500s and was revealed over several years by angels to two men: a scientist and adviser to Queen Elizabeth I, John Dee, and an established occultist and spirit medium named Edward Kelley.

She taught me about high magick — or ceremonial magick — a very formalized and structured approach, which is steeped in complex rituals drawn from numerous academic magickal texts. This is the magick of robes, athames, altars, goblets, and wands. Practitioners of high magick are historically well educated and are comfortable deciphering antique esoteric writings.

Then there is low magick, which has historically been practiced by plain "folks," which is why it is also called folk magick. Many witches practice this.

I began practicing a form called chaos magick when I was twenty-five and had recently moved to Manhattan from San Francisco. I'd never heard of it until I found a book on it in a West Village bookstore. Chaos magick is sort of a rebellion magick, an individualized, creative, nonstructured, untraditional practice. I was drawn to it because I had been unwittingly practicing it all my life; I just never knew there was a word for it. It originated in the United Kingdom with the work of Austin Osman Spare, a painter who came to reject Christianity and discovered more esoteric philosophies.

Aleister Crowley was an extremely influential British occultist who founded the Thelemic magickal order. He was a great admirer of Spare's intense, semi-insane illustrative artwork and introduced himself to the artist. In time, though, Spare came to dislike Crowley and began writing about his

124

own personal magickal beliefs. Much of his belief system revolved around the subconscious mind and the power of symbolism, in the form of sigils.

A sigil is sort of a logo that symbolizes that which the magickal practitioner desires. A contemporary British occultist named Peter James Carroll is credited with refining Spare's philosophical ideas, crystallizing them in his seminal 1987 work *Liber Null & Psychonaut*. This is widely considered to be the defining text on chaos magick, and it was the very one I found in the West Village.

It was hugely influential to me partly because it's so very British in tone. I could hear the silky accent in every sentence. This was at a time in my life when I would *absolutely* date *anyone* from anywhere in England and I would not be the one to break up, not ever.

I also liked the concept of compressing a desire or desired outcome into a single concise symbol, or sigil. Like the Nike Swoosh logo. Maybe it's because I was in advertising that this spoke so powerfully to me. The lack of ceremonial accoutrements resonated with me, too. I thought that the paraphernalia associated with high magick — the cloaks and wands and ceremonial knives — were ridiculous and had nothing to do with actual magick. This is something inherent in chaos magick: it's all about the intent. Chaos magick is about making things happen. It's not about pomp and ceremony. It's more utilitarian.

It was also flexible. You could incorporate candle magick or spells of any kind, even high magick ceremony, *if you wanted.* Some people love that stuff, and that's fine. But I'm not one of those people.

When I phoned my mother and told her about chaos magick, she bought the book and read it. "Well, of course this is very much what we have been practicing for hundreds of years." She also liked the word "chaos," because she interpreted it exactly the same way I did: cosmologically. It is from chaos that worlds are born, order is created.

Chaos magick took the ceremonial robe off magick and put it in jeans.

You enter what is called a gnostic state, which is an altered state of mind — however you reach it — and focus intensely and exclusively on only the condensed representation of the desired outcome — the sigil — until it is "charged." Once this happens, chaos magicians "forget" or repress the thought of what it is they desired. The

126

concept here is, our conscious minds mess with us. We are likely to self-sabotage. We are prone to doubt. So immediately, the meaning-loaded sigil is launched into the subconscious, where the magick can occur without interference or hindrance from the pesky conscious mind.

Chaos magick demands that you shape-shift. If what you're doing isn't working, do something else. And if that doesn't work, do something else again. Until something works. The point is to get the work done. It's very pragmatic magick.

Back in 1990, the internet was made out of paper and it was called *The Village Voice*. It had a rich and active classified section, but there was no search function, so you basically had to read everything, manually hunting for that one keyword. And I found it: "chaotes." That's how many practitioners of chaos magick refer to themselves. I was searching for others who had discovered this form of magick and were curious about it. I found a group that was meeting on a Friday night at an apartment on Bank Street. The West Village was mostly four-story brownstones or brick town houses, with a few out-of-place stucco buildings, and this was one of those. It was a dirty pink walk-up. The ad in the *Voice* said to come over any time between nine and midnight, so I split the difference and arrived at ten thirty. I rang the intercom, and the guy on the other end sounded surprised, like he wasn't expecting anybody. I mentioned that I'd seen his ad in the *Voice*. There was a meeting tonight for people interested in chaos magick? He didn't actually say anything, but an instant later the door buzzed and I opened it. I climbed four flights of stairs to find three doors, but one of them was open. I walked in.

"Shut the door behind you," said a disembodied voice. It was so dark, the only light came from the street lamp outside, filtering through a grimy window. And it smelled weird. Like Doritos and unwashed balls. Which, as I passed through the hallway and the kitchen and then entered the main room, suddenly made perfect sense. Because occupying various chairs and sofas were a bunch of "sky-clad" dudes, limp dicks in their hands. Gerald Gardner, the British occultist and father of modern-day Wicca, most likely lifted an Indian phrase that translates to "sky-clad." Naked, wearing only the sky.

These sky-clad guys all had that Radio Shack look about them: thick, D-shaped

glasses, all probably computer program-
mers.

I was in exactly the wrong place. "Yeah, I
made a mistake, sorry," I said as I turned
around to leave. One of the Radio Shack
dudes grabbed my arm. "Hold on. I know
this looks weird and shit, but we're trying
to challenge ourselves. We're trying to break
through our limitations."

I glanced around the room. "Looks like
it's going well," I said.

"We have to try," said a guy from a
scratchy plaid sofa. "Come, join us. It's
about stepping outside who we think we are.
It's about being able to be or do anything."

I said, "Look, I'm not as well versed in
chaos magick as you guys. To be honest, I
really don't know much about *any* kind of
formal magick at all. I mean, this sounded
right, at least on paper." I refrained from
adding, "But you all seem straight and you
have really weird dicks and this is depressing." It occurred to me that I was blindly
thinking I needed to belong to something,
to anything. Why would I need to name
what I am? And why would it be the same
name used by anyone else?

On the way home I thought of something
my mother once told me: "When you're
born with it, you don't have to learn how to

129

use it; you have to learn how *not* to."

What I had learned was not to use it with a bunch of smelly naked dudes in a pink walk-up.

The problem is, Christopher can't really *see* the house, because the current owners have furniture and decorations that distract him and get in the way of his being able to absorb its perfectness. I did get a slight chill when he mentioned the low ceilings, but the place feels so perfect I am willing to live an entirely stooped life.

If he could see the house empty, he would appreciate it. If only he could block the *yellow* and picture it repainted the color it should be and always should have been: black. He needed to visualize our dogs in that house with a new, third dog (one we both now wanted because neighbors in our Battery Park City apartment building had one and she was nearly unbearably sweet: a Great Dane).

As he sleeps, I try to sharpen my focus, to clarify what needs to happen in order for him to see and love the house. Magick fails most often because of a lack of precision in one's vision. You have to know *exactly* what you want.

Writing helps me focus, so this is what I

130

do. I type these words and then as I gently stroke his head while he sleeps, I whisper them into the bones of his soul:

In the night while sleep claims thee
Appears a fox from behind a tree
He eats the bunnies off the walls
He swallows the sofa
And devours the dolls
As he slinks through the house the
    furniture hides
He leaps through a shadow
And he lands outside
A waning crescent is the moon
Tonight
But in three days, new
And out of sight
Through the fox's eyes ye shall see
The house drained of yellow
And as black as the bottom of the sea

I climb out of bed and open the dresser. From the bottom drawer I unwrap a black candle from tissue paper. I choose it because black absorbs everything. It conceals, it hides, it cloaks. Black also makes you look thinner, and if you have black skin and you wear black, you have won visual lotto. Black is awesome.

Black also represents the subconscious mind.

Black is all the colors and none of them.

Using a sewing needle so thin I have trouble holding onto it with my caveman fingers, I carve the spell I wrote along the side of the candle, from bottom to top. *Next time,* I think, *come up with a shorter spell.*

When I finish, I place it in a pewter candlestick, set it on Christopher's bedside table, and light the wick. I work on a writing project (a euphemism for "I scroll through jewelry sites") while the candle burns all the way down, and I blow out the last bit at a little after four in the morning.

I don't mention the house the next day, and neither does he. Nor does he ask me if I've found any more properties. Rather, our life returns to what it had been before we saw the Cheever house: as if we'd never contemplated leaving the city at all.

A couple of nights later we are out with the dogs for their last walk on the esplanade along the Hudson River when Christopher says, "There's no moon."

I say, "There *is,* but it's a new moon, so we can't see it."

"Oh," he says in a tone that suggests he is surprised I know this.

Back inside the apartment, after we both

132

get bottles of seltzer and climb into bed, Christopher suddenly asks, "Do you still have the link to that yellow bunny house? Send it to me."

I feel a smile begin to form, but I don't dare allow it. "Um, yeah, I have that link somewhere, hold on." I sound so casual. But I am so not.

I can hear him clicking through the pictures, and from the corner of my eye I see him raise his laptop really close to his face.

"I had *not* noticed this before," he said.

"What's that?" I asked.

"The sunporch. It's amazing."

"Oh, that was one of my favorite rooms, even though it was clearly added on in, like, the 1940s. It's like being in a treehouse, the way it's built up so high off the sloping lawn."

He continues to click through the slideshow. "And the yard — the *land* — it's insane. It's *so* beautiful."

"Right?" I said.

He clicks a couple more times and then says, "The yellow is horrible, though."

I turn around in bed so that I'm facing him. "I *totally* agree. The first thing we'll have to do is paint it. And you do know what color it should be, right?" I ask him.

"Black," we both say at the same time.

*Now that's more like it.*

"Oh my God," he says. He is looking at a picture of the landing at the top of the stairs. "My brother has the same wallpaper in his house."

"You're kidding."

"No, it's exactly the same pattern. I'm sure of it. I recognize the boy in the hat on the ladder, the girl with the basket holding the branch. It's the same."

It is a toile wallpaper I'd noted before that I didn't hate. What were the chances both sons would end up living in antique houses with exactly the same old wallpaper? If the husband of one of the sons is a witch? One hundred percent.

"You know something," Christopher says, "the more I look at this house, the more I realize it's spectacular. It could be very *us,* you know? I think I was just distracted by all the *crap.* But the house itself —"

I wait. When he says nothing more, I say, "What?"

He slowly turns to face me. "You were right all along. This is it. This is our house."

I smile at him. "It is. It already belongs to us, is the thing. I already see us living in it. I've seen that from the first moment I saw the first picture, even though I hate yellow as much as you do. We already live in the

134

house. We're not at that point in time yet. But it exists."

"We could get a Great Dane," he says excitedly.

"Without a doubt."

He grabs his phone and leaves a voicemail for the real estate agent, ending with, "We would really like to come out and see it. The sooner the better for us."

Christopher would have come around and seen the true nature of the house on his own. My silly bit of candle magick had absolutely nothing to do with it. Maybe.

I suggest we start searching for a Great Dane immediately in case there's a perfect rescue, or a litter is on the way, in which case we could coordinate moving into the new house with the arrival of a puppy. This seems entirely reasonable to Christopher, who immediately begins scouring the internet. He gets a little weepy over the few available rescues in the area, which are all geriatric (meaning age seven for the breed), and most have health problems. "I'd love a rescue, too," I say, "but let's not move a blind, one-hundred-eighty-pound dog with hip dysplasia out to the country with us."

"Yeah, we don't need another broken dog." This is a not even slightly veiled reference to the Bernese mountain dog I got him

135

as a surprise gift years ago, a big, sweet, beautiful animal who needed massive and expensive surgery on both front legs before she even turned eighteen months.

He finds a litter in Ohio with the most adorable puppy. He's brindle, a fairly rare Dane coat, with the temporary name of Remington. I see one of his fawn-colored brothers is Winchester, and while they aren't able to give bolt-action rifle names to the entire large litter, I'm pleased that there's no sister AK-47. They're only a few weeks old, so it will be several more weeks before they will be able to leave the litter.

"I need to grill this breeder to make sure it's not some puppy-mill scam. People are already going to hate that this isn't another adoption."

I nod. "Yeah, do it."

The next day he calls me from the office, a rare occurrence. A note of alarm charges his voice as he shouts, "When did I turn into you?"

"What?" I ask, slightly alarmed myself. Had something gone seriously awry with the candle spell?

"I called the Great Dane owner and it was more like she interviewed me than the other way around, because it turns out she's great and she's not going to place one of her

136

amazing dogs with just anybody. But I guess I passed because I sent her a deposit."

"That's great!" I say. Isn't it? "The timing could work perfectly."

"Uh-huh. *Could.* Except not only do we not own the house, *we haven't even seen it in person.*"

He is correct. But it is a minor point.

"I'm supposed to be the realist," he continues ranting. "*You're* the one who does things like writing real checks for imaginary dogs to go in even more imaginary houses, so when *exactly* did I turn into you?"

If we don't get this house, we will end up living in a studio apartment with three dogs, one of which will be a Great Dane, which could conceivably outweigh each of us and occupy a significant percentage of the square footage.

Except we will get the house. We already have the house.

For somebody who had never even experienced a coincidence in his life before meeting me, Christopher now knew that my seemingly irrational behavior was frequently warranted. "It's like insider trading," he says. "Except supernatural."

"Kind of," I agree.

The first time it happens is about a month

after we become romantically involved. (We'd already been professionally involved — he was my agent — for a decade.) One morning I wake up and tell him, "I had a dream about a red accordion."

He says, "Oh my God, that is so weird because I own a red accordion."

He is completely amazed, but I'm not. I'm like, "Yeah, and?"

To him, it is mind-blowing.

He leaves for work and a half hour later calls me, breathless.

"I just got off the subway, where a guy was going from car to car . . . playing a red accordion. I've seen people playing before, like the blind guy at Grand Central with a button accordion, but I've never seen anybody strolling through the cars with a red Italian one, mother-of-pearl exactly like mine, coming right at me. Spooky."

*Not spooky. Normal.*

"He was playing 'Paint It, Black' and I gave him twenty bucks."

Witchcraft with a touch of Christopher.

The first time we take a road trip, we're in endless Pennsylvania and Christopher is in the fast lane, but the car to our right is keeping even pace. I am staring at the right rear wheel, hypnotized, just watching the design

138

of the hubcap seem to liquefy as the wheel spins.

"What are you thinking?" Christopher asks.

Without turning to face him I reply, "Nothing. I'm staring at that hubcap."

I look over at him as his eyebrows shoot up in alarm. "Holy shit!" he shouts. "Look!"

I turn back and the hubcap has slipped right off the tire and been left behind, still rolling on its own behind the car.

"You made that happen," he says.

Another time we are in bed with our laptops, TCM on and, as always, muted. I am scrolling mindlessly through pages of jewelry on one of my favorite antique websites, and for no reason I ask, "How well did *Rhoda* do in the ratings? And did it win any Emmys?"

Christopher checks IMDb and Wikipedia — because apparently that's too much effort for me to exert myself — and reports, "*Rhoda* actually had huge ratings at first. In fact, the highest *The Mary Tyler Moore Show* ever reached was number seven in the third season. But *Rhoda* was number six in season one. Seven in season two. Then she plunged to thirty-two in season three. But the wedding episode was massive, half of America watched. And yes, she won Emmys, four of them."

I enjoyed knowing all of this. "I like her," I said.

The next day, Valerie Harper announced that she had brain cancer and only three months to live.

"So *that's* why I was asking about her," I say. "She must have been up half the night thinking about her statement today, and somehow I must have heard her."

"I don't understand this," he says.

Something else he doesn't understand but no longer questions is my frequently accurate, fully unaccountable ability to find lost objects. In truth, I'd never known this about myself, but then I've also never been with somebody who lost so many things.

"Damn, my keys?"

And there they are: I can see them resting inside his left shoe in the closet. I tell him, he looks. "Wow, that's amazing!" I hear from the closet, and he reappears, keys in hand.

It doesn't always work. Sometimes I simply guess and this invariably fails. But if I actually *see* the misplaced thing, it always works.

"Can you help me find my sunglasses?"

I stand frozen in place, staring unfocused at the floor. "Ummmmm," I say. Until: "Did

140

you check the inside breast pocket of your blue suit jacket?"

"Oh my God, I forgot I even wore that. Thanks!"

He comes to rely on this unexplainable ability as though it is the most natural and familiar thing in the world, like being tall enough to reach everything on the top shelves in the kitchen — which I am and he is not.

# HAIR OF VENUS

Although she allowed me to watch it, my mother was not a fan of *Bewitched.* "Oh, but *why* do you love this show so much?" she said as soon as she heard the theme song's opening harp flourish.

"I don't know, I just do," I replied flippantly.

But this was a lie. *Bewitched* represented what I felt being a witch *ought* to be, versus what it actually was.

A small color television sat on the laminate kitchen counter in the corner above the dishwasher, right below the double cabinet in which my parents kept the cartons of cigarettes they bought in bulk out of state, where the taxes were lower.

When Endora entered the room in a cloud of purple smoke, I sighed, "I wish *we* could do that!"

My mother absolutely despised being compared to Endora, but she was very much like her in many ways. Even as she explained why we couldn't appear in a puff of smoke, she waved her arm in the air and spoke theatrically. "We've already talked about this. It just doesn't *happen* in the ordinary physical world. We must use things like our feet and cars and airliners."

I wanted to be able to wrinkle my nose and have the dining table instantly and perfectly set for a full Thanksgiving dinner, complete with one of those wicker horns in the center with fruit spilling out, even though I hated fruit and would never eat it except in flattened Roll-Ups form.

How ideal, I thought, to stay home all day and make ugly things in the world vanish, change the color of the car, or turn people into lizards while my loyal and dedicated husband went to his office job and made money. My mother saw Samantha as a bad influence on me, like I was hanging out with Robbie Norwalk, who sniffed model airplane glue and was still in the third grade even though he was about seventeen, had a mullet, and listened to Alice Cooper.

*Bewitched* was not influencing me. I knew I couldn't make a devil's food layer cake appear by blinking at the kitchen counter. I was not happy that I couldn't do this, but I understood that I couldn't. It wasn't like I would watch an episode and then go stare at the back of my brother's head, trying to turn him into a donkey. But if I could have done that, I would have given up TV forever.

The show presented a positive image of witches and witchcraft. Samantha didn't ride a broom (except sidesaddle in the animated opening credits) or have a long, ugly nose with a wart on it. She was perky and blonde. She drove a blue convertible. She wasn't being burned at the stake; she was serving a molded chicken liver and apricot gelatin salad at a dinner party for one of her husband's clients.

Uncle Arthur was the first gay man I'd seen on TV. Even though nobody actually came right out and said he was gay, it wasn't like he was trying to hide it. A gay male witch on TV. If you were black, you could watch black people on TV, but they were going to live in the ghetto and be poor. You couldn't get both black and rich, not until *The Jeffersons,* years later. If you were Hispanic, you had a few commercials (mostly taco shells and coffee). If you were from the Middle East, like Matek, the new kid in my class, you absolutely had to wear a white turban in the desert. And that was about it. So seeing a big queen doing magick on my favorite show was amazing. I never thought Samantha appreciated Uncle Arthur enough, though. That man would have done *anything* for her, and she was always kind of a worrywart killjoy. I would have begged him for diamonds the size of basketballs and little brass cricket boxes from "the Orient" filled with scorpions that I could bring to school and hide in the desks of the kids I hated (all of them).

It occurred to me that if Samantha were the kind of witch who could freeze a room-ful of people in motion, she probably could have cured diseases and lowered gas prices. Such grand gestures on a global scale would have drawn attention to her, though, and eventually she would have been outed. And Samantha Stephens was in the closet. She was my original "don't ask, don't tell," but even still, she had an effortless suburban chic vibe.

Witches had always been portrayed as creepy old ladies with hairy moles in black tattered dresses tossing bat wings and cat heads into boiling cauldrons. Finally, here was a witch who cared about upholstery and interior design in general, not baking little girls and little boys in her ghoulish, grease-stained stone oven. *Bewitched* was the first television evidence — proof — that a witch could go to a grocery store, marry an ad exec with a sharp chin, and not have the world know who or what she really was.

I totally got that I couldn't snap my fingers while standing in the kitchen and end up in the court of Louis XIV of France. But I *could* stand in the kitchen, snap my fingers, and in a week or so meet "entirely by chance" a professor of French history, or one of his descendants would sign up for one of the poetry workshops my mother was beginning to teach.

Most important of all, I saw that I could be a witch and have a kitchen with all the latest and most stylish appliances. Sam had a Frigidaire Flair Custom Imperial range.

I also watched *I Dream of Jeannie.* Though she was a "genie," Jeannie was also pretty much a witch. A bottle witch. And it was the bottle I loved most, specifically the interior. I wanted my bedroom to look identical to Jeannie's bottle: all cushions, tufted fabric walls, and no windows or sunlight. I love the moon, but you can have the sun. Perfection.

Jeannie also depressed me because she was *so desperate* for Tony to love her and approve of her. He was a work-obsessed military man who in retrospect was probably on the spectrum; he would tolerate her, but he would never love her. She just wasn't

146

bright enough to interest him, and Jeannie was either too sheltered or too stupid to know. She was a doormat but a super-happy one.

Starting in the late '50s, witches began being portrayed as perky, their magickal abilities usually used for the procuring of a man or the improvement of his lifestyle. *Bell, Book and Candle,* with Kim Novak, was a movie I watched more than once when it came on late at night. I wanted to like it, but it sucked. Kim Novak was such a bad actress she almost couldn't speak a complete sentence. And why would she have to lose her magickal powers if she fell in love? That part is not only wrong but downright damaging to a young witch's mind.

It was different with Samantha. Darrin didn't want her using her magick, not ever, though she still had it. Hers was more an issue of self-control. And when she used it to his benefit, he forgave her, grudgingly.

I also loved that there were two different Darrins, as if Samantha were displeased with the first one, so she turned him into the second one. The two Darrins were almost the coolest thing about the show, especially because it was never addressed in any way. Neither was the fact that there were two Gladys Kravitzes (an original thin one and a plumper replacement), twin girls as Tabitha (child labor laws), two Louise Tates (unless Darrin's boss got divorced and married a woman with the same first name between seasons), and two Frank Stephenses, Darrin's father (though they didn't line up with the two different Darrins). With its first two seasons in black and white and the rest in color, no other show taught me so many lessons in duality — with bonus points for the household's rampant alcohol consumption. That information came in handy later in life.

By the late '60s society was no longer afraid of witches, because people no longer believed in them. They were already worshipping the newfangled office computers and LED watches. Therefore, TV executives could create sexy witches and mischievous witches, not to mention male witches they called *warlocks,* and put them in front of the nation.

Except it seemed that people secretly *did* believe in witches, which was a little bit spooky and threatening, so the cute witches also had to be made powerless. Even though every rational person knew *witches weren't real,* a primal, tiny voice asked, *Were they?*

# DEAD MAN'S ASH

It is the first thing we notice when we pull into the circular crushed gravel driveway in the Zipcar crapmobile rental: How can you miss it? Standing at least one hundred fifty feet tall, it is almost as high as the Leaning Tower of Pisa. I've never seen such a massive maple tree, and I grew up in Massachusetts, where maple sugar houses are as common as hookers used to be in the meatpacking district of Manhattan back in the '80s. The tree takes me by surprise, because there aren't any pictures of it online, yet it is the centerpiece of the landscape surrounding the house.

The canopy spread is so massive, it is like a storm cloud has settled over the oval front yard, plunging it into shadow, so instead of grass, we are looking at hosta and moss. The tree must be twenty or thirty feet in diameter. This isn't a tree that makes you say "wow" when you see it; it makes you say "holy shit."

Even if you were a nun, I think that's what you would say.

It is undeniably awesome, an impressive beast.

And I hate it.

This feeling is instantaneous, automatic. Like a dog whose hair rises in alarm along his spine when he confronts somebody with a meat cleaver behind his back. This tree's obvious majestic beauty conceals its deeper truth: it will kill us unless I kill it first.

I gaze up the skyscraper height of the tree, and all I can see is how it's at the perfect height and angle to bisect and crush the house when it falls, spearing anyone or anything in its way. *You may be centuries old,* I think, *but I am a witch.* The maple is gorgeous and impressive and historic and Christopher is in awe of it, I can see that on his face.

There is a second tree, equally jaw-dropping and not at all ominous, tucked in a corner right up against the house. Ivy winds up this tree, wrapping all the way around the massive trunk and along the branches toward the top. An old black iron lantern with amber glass is attached at eye level, vines snaking around it, like an illustration from a Grimms' fairy tale.

Then there is the house. It is so spectacular I can't even find words. I manage to say, *"Home."*

"We don't even need to go inside," Christopher says, his eyes traveling the length of it, then down to the cottage by the water — an actual burbling fucking brook. "It's phenomenal. I was so afraid the pictures made it look good, but they can't do it justice."

The property is so beautiful it looks like a park or a WASPy private club that has an unwritten "No Jews, Gays, or Mexicans" policy.

It is seriously landscaped, but it doesn't have flower beds spread with tumbled white marble stones, or in-ground lighting fixtures, or a man-made "water feature." There is no free-form gunite pool — though in addition to the brook, there are two flowing streams that run through the property in the back, merging at the end of a large field, where cattails grow over my head.

"Look at those streams," I say.

"That's called a swale," Christopher replies.

"How do you know that?" I ask.

He shrugs. "I know things."

*Ha!* I think. *Not as many things as I know!* Simply looking around at the mossy old stone walls, the dignified trees, bushes, and flowering shrubs, the lilies and roses and ferns, is overwhelming. It seems like a place a person is not allowed to actually own but can visit after paying a small maintenance fee and promising not to leave behind any litter.

"It's perfect," I say, not even trying to conceal the wonderment in my voice. "When the real estate agent gets here, let's just tell her we want to sign the paperwork now."

We park in front of the barn, which is also a two-car garage with a horse stall overhang where the current owners, an older couple named Harold and Elinor, have firewood stacked.

The maple tree catches my eye again. I project my thoughts at it: *I don't trust you.* I have never experienced personal feelings for a tree before. Feeling mistrustful of foliage seems like the first sign of an oncoming mental illness. I could be turning into my psychotic mother.

I stare at the tree. There is a dark crevasse in the center of its trunk, almost like a sideways, toothless mouth. *Hello,* it seems to grin, *I want to murder you.*

I almost say to Christopher, "Does that tree look like it's going to fall over onto the house?" but I don't, because he will only remind me of the time I was obsessing about the roof pool caving in and crashing through our apartment when we didn't actually *have* a roof pool.

A car pulls into the driveway, and a well-dressed woman with hair like Kathleen Turner's in *Body Heat* steps out. This is Maura, the Realtor. We are all about the same age. Christopher introduces himself and then says, "This is my husband, Augusten."

Maura gives me a huge smile and shakes my hand. "Yes, I know."

Initially I find it an odd response, but then I figure that since Christopher gave his name when he contacted her, she'd googled him and found me. But I ask her if this is what happened and she drops my hand like I am trying to give her a turd.

"Gross! No! I would never do that. Google a potential client? That's disgusting!" She is animated and hilarious. "No," she says, and gives me a direct look. *"I know you."*

It feels like she's telling me more than "I've read your books," but she moves on, smooth and professional.

"Isn't that tree amazing?" she says.

"Yes!" I lie.

I expect she is looking at the devil maple, but instead she is gesturing toward the massive ivy-covered one up against the house. "It's a prize-winning honey locust and it's probably two hundred years old."

I feel a wave of envy of Maura, because I am not so friendly and outgoing. I am reserved and standoffish, which makes me come across as superior. I don't consider myself to be, but I look and act as if I do, and knowing this about myself only intensifies the behavior. I've always been socially awkward. Autism runs in the family like detached earlobes. I obviously got sprinkled with enough of it to make me come across as a horrible snob. I wish there were more opportunities to turn this to my advantage, but so far, no luck.

We stand on the driveway talking for nearly fifteen minutes, which is semi-torture because I hate standing in one place. Finally, sunglasses parked atop her head, she says, "Let's go inside. It's unbelievable and very special, as you shall see." There is a formality to the way she speaks that is at odds with her engaging manner, and the combination is fascinating.

As we start toward the house, Maura rummages through her large black shoulder bag for her phone. She scrolls through photos, finds something, and smiles. "Here, I have to show you this."

It is a photograph of me, standing next to a very pretty young woman in a place I instantly recognize: the Atlanta campus of the Savannah College of Art and Design, where I have taught. "That's my daughter," she said. "She met you when you came to her school. She texted me this picture the other day."

"Wow," Christopher said, "that's kind of weird and amazing."

Maura smiles like it is no surprise at all. So she *had* been expecting me all along.

Maura, I sense, comes with the house and could possibly be its best feature.

It has been on the market for over a year. Harold and Elinor already have several other homes, so they never used this year-round, and they have recently purchased a cattle ranch, complete with several hundred head of cattle, all of which are mooing for their time and attention. (I find it bewildering that a cattle ranch was at the top of Harold's bucket list. Who retires so they can slaughter huge numbers of one-ton farm animals?) In any case, at this point they are in a hurry to unload the yellow house. The negotiation is fast, the price is at a "please don't wake me from this dream" level, and we have an estimated closing date about a month away.

Which is when the Great Dane puppy Christopher has located will be ready for delivery from Ohio (a town less than fifty miles from one of Harold and Elinor's other homes).

It is like a real estate hallucination. This beautiful house is so old there are hatchet marks in the timber joists in the basement. Hands made this place, not machines. Hands and tools that didn't plug in.

Thick plaster walls, inch-thick chestnut floors, leaded-glass windows wrinkled with time, softly violet because of the lead. Rooms and more rooms, and bookcases built into corners, hidden inside closets, a secret back stairway, pull cords instead of light switches, everything formed and made by hands belonging to people who belonged to their lives: us but not us.

And the land: rolling green grassy hills and stone walls, weeping willows, pines as tall as office buildings, apple trees, flowing water, a chunk of raw topaz the size of a softball by the side of the river.

A perfect little cottage right at the water's edge.

Rosebushes, wild raspberries, bees.

The stars at night.

The moon.

156

Sometimes you just know.
We knew.

SCORPION'S TAIL
==

I was seventeen and had no interest in boa
constrictors, alligators, guinea pigs, or tropi-
cal fish. Yet each Saturday, I found myself at
a store called Exotic Pets and More. It was
the "and more" that I was interested in.

He was the clerk, and nearly old enough
to be my father, maybe thirty. He had thick,
dark brown hair, hit with gold at the ends,
and he wore it swept back from his face.
His arms were muscular, his body stocky.
He never smiled. Somehow, the fact that he
never smiled made him sexier. He was serious because there was a live alligator in the
store. There was a nineteen-foot-long boa
constrictor twelve paces from the cash
register. Of course he never smiled. A joke
here or a prank there could mean being
swallowed whole. This was rural Massachusetts, so rural that there wasn't even
any neon in the area, yet there existed this
exotic pet store, staffed by this exotic male,

more masculine and capable than any man I'd ever seen.

Every Saturday, I rode my bike or took the bus to the store in Hadley and I pretended to be fascinated by the fish. I spent hours apparently gazing into the glass at the colorful creatures when I was, in fact, staring nonblinking at his reflection in the aquarium glass.

When he stepped into the "reptile room," I always followed. The light was different there, ultraviolet and unnatural, and the temperature was noticeably warmer.

My hope was that he would talk to me. Someday he was going to say, "Can I help you?" or, at the very least, "So, you're interested in snakes, are you?"

And things would carry on from there.

But he never said this or anything else to me. He merely went about performing his tasks: feeding the fish, cleaning the aquariums of the giant bullfrogs, adding fresh cedar chips to the rodent cages.

Sometimes a true customer would enter the store, not a predator like me. He would give them what they needed, often expertly netting a tiny fish from a tank and depositing it into a plastic bag filled with water and knotting the top. Other times, he'd simply point the person in the right direction.

What kind of a man would work in a store like this? I wondered. Certainly he could have worked at a fast-food restaurant, or been a bartender, or sold record albums. He could have gone to college, perhaps even earned a graduate degree, become a doctor. He could have fixed sports cars, predicted the weather on the radio, or been the man to replace the heel of your shoe. But no. He worked in a tiny store in New England selling creatures that had no business being this far north of the equator.

What was his deal?

He was the first truly mysterious man I'd ever encountered. Up to this point, the ones I'd met or seen or had crushes on had been, somehow, quantifiable. There was the clerk at the twenty-four-hour food mart: an obvious student. The guidance counselor at school: an authority figure. This man was an enigma. His face was deeply tanned, and not from the same sun that I knew.

One Saturday, I decided I had to know more. Or, rather, I had to know *something*. I had to engage him in conversation. It was clear that he was content leaving me alone. If I was ever going to get him to fall in love with me, I had to impress him with my love of nature and thirst for knowledge. I would go to the store and I would say, "Can you tell me something? Do boa constrictors have teeth?"

When I opened the door, a young woman was behind the counter. I approached her and said, "Hi. Um, the guy? Who works here. Is he around?"

"Paul?" she said. "No, I'm sorry, he's not. He's gone back home."

"Was he sick or something?"

She smiled. "No, I mean he *moved* back home. He was only here for the summer."

I felt tricked. "Oh. Wow," I said. "Because I was going to ask him something. Where does he live?"

She looked at me curiously. Why was I asking this? She said, "I'm not sure. I didn't know him that well." Then, "But maybe there's something I can help you with?"

"No, thanks," I said and left the store.

I stood outside and looked across the parking lot, at the vast cornfields beyond. There were hundreds of acres, yet they seemed so small. This was the only geography I had ever known, and I realized I knew nothing. Nothing at all of the world. I had seen the Atlantic Ocean but not the Pacific. Not the Indian Ocean. Never a glacier, or a desert or a true mountain. I'd never seen a monkey that wasn't on television and dressed in a plaid jumpsuit. There were

161

colors and aromas I couldn't even imagine. People in India wore dots on their forehead. I knew this. But why?

I was minuscule.

And he was gone.

These two facts seemed related. As I stood there in front of the store, looking at my bike leaning against the side of the building, I felt a profound sense of loss. He was gone and this had changed my life. Or, rather, my life would now *not* change because he was gone. Before, every Saturday there was the possibility that he might say something to me. That he might be wondering about me the same way I was wondering about him. That eventually he might speak, and I would recognize in his voice something familiar in my cells. And he would recognize the same thing.

True: probably not. Also true: possibly.

And possibility was my fuel. It was the One Thing that prevented me from slitting my wrists on any given horrid day. The fact that at any moment, everything could change. As easily as you could be hit by a car, so you could be carried away by one.

Now there was one less possibility in my life, and I felt the loss of it. I went home and I carried him with me in my head, and I itched on my insides, madly, because I

162

would never know any more about him than I knew at that moment: nothing. I had made a huge mistake. I had not taken that risk and spoken to him first. I had been afraid and then let myself be invisible because of my fear.

From then on, I would take every risk. In fact, I would hunt them down. I would find the thing with the sharpest edges, the longest teeth, the thing that scared me the most. And I would chase it, and even though I would be afraid, I would catch it. In this way Paul, the guy from Exotic Pets and More, did take me away with him, change my life, make my world blow up to a thousand times its size.

I thank him for it.

Sometimes the most powerful thing a witch can do is . . . nothing. Not try to seize control. Not insist on leading. But rather, listen, follow, allow.

It's what my aunt Curtis called Making Allowances for the Universe.

"Witchcraft is the most natural thing in the world," my mother said, on one of the many afternoons when she painted and I watched and listened. "And I mean that quite literally. To be a witch is to possess a keen and unique sensitivity to the natural world. Not merely the top layer that every-

163

one can see and understand, but those layers beneath, where the machinery that drives the universe resides."

I never liked maps. Folded up, they were the size of dinner napkins, but unfolded, a map had the surface area of a dining room table. In the car, often your choice was either stop and open it or keep it folded and look through the windshield; you couldn't do both at the same time. Maps were infernal, unholy things but not just because they were unwieldy. What I hated was that they decreased the possibility of a wrong turn. Maps reduced chance. They put you in control, and that felt dangerous.

When my dog, Brutus, who had been a gift from Uncle Mercer, ran away from home, my mother's friend Helen said she would drive me around so I could place photocopied Lost Dog flyers in local mailboxes.

Helen was surprised that I did not want to use a map. "We can be much more organized and plot out where we need to go," she said.

But I was determined. "No, maps won't help us," I insisted. "If we're going to find him, it'll be because we made a mistake, not because we made a plan."

Helen was pretty easygoing, and after all, it was my dog that was lost, so she shrugged, climbed behind the wheel, and said, "Okay, where to?"

My methodology was to slide a flyer into all the mailboxes on our street, then turn right at the end of the street and put flyers inside those mailboxes, too.

"Now what?" Helen said when we'd reached the end of the street. We faced a fork in the road. "Right or left?"

I said, "Turn right," but as soon as she did I changed my mind. "No, left."

She braked and swung the car around. We placed more flyers in more mailboxes, made more right turns, then more left turns. By meandering aimlessly we'd managed to reduce my stack of a hundred flyers to only a dozen.

We were probably five or six miles from my house, and traveling along a road that was unfamiliar to me. As we passed a large rock in front of a wooded area, I felt a peculiar certainty: *Brutus has seen that rock.*

I said to Helen, "Make the next right. We need to get over there," and I pointed to the woods on my side of the car.

We came across a narrow dirt road on the right. As we bumped along, I wondered if this might be one of those service roads that ran near power lines and rivers with no houses at all. But eventually we came across a mailbox, black. The driveway went way back into the woods, and I couldn't see any house. But there must be one, I figured, so I opened the door and slid a flyer in. Helen continued down the road and after five minutes we came across another mailbox. Once more, I could see no house, only a long driveway. I slid a flyer in the box. We continued down this odd little unpaved road, placing flyers into mailboxes until I had none left. This bothered me, because I knew there had to be more houses.

"Well, we handed out a whole bunch of them, so at least that's something," I said to Helen.

She drove me home.

That evening the phone rang and my mother picked up. A woman had received one of my flyers, and she was almost positive that her next-door neighbor had found my dog. "He's been living there with them for two days. He's been eating leftover Thanksgiving turkey." She told my mother, "They didn't get a flyer, but we brought ours over and showed her the picture. We think it's your dog."

It was. He was at the very end of that little dirt road. The next-door neighbors had received my last flyer.

While Brutus slept on the shag carpet under the coffee table — a favorite spot — and my father sat at the kitchen table grading student papers for the philosophy class he taught at the University of Massachusetts, Amherst, my mother sat beside me on the sofa. "So, what do you believe brought Brutus home? Many people would say you were very lucky."

"It wasn't luck," I told her.

"No?" She lit one of her slender brown More cigarettes. "Why not?"

"Because I didn't hope. I knew. I knew we could find him. Or it was like a command that instantly turned into a fact — we would find him, there was no question. And I even had this funny feeling when we ran out of flyers."

She looked at me pointedly.

"Helen wanted to use a map. But" — my mother, who shared my contempt for maps, shook her head and frowned — "I told her, 'No maps.' Instead, I guided us. Very random."

"Yet exceedingly specific," she said, glancing at Brutus sleeping soundly.

"Yes. To within a couple hundred feet."

"Well done," my mother said.

# DEVIL'S EYE

These are our last weeks in Manhattan. I ought to enjoy them. Closing on a house takes time. There is an endless course of bank paperwork, which, Praise Our Lady Jesus, Christopher is handling; home inspections are scheduled, closing dates set, movers booked. There are boxes to be packed, and a Great Dane to be picked up from the airport. I am anxious. I want him here, now. I want everything packed, with the movers driving it away.

It is at times like this that I feel impatience as an actual disease.

I am emailing my friend Kevin about snapping turtles. He owns a house in upstate New York that abuts a nature preserve. In the past he's sent me pictures of deer and bears in his yard, but he lives across the street from a wide stream, so I have to ask about snapping turtles. All he says is, "I think they bite and don't let go — you gotta be careful and look out for them." Even I know that. Somebody already told me they can bite a trash can lid in half. Beavers, too. Beavers are made by Satan to anally penetrate your dreams. I have watched every video on YouTube about beaver attacks, and I have no shame admitting that I wish it were not only legal but required to kill all beavers on earth. I am a very bad witch. A witch is by definition one with nature. But *you* watch those videos and tell me if you wouldn't feel safer if all beavers were coats.

I can't get freaked about nature, because I'm going be surrounded by it. This town doesn't even have a . . . town. There's a Stop & Shop and some gas stations, but it's no Westport. I'm kind of getting the feeling that it's a Connecticut hillbilly town, yet I am so excited that I can't stand it. I feel like I'm seven years old again, ripping the doors open on my mother's Advent calendar one after the next to speed the arrival of Christmas.

I watch a thrilling video that has gone viral of a woman in China being swallowed whole by an escalator at a mall. As she reaches the top, a metal panel gives way and her legs plunge down. She is carrying a toddler and manages to hand him off to onlookers at the moment she begins being swallowed, exactly like in *Jaws.* It is quite shocking, so I watch it several times.

I am so neurologically malformed that I find this video a delightful respite from the tedium of waiting. It is like a light snowfall in the middle of the hottest summer day. I feed off atrocious news stories the way most people today consume kale. Nutrition comes from abductions, electrocutions, capsized boats, and freeway pileups. I can't blame it on New York, either, because I've always been this way. I don't want to cause these awful things to happen, so *technically* I'm not a monster, but I sure do enjoy watching. It takes extreme horror for me to feel better about my own life. Which, now that I think about it, is what people are always telling me that I do for them, so screw it.

The video is also relatable, because if we'd bought John Cheever's house several months ago, that woman on the escalator would be us. We would both by now have tetanus and casts. I honestly don't know if we would have a roof yet. We could be living with dirt floors. We definitely wouldn't have rewired the house. An electrician our friends had recommended to inspect it told us that millions of people live with old cloth-wrapped wiring, and that if we didn't touch it, we could probably keep using it. I asked, "What happens if we touch it?" — knowing I would be compelled to touch the cloth-covered wires wherever and whenever I encountered them.

"They'll crumble, and that could start a fire."

It's possible — likely, even — we would be in the burn ward of a hospital in Ossining, if the town even has one. It must be said: I'm pleased not to be living in Ossining. I thought that the downtown area was awful, with all the charm of a solitary brick and with insanely high taxes. All for the privilege of living near a prison that *doesn't even have their electric chair anymore?* If we're going to remain a nation that administers capital punishment, we owe it to ourselves and the offender to provide *capital* in the sense of *excellent* punishment. And nothing says excellence like a rickety old chair wired with cables and electrodes.

Of course the closing is pushed back a month, so we will be housebreaking a Great Dane puppy in the city. And by we I mean Christopher will be housebreaking a Great Dane puppy in the city.

We pick him up one morning from LaGuardia. The baggage claim area pages

171

Christopher, and we slip through a shiny silver door off to the side of the conveyer belt. The woman at the desk presents him with a flourish of her hands, as if we've just won him, which actually feels quite accurate.

"Here's your baby." She opens the door to his crate, but he doesn't come out. She leans forward to make sure he's even in there and says, "Aww, he's shy."

We are finally able to coax his head out — inch by gentle inch — and when he believes we won't eat him, the rest comes tumbling out at once, all heavy bones and steak-sized feet. I had been expecting a mess inside the cage: feces smashed on all sides, his coat drenched in urine and vomit. But the interior of the crate is spotless, and he smells like he has been massaged with sandalwood oil.

We carry him outside to the single patch of grass beside the cement parking structure, where he proceeds to recline. I say, "You have to get up and pee," and miraculously, he stands and wobbles around like he'd been drinking on the flight, then he squats down and pees. We have named him Otis, and this is the perfect time to start using it. "Good boy, Otis, you are such a good Otis boy for peeing."

Christopher and I are stunned to have a dog do exactly what we want. And on his first day in New York City, at only nine small weeks, outside baggage claim at one of the world's busiest international airports. Already he is better trained than our other two dogs. Put together.

I hold him on my lap in the car and I would testify under oath: that dog grows heavier by the mile. He physically develops in my arms between the airport and the Upper West Side.

Once we reach Christopher's apartment, I text my friend Suzanne that he is the biggest puppy in the litter, and she replies, "Of course he is. That's so alcoholic. Make mine a double!"

This is painfully true.

Christopher and I decided that I would stay downtown with Wiley and Radar and he will be uptown with Otis, both to housebreak him and to give him a chance to be a spoiled only child for a little while.

Even though I am several miles away and Christopher is doing the actual work with the puppy, I am in a state of constant housebreaking stress. *Does he pee on the carpet? He's not wetting the bed at night, is he?* When Christopher tells me about Otis having an accident in the elevator, I yell, "This is a nightmare!" and with something approaching Dick Voice, he replies, "A nightmare for . . . ?"

I know that under the best, lowest-stress circumstances I am an absolute horror to live with, a halogen-illuminated fountain of anxiety, control, and catastrophe. Mental health would be nice, but there's not time for that, so I do the next best thing: on a walk along the Hudson to loosen the phlegm in my chest, I stop at a deli and pick up a sack of twelve oversized butter cookies with multicolored sprinkles.

Manhattan isn't cool anymore, I tell myself back at the apartment, cookie crumbs in my chest hair. All the coolness has been caught in the folds of Brooklyn, where it's now competitively cool and youthful. Due to my age and physical imperfections, I have to live in Connecticut, where the state motto could be, "As long as you don't mind Lyme disease, we'll have you!"

We have purchased a mystery. Even witchcraft can't tell me what will happen. Years from now, in retrospect, will I have improved our lives? Or destroyed them?

Leaving Manhattan, I feel a sense of melancholy blended with excitement and tinged with disbelief. Nobody actually *leaves* New York City; they fight and compete to get *in*. It turns out that I will not drop dead on one of its streets or in a coffin-sized apartment, but that I'll quite possibly drown in a river in my own backyard or perhaps be the victim of a home invasion.

We've all been staying uptown at Christopher's. Before the downtown apartment can be listed with a real estate agency, repairs must be made, and it is to be repainted a neutral beige, the floors sanded and refinished.

I am tasked with going downtown to throw away the things I'm not taking. Honestly, I could just as easily walk away and leave them burning behind me, as I am wont to do, but the movers are doing all my packing and I don't need them boxing up my dental floss and ratty old dish towels. When you hire professional movers to pack, they pack everything, even the trash. If you leave a plate of buttered toast on the windowsill, expect to open a box three weeks later and find that toast and that plate wrapped up together in thick gray paper. I learned this life lesson the hard way many years ago.

I'll turn fifty shortly after the move. I did

not freak out when I turned twenty-five or thirty. Even forty didn't seem like much of anything. But fifty is different. Not because it's a major number, but I feel like this is the year my body has turned against me. Every Lay's potato chip remains with me permanently, part of an ever-expanding tube of fat around my waist. One morning for no reason my right knee begins to hurt. It is so cliché. I'm not even a runner, I'm a sitter. As I'm googling "knee cancer," I notice age spots on the backs of my hands. This is ridiculous — all these awful blinking neon signs of oldness suddenly upon me, like I've left the windows open and they all flew in and settled on me overnight.

My next search term, "best spiked dog collar," brings up a lot of items for humans before I find the canine section.

"What's that for?" Christopher asks, side-eyeing my screen.

"They're mostly used to protect against coyote attacks, but I want some for Wiley in case Otis lunges with his toaster-oven mouth and clamps down on Wiley's tooth-pick neck."

I have become a source of stress for Christopher.

"Am I driving you crazy?" I ask.

"Little bit," he replies.

It is the omission of the article "a" that makes me ask, "What does that mean, 'little bit'?"

He says he is worried about the move, about closing on time, and about money, and he doesn't need to add the worry that one of our dogs is going to kill another.

I know my anxiety is based on neurosis and has no basis in reality, but it's a runaway freight train of stress and dread and I cannot stop it.

When I tell him this, he says only one word, "Buspar," which is the anti-anxiety medication his friend told him recently she uses to calm her dread of absolutely everything. This remark only coats my misery with annoyance.

Instead, I realize I must accept the possibility of Wiley's death in advance of its actually happening so that I can function. I have to let him go. It is a recurring pattern in my life. I am always letting things go, whether friendships or the basic maintenance of an apartment; I cannot count the number of times I have started over from scratch. Wiley's death fits — perfectly — my longtime cycle of dysfunctional behavior.

I finally tell Christopher, "This is worse than being in rehab."

I don't think that comment goes over so well.

I know he thinks I am being sarcastic and an asshole, but only half of that is true: I wasn't being sarcastic. I'm trapped inside a box of fear, and no matter how I claw at the walls, I can't climb up and out. The only thing I can do is watch seven seasons of *Kitchen Nightmares,* one episode after the next. I just have to get through this day. If I remind myself that there's another day tomorrow, I experience a sinking sensation in my chest and a pulsing pain in the back of my head.

I go through this again and again; the play is the same, but the cast changes. It's all about me being terrified and anxious because some terrible thing is inevitable. Impending doom is perfectly logical. When I'm locked inside this moment, the feeling appears so cloaked in truth and rationality that a switch engages inside my head that says, *You've been this way before . . . but this time it's real, and it's serious.*

Surely I will look back on this period as an insane, dysfunctional interim. I might even joke about how crazy I "was" and tell Christopher, "Next time I'm like that, punch me in the face." I don't understand how to pull back and allow things to happen, allow the dogs to "be dogs." It's like I have a horror obsession, terror running on a loop that I hate but I can't get enough of it.

So many wonderful things are about to happen to us — my God, we're moving to a stunning vintage home and we have a floppy Great Dane puppy! — and my reaction is to be stricken with insurmountable anxiety, immobilized by fear, clutching at every close call, checking the margin of error between Wiley's fragile throat and Otis's maw. It's as if I enjoy this, except I don't. But it buzzes when I realize that this is happening on the cusp of wonderfulness.

That knowledge seems diagnostic.

Something has engaged within me, and I believe that thing is love. It has replaced the fear.

The way Otis gallops toward me and, because he lacks the ability to brake, crashes into me and buries his face in my chest, is magnificent. His sweet, expressive eyes and high cheekbones, his black snout and sailboat ears — the entire package of him is irresistible.

This afternoon I lay on the couch with him on his back between my legs and across my stomach and chest. He fell asleep instantly, so heavily, his great paws bending over and flipping at the joints, his rear legs curled forward. He compresses his body into a space that is much smaller than you could imagine, given his mass.

Yes, this is the falling-in-love stage, which gives me a new window to peer through: I can train him not to eat Wiley by communicating with him directly. He listens.

In the elevator I am holding him across my shoulder like a chimpanzee and he is licking my ear, the side of my head. He nibbles my earlobe and I say, "Ow." I don't say it loud, because it wasn't hard, but he stops and draws his head back. He looks kind of stunned, like he's bitten down on a bumblebee.

I find his switch. If I press the back of his neck with my fingertips, he falls asleep almost instantly, even if he's sitting up, in which case his front feet will begin to slide forward until he kind of topples over to one side and lands on the floor, which will then wake him up again.

For reasons Christopher and I and the laws of geometry cannot explain, the bed is less crowded at night with three dogs instead of two. Even though Otis occupies the most room, he's able to contort his form to whatever space is available. Last night he slept on his back at the foot, with his gigantic legs splayed, beneath one of which Wiley was curled into a ball. His top half was twisted around, and his head came to rest on Christopher's thigh. It seemed an impossible position for any living creature to assume, yet there he was.

In the morning I leave for downtown trash day. As I enter my soon-to-be ex-apartment, I'm struck by how amazing the place smells. It's filthy, but my significant inventories of witch herbs and candles have been blossoming into a confusing but lovely herbal aroma.

I have drawers upon drawers of colored tapered candles: green ones in case I need to perform a candle spell to increase the cash flow, black ones so that I can banish negative energies. There is also an apothecary of herbs that have been used by witches for hundreds of years. Some of them, like rosemary and sage, everybody has in their cabinets. Others are toxic. I have small glass bottles with cork tops filled with cemetery dirt, tree bark, thorns. There is a vial of Van Van oil from New Orleans with tiny bits of pyrite at the bottom.

None of these things in and of themselves cause magick to happen. Rather, they all make the process entertaining, they look cool, and they amplify focus. For example, in candle magick, you might write an inscription up the length of the candle, exactly as I did with Christopher when he was unable to "see" the house clearly for what it was. It could be a spell to attract romance to your life. The act of carving the words into the wax clarifies what it is you seek. The magick occurs in my mind; the carving and burning of the candle only serves to underscore, to magnify my intent. A witch requires nothing man-made to generate magickal phenomena. These extra components can just be nice to have. And they smell good.

Because I am me, I am throwing things away and then adding the same items to my clinically obese online shopping cart. I'm dumping the dregs of all the herbs and spices, but Christopher doesn't want to order more yet. "We had too many, so let's wait and buy what we need once we're there. There was a jar of cream of tartar that was old enough to vote."

I try to be a good recycler, which means I put all the little jars into one plastic bag (which itself will never decompose), and all the powders into another for trash (doubling my landfill footprint). Walking down the hallway with a huge sack of empty bottles all clanking musically against one another, I feel like a rogue reindeer, an anti-Christmas messenger only briefly landing to drop off my North Pole trash.

Back inside my apartment, the bag with the loose spices splits open as I hoist it. What seems like ten pounds of curry powder, turmeric, coriander, and fenugreek comes billowing out in an actual cloud. Now the apartment smells like I kidnapped a young girl from India and have been forcing her to cook in institutional quantity.

QVC is on in the background, a soundtrack compounding my frenzied mood of EVERYTHING MUST GO, EVERYTHING NEW MUST COME.

What must the neighbors think of us, the two weird old guys at the very end of the hall?

Like during the period when we binge-watched *Call the Midwife,* where on every episode at least one woman (usually several) undergoes primitive childbirth, so there is lots of screaming and crying and shrieking. Which, if you don't have the visuals, could be misconstrued as porn.

So we are the fags at the end of the hallway watching straight gang-bang porn nonstop.

Almost nothing, though, tops the Vanessa Williams Incident.

I don't even remember the point I was trying to make about her, but it required that I play "Colors of the Wind," her Disney anthem, on my laptop at full volume at three in the morning. The song ended, and there was polite yet firm knocking from the neighbor on the other side of the wall.

Christopher, who regularly travels to Brooklyn to see cool bands and does not care that he is the oldest guy in the place by decades, was beyond horrified. "We have to move," he said flatly, not knowing that in a few short months, that was exactly what we would be doing.

After six hours of purging, and then packing the things I don't want the movers to touch, I am ready to leave this apartment in Battery Park City. We have been informed by our real estate agent (a glamorous friend of Christopher's, an actress he made friends with at a dog park, like in a *New Yorker* short story) that once it has been painted, spit-shined, and staged, it should sell within a week.

I take one last look around. We laughed so hard here. We had so much sex here. We lived so much life here. We began here.

But we will expand *there.*

I need the apartment to sell immediately. As I stand by the front door, goose bumps rise on my arms. A sensation of momentum starts running through my body, energies gathering, almost like orgasm. "Sold," I say, and instantly I am drained of the energy. I know as I close the door and lock it that the apartment will sell the moment it is listed.

With a nylon shoulder bag filled with diamonds, rubies, emeralds, witchy herbs and spices, an antique magick wand, all my necklaces, rings, and pendants, I hail my last cab. "Seventy-Ninth and Amsterdam," I tell the driver one final time.

Tonight is the end of our Manhattan. At eight tomorrow morning we drive to Connecticut. Christopher will drop me and the dogs off at the house while he goes to the lawyer's office for the closing.

We order our last pizza. It is merely *okay.*

We sleep fitfully.

In the morning our eyes sting.

# EAR OF LAMB

While Christopher is at the closing, I am at the house with the dogs, all of whom are sleeping. The puppy is so perfectly behaved, not peeing once indoors. Earlier, he walked over to the kitchen door and sat. I put his leash on and led him outside, where he took four steps and then peed.

A breeze is flowing through the rooms, the thick old plaster walls are cool to the touch, and the house itself is tucked beneath its own tree-formed umbrella of shade. Sunlight floods the field and across the brook, where it lands dappled by the trees on the pine needle–covered earth. It's so beautiful and soothing that I'm not sure what to do, so I do nothing but sit and then sit some more. The concentric circles of dread and anxiety and fear in which I usually find myself trapped are gone. Instead there are trees — also sky and light, and a sound I have to think about before I can identify it: silence.

If we had rented this place for a week and I saw this view, I would want to come back every year. Except we own it. I think we own it. *Do we own it?*

At that moment Christopher sends me a text from the lawyer's office: "We own it."

An hour later he arrives with bags of groceries and an emergency set of Jaclyn Smith sheets, which we can place on the mattress Harold and Elinor left behind for us. Harold and Elinor show up, too, right after Christopher. The huge moving van Harold has rented and packed and will drive himself is still in what is now our driveway.

Christopher pulls me aside and says, "Guess what Maura told me? Earlier in the year, the house was under contract and the deal fell through. Harold and Elinor were really upset and angry, and then one day Elinor called Maura and said she'd had, like, a vision. That a gay couple from Manhattan would be the buyers and they just needed to wait for them to materialize."

"No way."

"Uh-huh. So when I left a voicemail, Maura told Elinor, 'I found them,' and everything fell into place."

By my reckoning, Elinor's "vision" probably happened right around the time I started pushing Christopher out of the city with my mind. She and I had apparently been communicating in the ether. Her message was strong enough that I started my work in earnest, so maybe there was some witchiness to Elinor that she would leave behind.

We do a final walk-through with them, Harold explaining how to clean the boiler while Elinor gives us the lowdown on the neighbors. "There are only a couple houses within shouting distance, but whatever you do, don't shout at that one," she says, gesturing toward the back to a charming red Colonial across the brook and past a wooded area. "She's a retired opera singer, and if you let her start talking, she will never stop. I don't mean a conversation, I mean *talk*. Do not engage her!" Her fervency seems unwarranted.

Christopher laughs. "One of the reasons I'm thrilled to leave the city is that I had to have my neighbor across the hall arrested for harassment. He's one of the world's worst humans, so I don't think an opera singer should be a problem."

Elinor fixes him with a pointed stare and says, "No matter what, never invite her inside."

"Wow." His laugh isn't so strong now.

"That is the exact warning they give about Dracula and the Devil."

Elinor's eyes widen and she nods. "Anyway!" she chirps, back to her normal upbeat self. "We hope you have a wonderful life here."

Harold shakes our hands vigorously. "I've got lots of instructions and notes and labels everywhere, you'll see. And we left some other things for you, beyond what contracts say. We know how it is, being young and starting off."

They climb into their van, and as they're about to pull out of the driveway, Elinor sticks her head out the window, points to the woods, and shouts, "And remember, avoid her like the plague!"

I want to yell back, "Don't worry. We *are* the plague!"

They left quite a bit behind for us, we discover. Though we can only be considered "young" in comparison to the age of the house itself.

Later, Christopher ran around outside on the grass with the dogs, and now he's making porterhouse steaks on the cruddy old propane grill outside. I hear the screen door open and then smack closed, sounding exactly like a screen door ought to, and then he's in the kitchen, fussing with the oven

189

for baked potatoes. "Our first purchase is going to be a Weber," he mutters.

I'm sitting in the glass sunroom watching the sky fade to a faint blue. A small single-prop plane buzzes by over the trees, the first I've seen or even heard. For an instant I feel the machinery of worry kick in: *How low do they fly?*

After we bought the house, we studied it on Google Maps and saw that it was very close to a small airport.

"Great," I said. "It's going to be American Airlines Flight 587 all over again."

Christopher is not a connoisseur of plane crashes, so this flight number meant nothing to him. My friend Suzanne would have gotten it; she is the only other person I know who possesses encyclopedic knowledge of airplane disasters. In fact, she has the flight numbers committed to memory, whereas I have to look them up. "2001, remember?" I tell him, panic rising. "It crashed shortly after takeoff and everybody thought it was 9/11 all over again."

"Yeah," he says in the tone of voice he uses to neutralize me, "this is a little airport in the country. I don't think a passenger jet will hit our house."

He is right, of course. Plus, if a little plane *had* ever crashed on the property, surely

190

there would be a scar, a pit, on the land, and there is none. Suddenly it seems *fantastic* to live near a small airport. One of my best friends is a pilot with his own plane: he could visit constantly!

Christopher will leave in the morning and return to New York to meet the movers, who will load the contents of both our apartments Monday and then deliver everything Tuesday. This seems impossible to me, but they're a national moving company and presumably they do this trick all the time. Tomorrow is Sunday, and Christopher will be having dinner with one of his oldest and best friends, Billy. They've known each other for thirty years. All of this is wonderful, except for the part where I get left out here at the house by myself.

"Hey, are you okay?" Christopher asks gently. But because I am lost in a trance out the window, I startle and yell, "Jesus Christ, you scared the shit out of me!"

"Yikes, sorry," he says. "But you should see the expression on your face. You look petrified."

I sigh. "I'm sorry. I shouldn't make facial expressions. The truth is, being in the country freaks me out. It always has, even when I was little. So thinking about you being in the city tomorrow and me being here alone, I kind of dread it. It's like, where do most manhunts for escaped serial killers begin? In the woods." I nod in the direction of the dense trees out the window.

"So. Wait." Uh-oh, is that Dick Voice I hear? "You convinced me to move to the country because you were so unhappy in the city . . . and we've been here barely twenty-four hours and you're already unhappy in the country?"

"No, no, no," I say. "That's not it at all. I'm already much happier here."

"Yeah, you look it," he says out of the corner of his mouth.

"Okay, I'm not crazy about bears and snakes and cougars — wildlife. And I don't exactly *love* the idea of people standing out there in the woods, where it's dark, watching us inside the house, where it's bright. But I'd much rather have these country worries than my city worries. I was convinced every plane was going to crash into the Empire State Building. At least I don't have to worry about that anymore."

He laughs. "But we're living next to an airport and a passenger jet is going to fly into our house, remember?"

I hate being strapped down and buckled to my own words. "Well, I hadn't thought it through is all. I'm not worried about planes anymore." I decide not to add, "And for the record, I didn't 'convince' you to move. I put a spell on you."

On this, our first full day living in the country, I receive my inaugural box from UPS. "Wow, already?" he says. "I'm kind of impressed, because I didn't even think you knew your new zip code yet." It's true that I don't, but I *do* know how to google, then copy and paste.

Inside is one high-powered tactical flashlight that will light up the yard like the sun, along with two twelve-inch cans of bear-repellent spray, each in a handy canvas holster that hooks onto a belt with a Velcro strap.

Christopher laughs even harder. "Oh my God, it's your personal 9/11 *and* bears! I am going to have so much fun living in the country with you!" His eyes tell me he *means* it.

"The problem is," I say, "I'm a witch, so by worrying about things, I draw them to me, so then they actually happen. Like when I was on my first big TV commercial production in 1989 and we had to charter a flight on Anguilla Air. I walked around the plane and looked at the engines from the back, how one had actual metal tape holding something together on it. And I instantly visualized the plane falling. I didn't see a crash, but I sure saw a fall. So we get up into the air, and three-quarters of the way through the flight the ride is suddenly really bumpy, and the little phone rings for the flight attendant, and she picks it up — while the door to the cockpit smacks open, bounces, and slams with the lurching of the plane, and she screams into the phone, 'Oh my God, I can't tell them that!' So that's what I mean, I dread an event and then it happens, because I can conjure things. A normal person has the same worries and nothing happens. They need a Klonopin, but I need bear spray. Because once I start worrying about bears, they'll be in the yard."

"Wait," he says. "Go back."

"Oh, right. Well, we'd run out of gas is the thing. And the director, he also had his pilot's license. He turns around in his seat and goes, 'This is it, guys, we're going down.' But I *knew* we weren't. I couldn't see it, I couldn't watch it happen, therefore it wasn't going to. It was not within the realm of possibility. I ended up being the only calm person on the flight."

Christopher is shaking his head and says, "No, I meant go back further. To the part where you said, 'I'm a witch.' That part."

I say, "Oh."

It's like the silence and the air both thicken and swirl around and around us as we both wait to hear what I will say next.

"Have I not told you that until now?"

His head tilts slightly to the right. "Mmmm, I would say the answer to that is a huge no. I would remember if you'd mentioned it."

"Yeah," I say, "I guess I never said the actual words. But you know. You knew. Right?"

He cocks his head to the other side, like a puppy, thinks about it, and says, "I guess probably I did."

"Yeah," I say to him, "you had to. I mean, almost right from the start."

"I knew" — he stops, searches for the right word — "something. That you had something, were something. I guess I never put a word to it."

"Okay," I say, "so now you have the word."

"Yeah," he says. And he smiles. He nods. He's happy because he's from Ohio and he's pragmatic. He likes things that make sense, and this word explains everything he knows about me. It makes *perfect* sense. Unless you don't know me, in which case it's delusional, irrational, and absurd.

"I don't think you should be afraid of nature anymore," he tells me.

"No?"

"I don't think an animal on this property would attack you. I think you'd stare at one another and if you told it to go away, it would."

That seems almost witchily correct.

A partial inventory of items Harold and Elinor left behind: a back brush inside the shower stall, a plastic mirror also inside the shower, a wooden dollhouse with heart-shaped windows, a pale pink ceramic swan, a hoard of baskets, assorted kitchen plates and glasses, fifty-six thousand wine glasses, one skillet and one frying pan, several towels, a set of blue-and-white-striped sheets, assorted rusty tools. In the barn there is an unopened box containing very fine copper kitchen utensils and another box of unused grill utensils, pig fencing, green metal stakes to attach to the pig fencing, numerous scraps of wood, a Sucrets box, several bars of partially used soap, light-bulbs, a small Sanyo television from the 1990s, numerous pieces of furniture, an American flag, a flyswatter shaped like a daisy, an old jam jar filled with bobby pins, a window fan, an escape ladder for the top floor, bunny wrapping paper, one plastic window candle for Christmas with a flickering orange bulb.

They also left several Broyhill armchairs, and seeing the label makes me think of *The Price Is Right,* my favorite game show as a child and one at which I excelled as a stay-at-home contestant.

Why I knew the prices of Kikkoman Soy Sauce, Underwood Deviled Ham, and Pillsbury Space Food Sticks at the age of eight I cannot say, but I did, right down to the penny. If I had been an actual contestant on that show, I would have walked off the set with a brand-new 1973 twenty-four-foot Winnebago Chieftain with a Light Avocado and Willow Green Interior that featured glove-soft vinyl upholstery and teak vinyl-face paneling, plus the revolutionary convenience of a Glideaway bunk — along with an all-expenses-paid vacation to Acapulco, Mexico, a pair of his-and-her Jet Skis, and an Amana Radarange oven.

I *always* won the showcase.

It's because of this fond association I have with the Broyhill name that I don't loathe the wing chairs, which are, in fact, hideous in design, scale, and fabric.

I'm trying to pretend I feel at home, but I don't. I'm telling myself it's because our stuff isn't here yet, and while this is almost certainly true, another part of me worries,

*What if this is a horrible mistake?* What if the beauty of the house and land wears away like cheap gold electroplating, and all I'm left with is a wood house on a plot of nature? I don't have any evidence that this is the case, but I am certain there is nothing I can do about it, so we're stuck living inside my mistake for the rest of our lives with three aging dogs and Harold and Elinor's back brush.

I feel tremendous anxiety — my default emotion — and anticipatory dread about tomorrow when Christopher is gone and I'm stranded with three dogs. I can't let the dogs run free until we get an Invisible Fence installed and they are trained by miracle to respect its boundaries. To me, it seems like teaching a dog how to drive a car, but everybody swears it will work, that the dogs will understand and right away, too. Wiley hasn't understood a thing I've said for five years, so we'll see if electrocution works.

This is such an old house — which I always wanted — but every time I go inside I find another small thing that needs to be fixed, looked at, or let go of. I walk across the threshold of the library into the foyer and the board creaks and I think, Is this going to come up? But it's an old house and that's what old floors do, they talk back at your feet.

One of the screen doors doesn't close tightly, so that should be fixed. The dryer is on its very last tumble, and we need to buy a new one and have it installed — but does it even vent properly to the outside? I go to change a lightbulb in the beautiful antique lantern attached to the honey locust tree beside the kitchen, and the entire lantern falls off in my hands. Plus, there doesn't seem to be any electricity in the very top bedroom, a perfectly creepy guest room with twin beds. Either that or all the light-bulbs are burned out. Doors need latches, things need polishing, some things are too loose, others too tight. Will we be vigilant custodians of this house or run it straight into the ground?

Our city lives were very different. Christopher's apartment was filled with party favors, novelty gifts and cards, mementos, photographs of friends, and an entire life told in the form of books of wooden matches from restaurants that closed in the 1980s or broken pieces of pottery that were once whole and given to him by somebody special, pieces he's inexplicably kept. The box of one of his dogs' ashes was on the top shelf of his closet next to some old belts.

My place was filled with jewelry I purchased to soothe ever-flowing anxiety, attracted to the spark and sparkle like a farm animal to the sound of the hose being turned on, along with antiques I purchased rather than inherited and paintings by people who mean nothing to me. His has been a life of people and events; mine a life of obsessions and *junk*.

Christopher takes Radar into the city with him, so it's just me and Otis and Wiley. I'm aware of how old and solid and true this house is. Christopher and I aren't careful with things; we live hard. If we occupied a new house, we would destroy it within months. I know this because my New York apartment was brand-new when I moved into it. It had all the latest materials and finishes, and it got torn to pieces, with cabinets falling off the walls and the floors destroyed. Crappy new construction.

"This house has been here for almost two hundred years," Christopher had said. "What could happen to it?"

"Us," I replied.

The dogs and I are all lying on Harold and Elinor's sofa in the living room. Otis has a lap dog's personality in the body of a clumsy baby ox. The couch is surprisingly comfortable and of good quality, though it's not a thing of beauty. Tonight the three of us will just sleep here. My back is killing me, so it's better than having to hoist Otis onto the bed and then carry him from the second floor in the morning to pee, because he still can't really do stairs.

To make room for all the boxes and furniture, I have moved the sofa against the wall, under the windows. On the other side of this wall, outside, is the porch that spans the length of the dining room. It's chilly and dark and I want to light a fire because that would bring the room to life, but I want to save that for Christopher, first fire and all. Of course, he would think this was crazy — (a) that I felt the need to wait for him, and (b) that I need a fire and it's Labor Day. I don't have kindling, anyway.

I am reading a book on my phone when I hear floorboards creaking on the porch. Footsteps. I quickly turn off my phone to darken it.

More footsteps, like there might be another person. My heart starts racing.

Wiley and Otis remain sound asleep.

"I can't get in!" It sounds like the whiny cry of a teenage girl. She seems frustrated, pissed, and hopeless. She says something else, but I can't hear. Then she shouts in indignation, "My own house!"

Somebody fiddles with the door latch. All you have to do is press your thumb down and the door opens. What's there to fiddle with?

A wail of frustration erupts and again that same teenage girl cries, "I can't get in!"

Soon they'll start kicking the door. A horrible realization strikes me: *meth addicts.* Or desperate locals in the grip of the opioid addiction that's barreling through the country.

Suddenly it all makes sense: the sudden drop in price, why Harold and Elinor were so happy to unload it on us, even paying for a new septic system to make sure we didn't back out. Because they own multiple homes and weren't here very often, they must have returned once and found kids squatting, shooting up in the attic or the basement or maybe right here in the living room.

Now the kids were back.

Harold and Elinor are miles away in their moving truck, probably passing a paper bag of whiskey back and forth, whooping it up, French fries steaming up the front window. "Suckers!" I can practically hear Elinor cackling. "*We just need this gay couple to materialize.* Don't you wish you could see their faces when the meth heads show up?!"

And now it's *our* problem. Or, more

specifically, *my* problem, since Christopher is in the city.

I slide silently off the sofa, like I have no bones, and crawl across the room to where I'd set a can of bear defense spray.

I walk to the door, where again I hear the floorboards of the porch squeaking on the other side. I take a deep breath and visualize a blinding light surrounding me, protecting me. I swing open the door, fast and hard, practically yanking the old thing off its hinges, chemical weapon drawn.

Nobody is there.

I stick my head out the door and look left. Wall. Tree. I walk down the front stone walkway. Nothing.

That isn't possible, because I just heard them on the other side of the door.

I return to the porch, reach around, and flip on the light. Nobody is running away, either.

I pace on the porch for a moment to try to figure this out and then I freeze: the porch boards don't creak. The floors on the *inside* creak, not out here.

I run out onto the gravel driveway, listen.

Nothing.

I do not believe in ghosts.

I ordered one from a mail order catalog as a kid and waited six weeks for it to arrive, only to be outraged and homicidal when what finally arrived was a balloon; a small, thin white plastic sheet; a twist-tie; and a length of clear nylon string.

Sane, intelligent people do not see — or hear — ghosts. Because there are no such things as ghosts.

Apparently, just like there are no such things as witches.

As soon as Christopher returns from the city, I tell him about the meth addict on the porch who turned out to be a ghost.

"Wait, are you kidding me?" he says, dropping his bag on the kitchen counter.

"No. And it's also no to all the usual questions: Were you asleep? Had you been drinking? I'm telling you, it happened. So I spent some time on Google and I learned about Moll Cramer."

"Who's she?"

"Well, Moll lived a few miles from here and she was married to a blacksmith. This was in the seventeen-hundreds, by the way. But Moll and her husband didn't get along. It sounds like he had some problems with his blacksmithing business and blamed her, of course. He figures, she must be a witch. He kicks his wife *and* son out of the house — can you believe it? And Moll, she ends up building like a hut made of sticks in the woods. I guess she started to beg for food from neighbors. And because people were freaked out by her and thought she really was a witch, especially now that she was living in a stick shack, they gave her whatever she wanted. But then I guess some farmer turned her away when she asked for bacon, and the next thing you know, all his pigs die of cholera.

"But the thing is, there is no end to the Moll story, or at least I couldn't find one. Like, what happened to her? What happened to her son? Her asshole blacksmith husband? There's a legend that Moll's ghost still lives in the woods, and she shows up at houses and knocks on doors wanting things."

"So you think it was Moll?"

"I do. This morning after I took the dogs out, I drove out to that French bakery that Maura told us about? And I bought a little berry tart. And also a baguette. Then I walked into the woods and I found this moss-covered tree stump. God, our property is beautiful. Anyway, I left the tart and the bread on the tree stump as an offering for Moll. I want her to know she can come stay with us anytime she wants."

"God, I hope she comes back," Christopher says.

"But if it's Moll, I have a feeling she won't."

"Oh? Why not?"

"Well, you know, it's like a professional courtesy. Once she sees the tart and the bread, she'll be like, *Oh, this is from the man in the yellow house that's supposed to be black and he must be a witch.* And she'll leave us alone. A ghost won't pester a witch. Like a proctologist won't charge a dermatologist to examine a wart. I mean, a ghost might visit a witch, socially. But they wouldn't ever enter the house uninvited. If it's witch versus ghost, witch wins."

"Well, she better be quick if she wants that tart before a squirrel gets it. And maybe it wasn't Moll. Maybe it was a girl who used to live here."

"That's possible," I say. "We need to learn the history of the house."

"Wait," Christopher says. "Remember the box Maura pointed out? Harold said, 'It stays with the house,' and he left it in one of the cabinets in the office."

We find the old black wooden box with burnished steel hinges. There is faint printing on the side in gold letters, but it is so worn away that the traces are not enough for us even to guess at what it once said.

Inside are stacks of documents, an old magazine the house appeared in when an interior designer and his wife owned it in the eighties, handwritten notes.

We spread them out on the floor, which causes Radar and Wiley to step on them and then try to use them as napping surfaces. Otis, though, is frightened of the papers. He looks at them as if they might rise up in unison and smother him. He keeps his distance as we dive into the lake of the past.

Woodbury, Connecticut, a large area that is now split into about a half-dozen towns, was founded in 1672. Israel and Rebecca Curtiss, who eventually had eight children, were among the original fifteen families who arrived to "purchase" the land from the Pootatuck Indians. According to an 1854 book, *The History of Ancient Woodbury, Connecticut,* everything went *just fine* with that transaction, and there was *no trouble* with the tribe. (This 1,600-page tome was written by an old white guy, so it must be true.)

The Curtiss family crest shows a lion holding an azure shield in its right paw and features the motto *Sapere aude,* which translates as "Dare to know." That's an interesting phrase for a clan of Indian land-stealers, but since everything was *so great* and *entirely peaceful* with the Pootatucks, I can imagine the Curtisses as the progressive intellectual family in town.

It was the fifth generation of the family, then sawmill owners, that built our house, in 1820. A farmhouse across the way already existed by then, and shortly thereafter a brother built the home now occupied by a young family who moved in two weeks before we did. The houses even have official names: ours is the Jason Curtiss House.

All of this Curtiss information keeps pushing my thoughts back to my aunt Curtis.

Christopher waves a hand in front of my eyes. "Where'd you go? You still in there?"

I laugh. "Sorry, yeah. I was thinking about how . . ." I want to phrase it right without sounding trite, but I just go for it. "This house was our destiny."

"It is," he says, smiling.

Otis finally approaches us, and I hold my arms out. "You big baby monster, these papers aren't going to hurt you." I reach for his dinner-plate ears, mink-soft and hot.

"Hey, okay, here's something kinda weird," Christopher says. "Jason Curtiss had three wives."

"Whaaaat?"

"Uh-huh. The first two both died when they were thirty-nine. And the third one outlived him."

"Holy shit. What are the odds of having two wives die on you and at the same age? That is a serial wife murderer for sure."

"I don't know. It doesn't say how they died. Antibiotics weren't around for another hundred years. I think people just died earlier back then."

I pick up my phone and search. "Oh," I say, disappointed. "Life expectancy back then was thirty-seven years. Can you believe that? So I guess they died of old age. I would think if they had kids, some of them would have died. So maybe it's a dead Curtiss girl, pissed off that she can't open the door and go upstairs to her room."

"Though I also can't find any record of Jason having children with any of the wives," Christopher says, shuffling more papers. "One of the records shows that the house remained in the Curtiss family until 1936, but there were a lot of brothers and cousins in the meantime — Japhet and Cyrus and Simeon and a bunch of other antique names."

"Just because there's no record of children doesn't mean those three wives didn't have miscarriages or stillborn babies," I muse. "That ghost could still be a Curtiss girl."

"Yeah," Christopher says warily. "Let's,

209

um, hope for that."

We look through another pile, and I find a document called House History, which details the additions and structural changes made to the house over the years. *"Ho. Ly. CRAP,"* I say. "This area right where we're sitting with these papers?" I indicate the space in the living room that leads to the office. "It used to be walled off as a room."

"That's one claustrophobic room," Christopher says, and it does seem like it would have been sort of a tall coffin. "Like the hall closet Mia finds in *Rosemary's Baby* that leads to Ruth Gordon's lair."

"Just wait. It's a colonial feature that goes by two different names: the Marrying and Burying Room, and the Mourning and Borning Room."

"So . . . they had weddings in here?"

"Right next to the deacon's cabinet so he could get smashed before the ceremony."

"And the women gave birth here?" he asks.

"Uh-huh. *And* this is where they laid out the corpses for viewing. Definitely both of the wives, and we haven't ruled out their possible murders. And maybe some of those dead babies." We're quiet for a second. "I think one of those bodies was attempting a B&E here recently," I say.

"And we've gravitated to the one tiny section of our new home where they stashed the cadavers," he remarks. "That's macabre."

I give him a look. "And that's . . . bad?"

The same papers show that the 1936 purchase was to a Ms. Brown, who owned the house with her lady companion, Ms. Kaiser. They added the sunporch, which was designed by a somewhat famous society architect whose mansions still line the oceanfront of the Hamptons to this day. I love that super-tasteful lesbians from the 1930s — lesbian schoolteachers, even — made the most significant, beautiful, and recent renovations to the house.

Why can't *their* ghosts come back and visit? I'd let them in.

# EYE OF NEWT

By the time the movers leave, it's dark and they hate us. Every room is filled with boxes, looming nearly eight feet high. It is like stepping into a surreal cardboard funhouse. We have to slide the teetering towers around to make paths for ourselves and the dogs. It is moving day and we are already an episode of *Hoarders.*

The next eternity is spent cutting boxes open, breaking them down, and stacking them outside and trying to find places for things. Of course, you never open them in the proper order, so you find the wrong half of everything first. *Yay, the coffeepot!* Four days later: *Finally, the coffeemaker.*

The process of unpacking Christopher's belongings, which had been extracted from the deepest, darkest, and most unexplored crevices of the massive rent-stabilized apartment he had inhabited for more than thirty years, provide me with stunning revelations:

the first and most obvious is that he is not materialistic by nature.

In this capacity we are not merely different people but different species. I would sell what little remains of my soul to live the rest of my life in The Breakers, Cornelius Vanderbilt II's mansion in Newport, which was designed by Richard Morris Hunt and is my favorite physical structure in all the world. If Christopher won a $300 million Powerball lottery, he would change nothing about his life, including his old phone with a cracked screen.

As a result of his comfort without possessions, he owns little furniture. Aside from a pack of original 1984 Cyndi Lauper bubble gum, he has a Furby, every driver's license he's ever held, and all the belts he's ever owned. He also owns a trillion books and, in his words, "very few" CDs he's kept from a huge collection in the '90s, but by my count this would be about five hundred. Then there are surprises: a vast collection of gorgeous Frankoma pottery from Sapulpa, Oklahoma. Bowls, platters, vases, dishes; a giant quantity in muted earth tones. His first boyfriend, Harvey, left this — along with the apartment and everything in it — to Christopher when he died from AIDS in 1993. Frankoma is not a popular collector's item, which puzzles me because each piece looks like it could have been designed by Georgia O'Keefe herself, such is the strength of the art deco lines and the organic, feminine curves. He also owns handmade steel flatware that he bought on a trip to Thailand. "You went to Thailand?" I ask, flabbergasted.

You think you know a person, then movers come and deliver the contents of their closets, top shelves, backs of dresser drawers, and you realize you married a stranger.

Black leather jeans. He owns these? He wore these? When? With whom?

A turquoise electric Gibson guitar. "That belongs to Alice," he tells me. Alice is an actress he's been friends with since college. She's a Tony Award winner, and the white faux-fur guitar strap alone should have been enough of a clue it was Alice's.

A tiny sterling silver screw-top vial from Tiffany & Co. from the 1970s or 1980s, no doubt sold as a "pill container," was obviously for cocaine. Two Tylenol wouldn't fit in it, but a half gram of white powder would.

A week later, a third moving vehicle arrives. These are my belongings from when I was in my Wrong Relationship. I haven't seen any of these things in almost ten years. There are not only seven BlackBerry phones from the mid-early 2000s but also a PalmPilot from even earlier. Suddenly I'm drowning in down parkas, questionable shoes, Orvis vests (*vests?*), giant khaki pants, voluminous button-down shirts on hangers. Why did I have the wardrobe of an obese stockbroker from New Jersey? There are also T-shirts from LA with lots of fancy stitching embellishments, but mostly there is out-of-date technology: USB cables and phone chargers and routers, keyboards, emergency weather-band radios. Most of the batteries have swollen over the years in storage. When I close the barn door for the night, I imagine everything exploding, the building burning, flames leaping over to the house. Because I have envisioned this, it will now likely happen, so I go back outside with a large red bucket filled with water and dunk anything with a battery, mutant or not.

It takes about a week to unpack it all, break down the boxes, and have our belongings distributed around the house. It feels more like home with some of our familiar stuff around, but it won't feel like "us" until we really make the place our own and ditch Harold and Elinor's sofa, chairs, and house color. We have time.

One evening we are sitting in the living room, both on our computers, when Christopher yelps in astonishment, "Look at me, I'm browsing wall sconces!" He is scrolling through a page of antique lighting to replace the four made-in-China tin star-shaped fixtures in the dining room that are too tacky to look at any longer. "I'm a slag glass lamp queen! How did *that* happen?" he says, laughing.

He's always been happy, but this is different. It's a domesticated side I've never seen before. He is not only looking at sconces, but he wants to get a velvet sofa and he thinks we need rugs. City Christopher didn't care about velvet. City Christopher didn't even notice when I redecorated my apartment; a month later he said, "Is something different in here?" And I was like, "Um, there's an upright piano and two new sofas? All right here in the same studio apartment."

Country Christopher is buying antique portraits. I never knew he had such fantastic taste in paintings. He is drawn to canvases nobody else wants, frequently paying ten or fifteen dollars for portraits of odd-looking people, like a smiling little girl with serious dental issues. We intend to fill the walls with vintage oil paintings of strangers, plus monkeys (if they are wearing costumes but not if they read as racist, which is a fine line), and dogs that are peculiarly out of proportion (which they apparently had a lot of trouble getting right in the old days).

He loves going out at night with the flashlight and checking the property.

He seems calm. He looks fantastic.

I make a large fire in the living room. Christopher, who hates being hot, loves fires. He notices that the best part is the upward rise of sparks against the sooty back wall. "Like fireworks in reverse," he murmurs.

I loved fires when I was a kid, which I guess is not surprising at all because — *witches.*

Even as a little boy I lusted after a fireplace exactly like this: flush with the floor, a deep stone hearth you could stand on, a beehive oven on the side, dome-shaped and unchanged in design since the medieval period or maybe earlier. You can bake pies in it, bread. There is an iron swing-arm inside for hanging a black iron cauldron over hot coals for stew, and a second, smaller arm beneath it. Instead my parents had a 1970s brick fireplace with a tall, long hearth that made it impossible to get close to the fire. At least it burned wood.

I even begged my father for one of those artificial fireplaces for my bedroom that you plugged in and which fooled nobody. He wouldn't do it, though. "Why would you want such a god-awful tacky thing when we have a wonderful real fireplace in the living room?"

I also loved blacksmiths. Part welder, part jeweler, this profession was made up of big, sweaty men who had me burning with predatory curiosity. There was a blacksmith at the Leverett Crafts & Arts Center, and I was obsessed with both him and his gigantic bellows, feeding the huge, hot fire within his circle of brick, a hood above sucking away the smoke. He hammered rings for me out of iron nails and never charged a thing.

If the adults around me — like at school — knew how much I loved fire, they would have believed I was an arsonist, when I was actually the opposite. I like my flames inside of containers. A loose, wild fire running unbridled through the woods is the worst thing I can imagine. A house fire, my number-one greatest fear, would surely leave me with a melted face and shiny, brittle arms and legs. After I poke at a log with the long iron fork, I always tap it to make sure no lit embers are stuck to the back of a prong where I can't see.

To have this fireplace — to have *five*

fireplaces, plus a fire pit outside — is deeply satisfying.

Christopher and Otis and Radar are lying on the sofa, and after a few minutes Christopher is snoring softly. I love that he loves it here, and I love that making a fire was his idea. "It's Friday," he said, "so we can have a bigger one."

Even in the dark, the maple tree outside the window seems to cast a moving shadow. Or — and I know this can't be true but — it looks like it's taken three or four steps closer to the house.

Every time I look at it I want to chop it down. Think of all the firewood for Christopher! Maybe I can present it as a cost-saving measure. "It's actually environmentally conscious because we're using our own wood, not part of a forest that was ravaged for New Englanders to enjoy toasty winters." I tell myself, it's just a tree. A beautiful tree. You are being paranoid.

We continue to find more things left behind by Harold and Elinor. Today I removed a snarl of coat hangers from the closet and a plaster sheep from on top of a dresser. I cannot fathom why anybody would buy a plaster sheep with a thick seam from the mold running straight along the spine of the animal and down the center of its head, like a birth defect. That's a sheep you would put down, not honor in statuary form.

About a month ago I ordered an antique fireplace bellows from an online store, but it never showed up. Today I got an email from the seller telling me that he is so sorry the bellows hasn't shipped yet but that his girlfriend died recently from lung cancer and he is overwhelmed. He promises to send it out immediately.

My first thought is to write back and say, "Ooh, gosh, the bellows came from the home of a smoker? I didn't know that when I ordered it. Can I cancel the order? Also, sorry, RIP!"

But instead I thank him for the update and tell him I am sorry for his loss. And I am sorry, because the true loss is *mine:* it is a nice bellows, and every time I use it for the rest of my life I will hear the words "lung cancer, lung cancer, lung cancer" with every pump. I will think of his dead girlfriend as I blow diseased air onto my fireplace coals. I don't even want it in the house.

That's not my only unsettling shopping experience. After I unpack our toaster, which is in the very last box I open, I look at all its scars and stains and the chip on the plastic fake chrome handle and I think,

Why did we even bring this? It was cheap to begin with, and now it's abused *and* cheap. That's because it was *new.*

I don't like new things. They're made quickly and in enormous quantities, but even the best new item cannot compete with the average old one. A Model G Electrolux from the 1960s will suck the dirt from a carpet two floors below you; a twenty-first-century Dyson gently swirls small bits of detritus and redistributes them.

Surely eBay will have the perfect vintage Toastmaster.

A single search term and two clicks later, I find one for thirty dollars that has been professionally restored and is in flawless condition. It will last the rest of our lives and probably Jane Fonda's, too. Before I click the blue Buy It Now button, I hesitate. Something has disturbed me . . . but what? I look at each image again, and everything seems shiny and beautiful.

Then I pull my focus back, and I see what I had missed before in the first picture.

A crisp reflection.

Of the man selling the toaster. Sitting cross-legged on the floor, aiming his point-and-shoot camera right at the shiny surface.

He is wearing red bikini briefs and nothing else.

Obviously I can't buy the toaster, because his image will remain on the side of it forever. I would see his pale, plump, middle-aged hairless white legs and the bikini briefs and the overhanging stomach and the sad, downward-pointing nipples every time I toasted a slice of Christopher's homemade sourdough bread. Food poisoning, every morning.

Our crappy old-new toaster will stay.

It feels good to be surrounded by our possessions again, even if many of them could not be less familiar to me (a black trumpet?).

This is the right house and the right life, but it's weird because I've never had a home before; I've had addresses.

# QUEEN OF THE NIGHT

We had been warned, repeatedly and seriously, about the woman we'd begun calling the Soprano in the Woods, like she was a girl ensorcelled by a witch in a fairy tale. She has a lovely old house, more of an austere saltbox than ours, with many acres of grass fields sectioned by old stone walls.

Elinor told us her name was Veronique. Not Veronica but "vair-oh-NEEK," a former opera singer known as Vivi. ("Yeah, right," snorts Christopher, who is no aficionado but has a solid working knowledge of opera, "known by whom?") Her husband is a Frenchman she brought back duty-free after touring at some point in the 1980s, into what had been her mother's house and presumably the house she grew up in. (Because lots of girls from Cow Dung, Connecticut, are named Veronique.)

We google her full name, and to our surprise and delight there are a couple of recordings of her on YouTube. Unfortunately, they are just sound with a still photo as the visual — but what a visual: a young Vivi with raven-black hair whipped into a high bouffant and topped with a sort of braided cruller, her eyes lined dramatically with charcoal mascara, the lids dusted with lush emerald-green eye shadow. Large drop-shaped pearl earrings dangle from beneath her shoe polish coiff.

One selection is a live recording from Vienna in the '70s — again, sadly, with no video — that is so muffled and hissy that it seems the microphone might have been placed outside the theater. Every so often a sustained tone or a phrase breaks through, and those are impressive.

"Wow," I say, "she sounds good. Shouldn't she be more famous?"

Christopher shrugs. "It's a tough world." He squints at the photo. "Maybe it was her hair."

He could be right. Poor Viv, I think. If only her locks had been the color of the moon instead of a lump of coal, she might be an icon.

"Also," Christopher says, "I thought she was a soprano. She's a mezzo-soprano."

"What's the difference?" I ask.

He thinks for a moment then gives me the

answer I'll understand. "Mezzos have lower voices and not as many starring roles."

Perhaps it wasn't her hair that ruined her career, but that she couldn't hit the high notes. It's impossible to say, though we are biased, because there is almost no available information about her, so how revered could she have been? She'd had her brief moment, and now she lives a quiet life in rural Connecticut, where she plays the role of nosy neighbor. "You know the type," Elinor had said, "like Gladys Kravitz from *Bewitched*."

About two weeks after we move in there is a soft knock on the door. This sets off a chain reaction among the dogs, who bark as if it's a terrifying intruder who will also give them all the cheese they want. Christopher finds a timid older man standing well away from the door, lest the beasts lunge through it and clamp onto his throat. Christopher pushes the dogs back. "Don't worry, they're friendly. Too friendly, that's the problem." He squeezes out a crack in the door and stands with the old man on the porch while I watch to try to listen from the pantry window. I can't hear anything, but I see the man give something to Christopher, shake his hand, and walk away.

Christopher steps back in and shows me a calling card, like this is Edith Wharton's Gilded Age Manhattan. He's slightly puzzled. "I get the gist, though I'm not sure everything he said was English. But that's Vivi's husband." Then, tentatively, quietly, "Ooguh."

I pause. "Did you say 'ooo-gah,' like a Model T horn?"

"H-U-G-U-E-S."

Spelling at me is like doing math at me, so I remain silent and blank.

"It's . . . Hugh? I think? In French. So maybe just . . . 'Oog.' Anyway, that part was definitely not in English." He reads the note that accompanies the card. "She is welcoming us as new neighbors and requesting our presence at an intimate fête in honor of her birthday. This Saturday at seven p.m. It is requested that we bring no gifts."

"Oh my God," I say. "She's having a birthday party like she's a seven-year-old. Has she invited all the neighbors? Will there be games?"

"Since 'all the neighbors' is exactly one other house, maybe. Or it might be like Norma Desmond's New Year's Eve party in *Sunset Boulevard,* with an orchestra and us as the only guests. But she doesn't call it a birthday party, because she's a legendary mezzo-soprano. It's a 'fête in honor of my birthday,' " Christopher says.

I lean back against the refrigerator. "We've already learned so much about her. That this is to 'honor' her birthday tells us she probably couldn't be bothered to pick up a pen, so she dictated. It's sort of a masculine hand — and look how shaky 'neighbor' is, but 'fête' is big and bold. And *French.* So in the privacy of their own home, where nobody is watching and they are invulnerable to outside judgment or opinion, he serves her. And as a person who leans ever so slightly in the direction of One Who Requests, I can assure you, if she's dictating her birthday invite and then making him come over here to hand it to us in person, she's also handing him her gum when she's finished chewing it, and he's taking it from her."

"Yeah, but to be clear on one point: you do more than lean 'ever so slightly in the direction of One Who Requests.' In fact, 'Vivi' would be a great nickname for you."

I pull the nicotine gum out of my mouth and hand it to him. He bursts out laughing. But he takes it and tosses it into the trash.

"Also?" I continue. "We only ever see him outside, and he's always doing chores: painting the trim, pulling weeds, mowing. She's kept him all these years as her private servant; more than that, really. He is occupying the role of her physical body. Like an understudy who stars in every single performance. Of course he can't speak English after living here for thirty years! He doesn't need to speak English, because he exists to serve her, not to speak to other people who are not her. He understands her hand signals and grunts and prattling and that's all he needs to know."

"Wow, and you got all of this from the invitation?"

"I did. And you will see that I'm right."

"So you're saying we should accept?"

"Oh, without question. Despite Elinor's *many* warnings, we have to go. Maybe she'll sing 'Happy Birthday' to herself and we can get it on video. We can leave any time we want, but we have to go, because we need to understand them."

"I agree," Christopher says. "Even though this is the part of the horror movie where people are standing up in the theater screaming, 'Don't go in! You're gonna die!' "

When Saturday rolls around, we shower and put on our finery, which is to say we wear clean jeans and collared shirts as opposed to years-old shorts and band T-shirts from the merch table. We walk along the quiet, dark road, across a bridge, around the dense grove of giant pine trees. As we approach we note that there are no cars at Vivi's yet. Perhaps "fashionably late" is also a country thing. Christopher is Swiss; he is never one minute late. I am not Swiss, but I am never late, either. Maybe it's good to be a little early — we can get a house tour.

"By the way," Christopher says, "I set an alarm on my phone for 7:45. We'll say we have to go pick up our friends in Roxbury." Which we actually have to do the next day, but by not specifying that part, it's not a lie, if not entirely the truth. Clever.

We ring the bell and wait for what seems an inordinately long time before Hugues opens the door and waves us inside.

"Ah, is so good of you to pay the visit for us. Come, Vivi is living. I bring you refreshment."

Obviously he meant "Vivi is in the living room," but a psychoanalyst might call that a reaction formation, a mask to conceal his truest desires. "Vivi is living!" he says, because deep inside, he wants her head on a stick next to the mailbox. That's what I want, and I haven't even met her yet.

As soon as we enter the living room, I get the first glimmer that the charm of the house's exterior does not extend to the indoors. The room is long but narrow, with bright inset ceiling lights from the '90s. Furniture is pushed against the walls, giving an overall feel of a dentist's office waiting area, and not a cozy one.

But there she is, occupying a queenly position on the sofa, positioned in the corner so she can view the entire room. The strategically planned arrangement of nearby chairs means nobody can sit directly opposite her. All of her interactions will be at a forty-five-degree angle, and only to the right side of her face — thus replicating the exact perspective to which visitors to her YouTube videos are treated.

She stands to greet us. Because I've been expecting her to be ancient and senile, I'm surprised that she's only in her early seventies, and when she speaks, it is clear she's "all there." Her eyes dart back and forth between us, sizing us up. She is stout and wearing a tasteful pants suit, her hair snowy white but still voluminous. It is easy to envision her younger self on stage in a Viking helmet with long braids, carrying a spear and shrieking her full face off.

Christopher says, "Happy birthday, and thank you for having us."

"Oh, yes, thank *you*," she says grandly, then she narrows her eyes and fixes him with a beady stare. No longer grand, she talks quickly. "I looked you up on the internet."

That's her line after "hello"? And she chose to google the one who is not a famously crazy bestselling author who has been dragged through the media for years?

Without hesitating, Christopher says, "We looked you up, too."

There is a pause. Because Vivi was trained to play to the back of the theater, the look on her face is quite startling up close. It registers, "I am pretending not to be waiting for a compliment." She knows the first thing that comes up is her singing, so she is silently commanding the next line to be, "You have such a lovely voice." But instead, Christopher says, "Is it time for the house tour?" He laughs to indicate he is kidding but not kidding.

"Of course," she says, a little acid dripping from the words. "Follow me." We are led into a room that contains an upright piano. "I teach my students in here," she says. I nudge Christopher and indicate with my eyes a framed photo on the wall: the same black bouffant and green eye shadow. Now that we've seen the real Vivi, I suspect this was her headshot from 1964. We follow her through another room to a flight of stairs leading up. Christopher raises his leg to place a foot on the stairs, and Vivi instantly shrieks, "No! Downstairs only!"

We both freeze and look at her. Christopher says, "Oh-kay, downstairs only," in his perfectly calm, reasonable tone that says he KNOWS you are INSANE.

It is a puzzling reaction of such alarm that I can't help but wonder why. The downstairs isn't exactly gleaming, so maybe the upstairs is much worse? Genuine panic has issued forth from her professionally trained mouth. Her fears have circumvented her years of rigorous study. I feel positive that naughty Vivi has something up there that she knows she ought not have.

We enter the kitchen, which had been "renovated" by her mother in the 1970s, but Vivi has recently "refreshed" it by replacing the cabinet fronts and adding a new laminate countertop. At the same moment, Christopher and I notice a small lidded Revere Ware pot simmering on the electric stove along with cooked spaghetti lumped into a fixed coil at the bottom of a colander in the sink. Who serves pasta with salmonella sauce as party food?

Vivi proudly displays for us where the fireplace used to be. It is now drywalled over, though the mantel remains and is used as an ordinary kitchen shelf for mugs and a jelly glass of pens. She is actually proud of her wanton destruction of an eighteenth-century kitchen and seems to think she should be praised for making "home improvements." I look at her, thinking, *What have you done?* Her smile dims somewhat as she continues to study my face. Perhaps she has psychic as well as vocal talents, so I focus my thinking: *You should be locked in the cell next to convicted child killer Susan Smith for what you've done to this house.*

So now we knew: the house looks lovely and historic from the outside but is defiled on the inside. Well, *downstairs only.*

Back in the living room I notice something quite interesting that I missed before: motion-sensor cameras, tucked into the corners. A surprisingly high-tech little gadget for a woman in her seventies.

Suddenly, it makes a great deal more sense that she doesn't want us upstairs. I have an intuitive confirmation that she has surveillance equipment up there. And I'm not talking about a pair of binoculars. Vivi would have not just a telescope but a directional microphone. She would have night vision.

Hugues shuffles into the living room. "Dinner could occur in soon."

Christopher said, "Where are the other

guests?"

Vivi said, "Other guests?"

Oh. Shit. Christopher gives me a quick glance that says, "I'll take *Sunset Boulevard* for a thousand, Alex."

"As you may be aware, I was an opera singer for many years," Vivi begins, as Hugues sets glasses of ginger ale on the coffee table in front of the sofa. I reach for my glass, which is plastic and greasy. It has been used before and then washed but not washed well. I raise it near my lips and pretend to take a sip. Vivi's not the only one with stage experience.

"I toured Europe in the seventies, and I was known for my Carmen all through the eighties, of course."

"Of course," Christopher echoes, neither politely nor impolitely. "That's really something."

"Oh, yes," she agrees, taking both of his noncompliments as raves, "to be so young and see so much of the world. To have sung in the best houses, well, it was a thrill."

"I'm sure," Christopher says neutrally. He really is Swiss.

I keep thinking, *Please let your alarm go off.*

Vivi sits a little straighter and taller in her chair and declares, in a most imperious tone, "Many men tried to bed me."

My face is frozen. I have no idea what it's registering, but I'm incapable of changing it.

We wait for her to continue, but in her silence she is demanding a response.

I glance at Hugues, who nods politely and smiles. Does he know what she has just said? Is he following any of this? He catches Christopher's eye and engages him in a separate conversation.

I turn back to Vivi and say, "These days, sexual harassment is a topic that's finally out in the open, and the new generation, they don't tolerate it." Implying, of course, the old generation — hers specifically — would tolerate it. Then brag about it three hundred years later.

She looks at me as if I am a fool, blathering nonsense and missing her point. She doesn't roll her eyes, but she lets me know precisely how hard she's resisting it.

"Pavarotti, the pig, he tried to rape me. Many times. Many men tried to rape me. Perhaps I should have allowed him to have his way with me. My career might have been different if I had."

Is she actually expressing regret that she hadn't slept her way to the top?

"Wait," I say. "Pavarotti really tried to rape you?"

"Of course!" she replies, indignant that I would question her. "I was a young girl and he was enormous, both in stature and in physical size. He pushed me down onto a sofa, but I fought him."

"Well, good for you," I say.

"Was it?" she asks. "You tell me."

It is such a bold challenge that I am tempted to give her a truthful reply: *No, it wasn't good for you, Viv. Your younger instincts were the better instincts. You should have let any of them have their way with you back in the Truman era, or whenever this was. You'd now be living in Katharine Hepburn's former house and you'd have a Kennedy Center tribute where Adele would say it was hearing your performance in* La Traviata *that made her want to sing.*

Christopher's alarm goes off.

"What is that?" Vivi demands in mock horror.

"Oh, that's my timer. We have guests visiting from out of town and we have to go pick them up." So smooth — Swiss *and* an agent.

"Leave?" she says, turning the word into three syllables. "But you've only just arrived, and we prepared a meal for you."

"I'm so sorry, but your note didn't mention dinner, and we hadn't planned on it," he says. "Maybe another time."

We stand but she remains seated, wearing an opera-sized frown.

Hugues escorts us to the door.

Vivi says icily, "But Hugues made the sauce himself, from his grandmother's recipe."

*Oh, were Hunt's Diced Tomatoes popular in France in the nineteenth century?* I want to say, because I saw the fucking can on her "refreshed" countertop.

We thank them for a lovely evening and walk down the road, admiring our house from this never-before-seen perspective. As we round the corner and turn into the driveway, I stare up at the majestic, monstrous maple, and it appears to be leaning in the opposite direction now, away from the house. Its leaves shake and there's a disconcerting "pop" that sounds like a log on a fire. What the hell was that? I'm about to comment that it looks like it's about to topple on the barn and crush everything in it when Christopher has a thought.

"We have to get in the car and go somewhere or they'll know we were lying." He is right. He runs inside and grabs the keys and we head to a dairy farm in the next town that has amazing ice cream.

Christopher asks, "Did you hear Hugues tell me he doesn't drive? He walks everywhere."

"Wait, he's been in America for more than forty years, and not only does he not speak English as well as Google Maps, he travels on foot *in rural Connecticut*?"

"Yup. Everywhere. The grocery store, which is almost nine miles, one way."

"This would explain why he's so trim."

"And I guess there aren't all that many places he needs to walk to."

"True," I say, "but there is one to walk away *from.*"

No communication follows, but there's an upstairs room at Vivi's house that faces ours, visible over the tops of the trees, where the light never goes on. I picture her seated in a chair slightly back from the window, peering through night vision goggles, headphones on, eavesdropping with her directional mic.

Late one night our landline rings. This has never happened; neither of us even knows the number, but the novelty of the ringing house phone compels us to answer.

Of course it's Vivi. "Oh, you *are* home. You always have your exterior lights on at night, but tonight you didn't, and I saw *somebody* with a flashlight walking around outside. I was going to call the police."

The *somebody* was me, walking the dogs before bed. She was correct — we had not turned on the lights, so I had grabbed a flashlight. From that moment on I have never once forgotten to flip on the exterior lights. If I don't, we'll have a cruiser in the driveway.

I don't like having her back there, but it's not like I want her to die. If that happens, her property could easily become a shopping center, and that would be horrifying. When an ambulance rushes by and skids over the bridge before pulling into Vivi's driveway in the middle of winter, I think the worst: an embolism has traveled from her leg to her heart. She's going to die, if she isn't already dead. Hugues will return to France and live with a spinster sister, and Vivi's acreage will become a Costco, Best Buy, and Petland, the trifecta of American civilization.

Because I can so clearly imagine uttering the words "God, I wish Vivi still lived over there," I know for a fact I will one day speak them. The moment I say this already exists. But not quite yet.

# FAIRIE'S FINGER

Beavers came in the night and ate all the trees we planted by the water.

As he is standing in the kitchen sipping his coffee and looking out the window over the sink into the backyard, Christopher says, "That's weird. From this angle, doesn't it look like the trees we planted are gone?"

I look out the window. This is no trick of perspective. "The trees we planted *are* gone," I say. I slip into my hiking boots and stomp down to the water's edge.

Sticking up from the dirt like five pointy wood boners are the remains of the willow, redbud, and flowering pear trees we bought from the nursery and planted ourselves last week.

I cannot believe it. If our trees are going to disappear overnight, why can't one of them be the Maple of the Damned?

In a rage, I storm back to the house. I say one word: "Beavers."

Christopher is raising his red Frankoma mug to his mouth when he pauses. "Little bucktooth monsters."

He sets the mug down and grabs his phone. He uses Swype instead of the tappy keyboard, so he's fast. Soon he is scrolling through pages: he also reads fast. "Okay, so two mistakes: we planted willow, one of their favorite foods, right by the water. And we didn't surround the trunks with wire. So it's partly our fault. But still. It also says if you see a dam, break it up, and I think that's what all those sticks and crap are at the far edge of the waterfall on the other side. I'm gonna go destroy it."

For a moment I consider warning him because of my familiarity with When Beavers Attack videos on YouTube. I want them dead. And made into bedspreads.

I watch as he breaks the dam apart with surprising strength. Even though he watches sports that he doesn't play, and hasn't worked out at a gym since he was young and single, he's a jock. He's a former frat boy and a runner and a swimmer, and you never outgrow those things, so in fifteen minutes that beaver condominium is floating downriver.

Sleeves rolled up, arms wet, pants splashed, big smile: looks like he's been doing this his entire life. When he comes back inside and washes his hands, he says, "We should dig up those stumps and replant them, see if they grow."

Is he kidding?

He reads my mind, or maybe he just sees my face. "I don't mean somewhere prominent, but an out-of-the-way place. Like over there." He points, and even though Christopher came with a factory-installed anti-compass and he's pointing the wrong way, I knew exactly where he meant.

There is a stretch of our property that runs parallel to a road on which trees block the view of our property, except for one small area. If you're going the speed limit of 40 mph, you can glimpse our land for a second or two, enough time to see a flash of green field, some arthritic old crabapple trees, and maybe a "Wait, was that a pony?" Great Dane.

It is here, in this blank spot beside a thorn-entangled embankment leading up to the road, that Christopher suggests we create a "Plant Hospital."

"You know, it's worth a shot," he says. "If they live, they live. If not, no biggie."

This is where we take the plants, bushes, and flowers that for mysterious reasons haven't worked out and died. Or almost died. The first thing we plant here is the redbud tree that was to be a centerpiece, replacing the huge juniper bush that had been there originally, possibly for centuries. Normally we would not destroy or remove an old thing, but that sprawling, patchy juniper bush was the exception. "It's ugly, and they catch trash. I don't want to look out at the prettiest view we've got and see that shit." Christopher puts on perhaps his inaugural pair of gardening gloves and goes outside the first weekend and rips it out by its nefarious, far-reaching roots. His arms are covered with so many welts and slices that two years later there are silvery-white scars, making him appear like a reformed cutter.

We buy several new bushes and trees and flowering perennials (a word I had to learn upon moving to the country), and, almost without exception, everything fails. A storm snaps a Royal Purple smoke tree in half, leaving a leafless stump.

Out of everything we planted, only two things survive: *verbena bushes.* On a far less significant scale, it is like having two beautiful children horribly disfigured in a terrible accident while the one who is the spitting image of your beady-eyed, pocked, and chinless grandfather makes it out first and unscathed.

I would have yanked the remaining dead stumps and tossed them back into the woods, because to me the word "hospital" implies conscientious, around-the-clock care administered by dedicated professionals who work double shifts. In other words, me. I have appalling visions of myself out there where the hose doesn't reach — and neither would two hoses screwed together — with heavy cans filled with blue Miracle Gro–spiked water, one in each hand. I can picture myself watering the hyacinth that hates us and killed itself for no reason, soaking the base of the replanted dead dogwood tree that is so absurdly beyond hope that a random stick grabbed out of the woods and stuck in the ground would look better.

But this is not at all what he intends. He envisions the Plant Hospital as a place of both second chances and benign neglect. In other words, what he is really suggesting is a Plant *Mental* Hospital, where the plants could be left and ignored. It is essentially throwing them away, only instead of actually winding up the old arm and pitching the root balls into the woods, we will dig holes and plant them so they can at least die with dignity, vertically.

The instant I plunge the shovel into the

ground, I snap through the buried line for the Invisible Fence. What are the odds? A bad omen, I think. Maybe planting dead things isn't giving them dignity. Maybe it is like having your dead mother stuffed with sawdust and sitting her on the couch so you don't have to watch Netflix alone. Maybe when a tree dies, you accept it and move the hell on.

Annoyed that I cut the line, I nevertheless dig the holes and plant those pitiful failed things. As we get replacement bushes, trees, and plants of various kinds, a distressing number of these also end up in the Plant Mental Hospital.

It is then that I remember Miss Regina's words: "Not when it's blooming, not when the ground is frozen." She had been talking about replanting trees and I am *literally replanting trees.* Thankfully, I am within the witch-approved time frame, so maybe Miss Regina would be proud of how I'm tending to my new life.

Maybe.

I never once water a single thing. I never go over there to investigate and see how things are progressing — or not. When I mow the lawn on the tractor, that area is off my established route. It's in a grassless section at the foot of an embankment that is a tangle of thorny bushes and Styrofoam Dunkin' Donuts coffee cups tossed from the windows of passing cars, poison ivy, and airplane-sized liquor bottles. Once I found a doll's head. Just the head, and the eyes were really wide, as if in terror, like the toy manufacturer had designed it with the appropriate facial expression knowing in advance it would be decapitated, her head thrown out the window into an overgrown bramble.

It is sunny all day and then on a dime the sky turns dark and shines like gunmetal, the clouds crack open with a rip of lightning, and it begins to pour — torrential rain. I mean India monsoon rain.

Christopher loves being in the house during a storm like this, whereas it stokes my paranoia about leaks and water damage. He sits and searches for new music while I put my raincoat on every fifteen minutes and circle the house with the high-powered flashlight looking for damage or potential areas of worry. I check the ceilings for signs of leaks. Every sound of dripping signals water penetration. I wish I could be injected with ape tranquilizers.

Then things like this happen: it's 2:00 a.m., still raining, and I can't sleep, but I figure I can eat potato chips, so I go downstairs and kill almost an entire bag while reading horrible news on my phone. On my way back to the bedroom, I submit to my neurosis: I'll just pop down to the basement to make sure it hasn't flooded due to the nonstop torrential rain.

At the bottom of the stairs is a lake.

I'm down there for three hours mopping it up because I don't own a wet vac (but you can bet I order one right there on my phone in the basement). I am moving heavy, soaked boxes out of the way, hoisting Christopher's accordion in its crocodile case up onto the white file cabinet Harold left behind. All the while, I'm thinking, Christopher has no idea this is going on. He's sound asleep upstairs in bed with the dogs, snoring away, and I'm down here in this pond I generated with my mind.

The following morning is stunning. The brook is flowing fast and heavy from the rains, glittering with sharp sparks of sun. Puddles mirror the sky. The dogs try to drink the clouds.

I'm thinking of my mother this morning because of the water, how high the brook is and how fast it's moving. She told me I could write down something I needed to be free of on a piece of paper, fold it four times, and tie it with a piece of white string. "Then throw it into a river, banish it from your life, let the river take it from you. I like to speak words when I do this."

I have done this many times in my life. By taking a person or situation or a trait of my own, folding it in half, then half again, and releasing it, I have banished each one from my life and thoughts. No river required.

The ritual my mother taught me is just that: a series of actions performed in a specific way. Neither the ritual nor the spell, if it is spoken, is the thing that frees you. They are merely symbolic actions to affirm your intention. It is *intention* that creates the banishing. It is choosing to be free that makes you free.

So when I said, "He will never have the chance to betray me again," he did not.

When I said, "I will never have another drink," I did not.

But it's work; it's always work. No pill, no spell, no ritual, no words, no wrinkle of the nose or wave of the wand can create transformation. Only the power of the mind can do that.

My mother has been dead since early summer, and I didn't visit her in hospice or attend her funeral. I don't even know if she

248

*had* a funeral or if she was taken out into a field and burned on a pyre. Maybe there's a headstone marking her grave. Maybe her ashes were scattered in a parking lot.

Though I hadn't seen her since the early 2000s, I have been thinking of her since we moved, because the half dozen of her old paintings that I own — her best ones — hang in rooms and hallways in the house.

My favorite is a portrait of my uncle Mercer that is in the sunroom, one that my cousin Leigh — the daughter of my mother's oldest brother — sent me after it had been in her family's possession for years. My mother painted it when she was a freshman in college, away from home for the first time. She missed her brother, so she created him on canvas from memory. No sitting, no photograph, just a vision. What's stunning is that it looks exactly like him, and even more that there's something *true* in her brushstrokes. I don't know how to speak Art World Technique, but I can tell you, the texture of his blonde hair makes you feel you could reach out and tousle it.

In the dining room is her toe dip into cubism: an angular portrait of my father that presents him both in profile and head-on, eyes an intense red. The colors are fiery, and she perfectly captured my father's duality: the friendly, sociable face he put on for the world and the cold, sadistic, and sociopathic side that only we got to see.

Beside the front door is the largest painting of hers that I own; it's also of my uncle Mercer, no longer a young boy but a man. She'd painted him quickly, in blacks and purples. Once again she captured him perfectly, but at this point she'd had instruction in painting, and I can see her fighting what she'd learned, trying to "unlearn" it by using bold, spontaneous lines.

On the wall along the stairway leading up to the second floor is one of her more interesting paintings of ancestors. This group portrait — I believe it's my great-grandmother, her husband, my grandmother as a baby, and two people I don't know — is executed on two different canvases, so the woman in the very center has half a face on each painting. Framed separately and hung close together, they make for an appropriately strange effect.

The last painting is also of ancestors, and it hangs in our bedroom, above the fireplace. A husband and a wife stand; he in a brimmed hat and jacket, she in a smock dress and an even larger hat. But their faces are missing. Either my mother never finished or she intentionally left their faces . . .

not quite blank, but indistinct.

I love these paintings, but I feel a small, pea-green sadness when I pass them, thinking of what she might have been, who she could have become but didn't.

I'm not tortured or torn apart. I don't feel guilty for giving her none of me, and I don't wish I could change anything that happened. I believe the only difference between my mother and mothers who kill their own kids is one really extra-shitty day. She didn't drive into a lake with me strapped to the backseat, but probably because she couldn't find her car keys.

It took me a long time to realize: I can love my mother — from a distance. I can love who she was when I was very small. She can be forgiven for the mistakes she made as a parent and even for the more terrible things she did. I can accept that she was mentally ill and under the care of a psychiatrist who exploited her and made her even worse. At the same time, I can dislike my mother. For fifteen years I hadn't needed to see her or speak to her or share myself with her. I didn't have to give her anything, not a moment of my life.

My mother had been a perpetual victim. Everything was always somebody else's fault. This sickened me, and I resolved to never play that role. But did I have an ongoing emotional connection to her, either good or bad? Hell no. I could work up more emotion for the horror maple tree than I could for my sad old dead mom.

# INNOCENCE

I start calling and texting Maura dozens of times a day.

"What are you doing?" I write.

"Waiting outside in pouring rain for clients who were supposed to be here a half hour ago and my new shoes are DE-STROYED, but whatever."

She has become my favorite person. I can't remember the last time I made a connection with someone like we've known each other for years. We're friends now, but I still contact her when house things come up, no matter how small. Aside from being a real estate agent, Maura has owned many homes. She knows shit.

When our vintage swing-arm lamp with a green glass shade is finally delivered, we need it installed. I call Maura.

And that's how we meet Eddie.

"He's . . . not for everyone," Maura says cautiously, "but I think he's for you." At least she finishes with certainty. She clarifies. "Another couple of gay gentlemen in town called Eddie to do some work and they were so horrified when he arrived, they called me and were very upset. They didn't want him in their house, they didn't want him ever to return."

"Those don't sound like our kind of gays," I say.

"No kidding," Christopher adds.

"Well." Maura laughs to herself. "Wait and see!"

A beefy, stumpy, mouthy Italian guy in his early sixties, Eddie is a former marine with a missing front tooth from when he contracted hantavirus during the renovation of a church.

"I was pulling the ceiling down and all this fucking mouse shit rained down on top of me, foot after foot of the stuff. I was covered with it."

He ended up being hospitalized and getting a terrible sinus infection that somehow resulted in the loss of a front tooth.

He's had two heart attacks, and he smokes Virginia Slim cigarettes — 120s.

The first day we meet I am really polite, even though he shows up in the most comical, falling-apart vehicle I've ever seen: a blue van packed with crap, the driver's seat more like half a seat and some springs, and a coat hanger for a door handle.

Because Christopher and I introduce ourselves with three-syllable, formal-sounding names, he shakes our hands and says sarcastically, "Edwardo," though he could not be more of an Eddie.

"Hi, Edwardo," I say. "Maura says you're amazing, so we feel lucky to know you."

"Yeah, I'm amazing, all right. Whattaya need?" He's gruff, impatient.

Rather than being taken aback, I'm relieved that I no longer have to make an effort to be — or at least appear — polite.

I show him the lamp. He whistles. "Sweet. What'd this set you back, coupla thou?"

"No, two-fifty," I say, not sure why I'm revealing my finances to this gap-toothed stranger.

"No shit?" he says, his eyebrows raised. "That's a good fucking deal. This is the real McCoy, not some Home Depot crap. Nice."

"It's to replace the tacky reproduction lamp over the range."

I leave it with him and he whistles for me like a dog when he's done. I guess Eddie is into whistling.

I look at it. "It's not centered."

"Whattaya mean, it's not centered? Of course it is."

"No, it's not," I say. And I show him how the base of the fixture is hanging over the left side of the molding.

"Ah, fuck me. All right. Give me a minute."

This time when he's done he calls out, "Yo, Princess, wanna come see if it's centered enough for you now?"

I can't believe it. Not that he called me "Princess" but that he has overcorrected it.

"Now it's too far to the right."

This gets him mad, I can see it. "It's not too far to the right, I measured. It's your eyes that are broken, Missy."

"Listen, you fat fuck," I say, "any moron can see that this base" — I press my index finger against the base of the lamp — "is now hanging over the right side of the molding. Whereas before, it was hanging over the left side. What I want? Is for the fucking base to be in the middle of the trim. Do you even have a brain in that body of yours, or is it all stomach?"

He stifles a grin. "Well, excuse the fuck out of me, ma'am. God forbid I should hang your precious gay lamp one millimeter too far to the right."

"You caveman, that's not one millimeter, that's a quarter of an inch and you fucking know it. Don't think your lazy slob ways are going to get past me."

I have found another new favorite person.

After this, I call Eddie "Fat Fuck." He continues to call me "Princess" and, also accurately, he dubs Christopher "Checkbook."

As I've done with Maura, I begin texting Eddie for every petty little thing that comes up, even the ones I am perfectly capable of doing myself.

"HEY, there's a weird shape wrapped in a blanket in the storage room in the eaves of the attic, can you come over and see what it is? Hurry!!!!!"

And he always does. I want to test the limits, so one cold, rainy day I text him. "I need some lightbulbs changed quick!!!" I get no response, so he draws the line somewhere.

In addition to Princess, he calls me Master, Asshole, His Royal Highness, and Dickhead.

Eddie may slightly resemble a warthog and have a salty nature, but he is also a very experienced all-purpose handyman who has also been a plumber, an electrician, a woodworker, and a mechanic. Eddie can pretty much do anything. He is also smart and good at improvising; when it is a project that interests him, he is an artistic genius.

The only thing about the house that has been a "flaw" is the bathroom off the master bedroom. It was "redone" in the 1990s and has a cheap, discolored fiberglass shower stall and the ugliest tiles from Home Depot. I hate this room. I tell Eddie I want him to build a room for the shower: tiled floor, ceiling, and walls. I want good fixtures and a thick glass door, and I want the existing tile ripped up.

This is our first big Eddie project. He estimates that it will take two weeks, and it ends up taking six. He creates the trim by hand to match the existing antique trim. They don't manufacture the old penny tiles I want anymore, so he finds a guy in New Hampshire who can make them. The bathroom doesn't look renovated. In fact, if we put the house back on the market today, I can imagine people peering in and saying, "This needs updating. Double sinks, rainfall showerhead, maybe a skylight." In other words, it's perfect.

Otis steps on Christopher's mother's foot and gives her a bruised toe, but other than this, Thanksgiving goes off without a hitch.

We have a full house.

His family aren't the sort of people who gush and make a fuss over things. They're smart, witty, commonsense people from Ohio but they're not materialistic so nobody is walking around pointing and going, "Isn't that candelabra art nouveau?"

His parents appreciate the house. Even if old houses aren't your thing, the setting is spectacular. They had been warned that the home has settled over the centuries, and that there is not a single true ninety-degree angle anywhere, and that the sloping floorboards make walking from one room to another feel like you've had an Ambien and a whiskey sour. But I also think they are impressed. Certainly they have to see that it is an improvement, and that their son is happier than when he was a city rat, which is saying a lot, because when has he been unhappy? Not even when he was getting chemo five years ago.

One persistent worry I'd had in the weeks leading up to their arrival is that Christopher's mother keeps her house so clean it's like an operating suite. Seriously, you could perform a kidney transplant on her living room coffee table and no infection would follow.

When we bought the place, Maura told us, "Old houses are great in one way; they absorb a lot of dust and dirt. They are very forgiving." This is completely true.

Nevertheless, I pull up the rugs, shove the furniture out of the way, and wax the floors on my hands and knees, using an orbital buffer to polish them like glass. There is nothing on this earth that shines like a fifteen-inch plank of two-hundred-year-old chestnut. The floors look amazing.

Still, it's impossible to remove all the dust and fine dog hairs. Then we have the twelve-over-twelve windows, which means ninety-six corners where little spiderwebs can form or dust settle. To truly, fully clean this house would take two weeks, full-time. The upstairs guest bathroom, the one with the beautiful 1930s tub, has old brass fixtures that ought to shine. And polishing brass isn't something you can do with one spritz and a wipe.

I think I found a workaround.

For me, the process of writing anything at all is clarifying. I can be muddled in my head, but as soon as I write about whatever it is, I gain perspective. Writing a spell is a way for me to be surgically precise with what I want to happen so that it can happen. Unlike Samantha Stephens, I can't magically make the house clean. But I *can* deflect attention elsewhere, and that's what this brief spell was intended to do.

The keen observer will not detect
One thing amiss, nor one curious speck.
Any aberrations to the eye
Will pass right by
And flow like water over stones.
A thing not seen is never known.

I jotted that down and cycled it through my mind as I prepared for the family's arrival. I swept with a birch twig broom and I sprinkled dried mugwort in the corners of the rooms because of its usefulness in astral projection — and I wanted Christopher's family to project far outward, not in between the floorboards, where the vacuum can't ever reach.

Of course nobody said, "So, what's with the cobweb in the corner above the chair over there?" — the one that I myself noticed I had missed with the vacuum. Then again, they wouldn't, so I will have no way of knowing whether the spell worked or not. That's another thing about being a witch. Sometimes you focus on creating a moment that was going to happen anyway.

I was cooking and setting down plates of food, taking cleaned plates away, refilling glasses, making sure there was enough ice. It almost reminded me of when I was sixteen and worked as a waiter at the

Ground Round in Northampton. I didn't want anybody to do anything at all except relax and enjoy, but in order for this to happen, I had to work like a maniac.

At one point I realized I hadn't checked my phone all day. The first headline in my news feed said: "After the Cranberries and Pie, Take Time to Talk about Death." I thought, Does NPR really want me to bring up funeral plans and wills to my eighty-year-old in-laws immediately after they said they liked Christopher's cranberry sauce, which he made with ginger and worried would be too spicy but turned out not to be?

Fat Fuck Eddie texts that he's bringing one of his "famous apple pies." He says it's a labor of love that he doesn't extend to just anyone. So that's sweet. Calling him a Fat Fuck to his face and reminding him that because he's had hantavirus he remains part rat has truly paid off. He not only fixed the screen door, replaced the rotten trim under the kitchen door, and rewired the exterior lights so that they now work, but we're getting a homemade pie.

It's difficult to imagine Eddie as a baker, but Maura tells me he has a refrigerated pie table, where he can roll out the dough and it stays cold. "That's like five, maybe ten grand," she says, "so he's serious about his pies." I had no idea.

He is thrilled to meet Christopher's family, who have already been briefed. Christopher needed to prepare them, because none of them has ever encountered a creature like Eddie, and to the unsuspecting, he could be a shock. But he is on his best "normal person" behavior. "There's five different kinds of apples in there," he brags. I just hope he didn't drop a lug nut in by mistake. All Eddie has to do is step into the kitchen, turn around, and leave, and I find tiny nails, bits of copper wire, screws, and washers on the rug. He's like Pig-Pen from *Peanuts,* except instead of dirt, he walks around in a cloud of hardware.

Eddie doesn't stay long. "Got to return to the Mrs., or I'll never hear the end of it for abandoning her on Thanksgiving to be here instead of home with her fat, lazy ass." So a little of the real Eddie slips out at the last moment, and I notice my brother-in-law's wife frown.

It is the best apple pie I've ever had, and it wins raves all around the table. Eddie is unique, as horrible as he is wonderful.

I immediately text, "Yowza! Best apple pie ever. Bring more." And he does. He delivers another one the following day. More confident now that he knows he was popular in pie form, he attempts to entertain Christopher's parents with the same dumb-blonde jokes he made one summer thirty years ago when he allegedly did stand-up comedy at some roadhouse in the Catskills. After four or five of these gems, his eyes fall upon Christopher's mother, who is, in fact, blonde. He says, "Oops. Open mouth, insert foot. Sorry, Blondie. No offense, but you're not natural anyway, that's Clairol."

She looks at him and smiles. "As long as we're being honest, you know your pie's not really all *that* great."

We all laugh over the audacity of her snappy comeback, and Eddie clutches his chest dramatically. "Aww, you're killing me!" he roars.

The endearing detail to me is how thoughtful it was of him to remove the pistol that's normally fixed to his hip.

Maura is pleased to have gifted Eddie to us. We didn't move here to make new friends, but the two of them are remarkable and not the kinds of people you let slip away.

"And he does excellent work," she says.

"Yeah, when he deigns to show up," I reply. "It is impossible to get him here before eleven, and then he always has to leave at four, and wouldn't you know it, he can't make it the next day or the day after that, and he's driving me crazy. Is he an alcoholic? He's got the beer gut of a drinker, that's for sure."

"Do you know about Eddie's kids?"

Eddie is a *father*? It is like she told me he is also a Calvin Klein model: impossible to believe. "No. He's mentioned a wife, but I can't tell if she's real. Once he made it sound like she was in prison. I guess I kind of always imagined Eddie living alone above an old closed-down gas station. Just him and his refrigerated pie table."

Maura explains that Eddie has two adult kids from his first marriage, and two kids with his current wife (who is not in prison and is very nice) who are both severely autistic. The older boy is nonverbal and can be physically aggressive and destructive. Eddie is always having trouble with caretakers — "mentors," they're called — to watch the kid. The younger boy is not only verbal but a savant.

Next time I see him I bring it up. "You have autistic kids?"

"Yeah," he says. "And the oldest is giving me a lot of shit lately. He destroyed the fucking sofa, tore all the stuffing out."

No stranger to spectrum disorders myself, I say, "There must be something annoying about the sofa. Is it polyester? Your kid probably hates the texture. He wouldn't destroy it if something wasn't wrong with it."

"It is polyester," Eddie admits. "It's kind of nubby."

Oh, I know exactly what such a sofa would feel like. It makes me shiver involuntarily and causes goose bumps to rise along the back of my neck. "Nubby is horrible," I tell him. "I would have destroyed it, too. Get canvas or leather or something smooth. Scratchy, man-made fabrics are the worst. He can probably feel the individual chemicals that make up the horrible thing. When I get a whiff of Diet Coke, I don't smell just one thing, it's a laboratory of chemicals, individually but all together. It's appalling. You have to be very aware of scientist-created substances and avoid them."

Eddie grunts and I am unsatisfied with his reaction. He doesn't understand that I understand. I must prove it. "Does he smash lightbulbs?" I ask.

This gets his attention. "He sure as hell does. How did you know that?"

"Because normal lightbulbs, the ones that people like you have, burn my skin. Haven't you ever noticed that we don't have any bulb over 20 watts in the house? And most are LED lights encased in amber-colored plastic, so they give off a warm light. They don't bother me at all. But halogen lights? Those are the worst."

"We have halogen spots."

"Well, I hope he rips them right down from the ceiling."

"He already did," Eddie says.

Eddie won't put his son in an assisted-living facility because he is (probably rightly) worried the boy will be abused by the adults in charge of his care. But one day Eddie shows up with bite marks on his shoulder and arm. Another day he arrives late looking completely exhausted because his kid was up all night and ripped the trim off every window in the house.

The other gay couple Maura mentioned must have looked at Eddie and seen a misogynist, racist, Trump-loving, gun-packing, motorcycle-riding Italian with a missing front tooth and wanted nothing to do with him. And while he is all those things and more, we love Eddie. Yes, he is a wart-hog from hell, but you can trust him. His heart is good and large and covered with surgical scars. And he can bake. Plus, he isn't really a misogynist racist; he is a misanthropic xenophobe. He hates every-one who isn't him or his immediate family or the one friend he visits in Arizona, and now us — and the dogs, who love him and are loved in return (save Wiley, who is incapable of love except for us, and then only sometimes).

It doesn't take long before the sound of either a falling-apart-piece-of-junk van or a motorcycle passing by sends the dogs into a frenzy of excitement. They deflate miserably every time it turns out not to be Eddie, including Wiley, because he's been deprived of a chance to bark incessantly.

Eddie is a temperamental, arrogant know-it-all who is also a craftsman of such rarefied talent, honed by decades of experience, that of course he's temperamental, because artists frequently are; of course he's arrogant, because he's either smarter than you think he is or he's smarter than you are; and he comes across as a know-it-all because, well, when it comes to houses or engines or anything mechanical, he pretty much does know it all.

Except you wouldn't think so if you saw the picture I took where his blue plaid shirt had popped a couple of buttons over the stomach as he bent over, lit cigarette dangling from his mouth, to open a red gas can.

# JOHN'S BREAD

Otis has made an effortless transition from softball-footed city puppy on a leash to free-range country beast.

From his perspective, it must seem that the world has suddenly righted itself, for now everything is at a scale that suits him. Those hard, narrow sidewalks peppered with scrawny, already peed-upon trees are gone. That cramped and noisy six-room Upper West Side cage is no more. His once wobbly gait has been replaced by authoritative strides. With a very low expenditure of energy he can trot from the far end of the field to the front door. But sometimes he runs and it is astonishing to see. Swimming pools of distance pass beneath him with each gallop across his acreage. At all times his face registers joy and freedom.

All three dogs are happier.

Phobic, neurotic Wiley had always hated leaving the comfort and security of the apartment and loathed going for walks, trembling on the end of his leash until we returned indoors. Now he is always the first one out the door, exploding across the field alongside Otis, surpassing him in speed, a tan blur streaking against green.

Radar tries to keep up, and it frustrates and embarrasses him that his legs are of inferior length due to his half-corgi genetics. He can run surprisingly fast but he pays for it the next day, limping and glowering. Radar misses nothing. He understands human language, both spoken and body. His personality is that of a police sergeant (the old sitcom kind, not the new riot-gear kind). He assumes a role of great authority and leadership, even if he is sometimes forced to do his job from the sidelines, where he issues commands to the others. Despite the pain, he is compelled to herd Otis, to guide him, to manage him. Although Radar is low-slung and close to the ground like a corgi, his German shepherd half propels him up, and he will try to take Otis down by the neck. Otis dramatically collapses onto the field and rolls onto his back, allowing Radar to wrestle with him.

Wiley knows better than to tangle with these two, but he prances around barking encouragement.

It is wonderful to see all the dogs running and playing so freely, but it is also alarming, because Otis is enormous and he is going to accidentally hurt one of the others one day.

It is obvious: Otis needs a playmate.

In the 2004 novel *My Sister's Keeper,* by Jodi Picoult, thirteen-year-old Anna Fitzgerald realizes she was conceived intentionally by her parents to be an organ donor for her sick older sister.

We need our own Anna Fitzgerald for Otis, a durable, tireless dog that won't end up with snapped bones or cardiac arrest after an afternoon playing in the field.

After researching breeds, we settle, at least academically, on a breed both of us are familiar with but neither of us has personally ever known: Rhodesian Ridgeback. According to the AKC, "The Rhodesian Ridgeback is a big-game hunter . . . imposing enough to make intruders think twice, yet swift enough to run with Greyhounds."

In other words, Hello, Anna!

Rhodesian Ridgebacks were bred to take down lions on the plains of Africa. That is exactly the sort of creature we require as a playmate for our rambunctious behemoth. We locate a litter on a horse farm in Massachusetts and drive there, though Google Maps has obviously been drinking because she keeps sending us off on maddening tangents.

We finally find it, a sprawling white house with acre upon rambling acre of bright green grass and a significant pond out front with birds gliding slowly across it. "Look at those beautiful duc—" I look closer as we approach. "Oh, no." My heart seizes. "Turn the car around."

"What?" Christopher says, pulling in to park. "Why?"

I point. *"Swans."*

We despise swans. They are bad omens for everything. The only people who hate swans more must be Donna Karan and her daughter, because the Central Park swans attacked and killed their dog. The reigning monarch of the United Kingdom technically owns all the swans in the country, and if I held that title, I would order them all beheaded and turned into duvets.

"Well," Christopher says, knowing he needs an angle, "we're not here to rescue a swan."

"No," I counter, "but these farmers are *swan people,* and I don't even know what that means."

In retrospect, we should have heeded the warning and gone home empty-handed. Instead, we greet Connie in her living room.

She has the sort of hair once referred to as a "hairdo" and that you almost never see in real life anymore: tall and blonde and vaguely egg-shaped, but with a fringe above the forehead and some sort of hair-braid belt around the very center, which I suppose holds it all securely in place but surely can't be real, can it?

Even from four feet away, I can tell that the ruby on the pendant she wears *is* real, and it looks to be a pretty good one. Retail price guesstimate: $14,000, if it is the two carats it appears to be and is from Burma, which the coloring suggests. If it weren't quite as purple, it would be worth much more. She has on cream slacks, a gold blouse, and black shoes, and she really pops against her pale blue wall-to-wall carpeting.

As we say our hellos, my attention shifts to the doorway, where a Rhodesian Ridgeback appears. I have seen posts on dog breed message boards that suggest certain Ridgebacks can be aggressive, but this one seems sweet, not made out of meanness.

Connie said, "That's Sasha, the mother. Why don't you follow me back and I'll take you to see the puppies."

We walked through the kitchen, where All-Clad pots hung from a black iron-and-copper pot hanger above the butcher block counter.

"You have an Amana Radarange Touchmatic II!" I blurt out, in the same tone of voice one might use to announce, "I know who killed JonBenét!"

Everybody stops because I have stopped and am staring lustfully at Connie's old microwave oven. "Oh, yeah," she says, "probably a little overdue for a new one."

"Oh, no," I tell her, awkwardly insistent. "You should never replace it. It's like a Mercedes Diesel from the 1970s — it will work forever."

"Yes," Connie says, smiling, "let's hope. Mostly use it for popcorn, anyway. Come right through here," and she leads us through a darkened dining room with a long, glossy mahogany-stained table, matching buffet, and china cabinet. The chairs are upholstered with gold-and-blue seats. Nancy Reagan herself could have picked out this tacky furniture, and in fact, Connie reminds me of Nancy. Rail thin, finely clothed — not my taste but polished. Her hair isn't as fashionable as Nancy's had been at the time, but then this is a working horse farm in the country, and she does have the clever braid wrapped around the center, so it's not like she isn't making the effort.

We arrive at a fancy pen/crate structure. "All of them are up-to-date on their shots, they've been checked over by our vet, and they're very healthy. There's just one bitch, though."

"Oh good, we're looking for a male," I say.

We couldn't feed a sweet girl puppy to Otis.

She opens the door, and five puppies run out. One stops at my shoe to chew on the lace. I step over it and into a carpeted room with a bar. Even though I no longer drink, just being near a bar, even one gussied up with a brass and white vinyl nautical theme, is a comfort.

Four puppies are now peeing on the carpet.

Connie seems unperturbed by this, as if the four of them are yawning. "They still have accidents now and then, but for the most part, they all know to go outside."

"Yeah, obviously," I mutter.

I kind of want to leave.

Christopher is bent over and playing with a puppy, the one that chewed my shoelace. "This one is cute." He is the only one who hasn't peed on the carpet, so there is that.

"That one has quite the personality," Connie says cheerfully, but I hear the words translated as "That one's an asshole dick-face."

When Christopher picks him up, I know *he is ours.* I also know *I don't want him.* But I have to want him, because this *is* going to happen.

Is it like that for everybody? I wonder. Sometimes you know something is going to happen, even though there are ample opportunities to prevent it. Even though you don't want it, you know it's inevitable.

Connie busies herself blotting her carpet with Listerine inside a former Windex bottle, the label worn away to white paper and glue. "This is the secret," she said. "Half Listerine and half water in a sprayer."

"Secret to what?" I wanted to ask her. "To looking like a former truck stop hooker who won the Massachusetts state lottery, or the secret to making sure nobody ever wants to visit your home again?" I can almost never say what I'm thinking at any given moment. I would have been stabbed to death years ago.

"What do you think?" Christopher asks.

I realize I am staring at Connie, watching her pad across the carpeting, bend over, and spritz in places she . . . imagined the puppies had peed? Saw them pee? Her spraying seems entirely random. Maybe it has nothing whatsoever to do with the pee. Maybe she just loves squirting mouthwash on her plush carpet?

I snap my attention to Christopher and the puppy. "Sure, why not?"

"Good, I think so, too." He looks excited, and this makes me happy.

"I'll take him outside while you deal with the Listerine queen," I whisper, eying the sliding glass door off the dining room that leads to a shit-peppered cement yard. I carry the puppy out and set him on the ground, where he immediately goes for my laces again. "No, now don't do that," I say in what I hope is a sweet but firm voice. "Can't you do anything else?"

I walk away knowing he'll follow, because that's what puppies do, but he doesn't. Instead, he begins to chase a large bumble-bee.

"Oh, hey, no, don't do that," I say as I scoop him up to save him from getting stung. I carry him over to a farther side of the cement lawn and set him down again. "You're coming home with us today. You're about to have a brand-new life," I tell him. I look over my shoulder to make sure I am out of hearing range. "We're rescuing you from her Listerine bottle," I tell him. "You owe us forever."

He looks right at me and pees.

"What a good boy!" I cry in amazement, petting him vigorously. "You are such a good boy."

We have picked the right dog, after all, the only one who didn't squat on the rug.

It is a sign. I feel enormous relief. I am going to love this dog.

He is going to be perfect.

On the car ride home he sleeps in my arms.

At one point I say to Christopher, "He's the most precious thing ever," as his little nose breath tickles the hairs on my wrist.

And this is the last nice thing I say about him until he is two.

# KING'S CROWN

Right before Christmas, I'm riding with Maura to look at a former dairy farm when she turns to me with a knowing smile and says, "I'm a witch, just like you are."

This remark comes out of nowhere: an owl flying into the grill of your car at night. It blows me back, pins me to the passenger seat. "What did you say?"

"You heard me. I said I'm a witch, like you."

I have never told anyone in my life, other than my husband, that I am a witch, or that my mother was a witch, or that my mother's line is populated with them, going way back.

I look at Maura and I see it myself. "Of course you are," I said. "That makes perfect sense." She knew from the start that we were meant to be in the house.

Beltaine: A Pagan Odyssey is the oldest pagan festival in the state, held on a farm five minutes down the very same brook

that's behind our house. That I unknowingly chose to share a river with the witches
and the Wiccans is an example of the
witches' Law of Attraction.

Often when we unearth an old can with a
pull-tab or a bottle from the 1940s, I will
tell Christopher, "Throw it in the river and
send it to the Wiccans."

Which has over time become abbreviated
to "Send it to the Wiccans."

As in "Did you see how Gunther gnawed
the arm of the chair in your office? Time to
send him to the Wiccans."

Wicca is a religion that began in Britain in
the 1950s — just like Doc Martens footwear. It has many "branches," or *traditions,*
and they all share a deep respect for nature,
and most Wiccans share the Wiccan Rede:
"An it harm none, do what you will."

Witchcraft, on the other hand, is thousands of years old and predates most — if
not all — formal religions. As I've explained,
it's not a religion. Rather, it's a trait, like
brown eyes. Or an ability, like being able to
do the splits. I've always considered it to be
inherited, but maybe it can be learned, in
which case perhaps it is all *craft.* It is art
and it is science and it is a complete mystery.
I've known people who are witches but who
have no idea, so you can inherit it without

knowledge or a family history of practice.

Being a witch requires no tools, no herbs, no spells. But if those things help someone, then they should cloak-and-wand all they want, but there aren't even any rituals that *must* be undertaken. A witch manipulates energy, near and distant. This is accomplished through conjuring, a form of creation generated through extraordinarily focused intent. It manifests within the witch as a feeling of *certainty.*

Some witches incorporate spells, herbs, rituals, and other tools into their practice. These can enhance or underscore one's focus. It is popularly believed that "spells" are "magic" and powerful on their own — that coming across an old spell in a grimoire, a book or collection of spells, and speaking it out loud could turn somebody into a rat or cause a demon to appear, for instance. Of course, that is fiction.

My first instinct is that if you have to look up a spell, you don't get it. If you decide you want one, it should come only from you.

Then I think, That's judgmental. I'm a writer. It comes to me naturally because I have done it since I was a little kid. When I compose a spell, it's something like a poem, a recipe, or a piece of computer code. I like a spell that rhymes, and I like an olde-timey dialect. But the most important detail is specificity.

It's not difficult for me to frame what it is I want to create or to change or to do using language, but some people can't express themselves like that. They can't sketch what's in their heart using letters. When they come across these words, though, these phrases, these spells, they can recognize when one rings true for them.

I define a spell as a *lens* that can aid in clarifying and maintaining one's focus so that *intent is transformed into certainty*. A *ritual* serves as an amplifier for a spell. A spell used in conjunction with a ritual can boost the magick by making the witch's focus — and intent — more powerful.

Witchcraft is *not* supernatural; it is hypernatural.

Witches are by default attuned to the thrumming network of connections that exist just beneath the obvious surface layer of reality we all experience. They are able to visualize an outcome to such a powerful and intense degree that something on the quantum level is triggered; a particle feels observed and thus decides whether it is in this state or that state.

That's my best guess at how it must work, but I don't know.

As I said, I would never believe in witches were it not for the fact that I am one myself. Even my extensive studies of the brain, physics, and cosmology have not enabled me to explain certain things I have experienced.

In 1998, when I had relapsed and was living in seclusion and squalor on Third Avenue, I was on the phone with my mother, and she told me she was near death. She believed she had suffered a small stroke and that another, fatal one was imminent. It had been nearly ten years since she had experienced a severe stroke, which paralyzed the right side of her body, altered her personality, and damaged the speech region of her brain so that she had to learn to talk again. I can remember calling her regularly and leading her through the correct pronunciation of the alphabet, from A through Z. "No, not see, zee. Try it again."

"You aren't going to die," I told her.

"How do you know that?"

"Because I know when you're going to die, and it's in the distant future. Do you want to know the year?"

My mother thought about it briefly. "Are you sure you know?"

"Yes."

"It's not soon? Mother died at seventy-five, and I'm sixty-three; I've never felt I would make it to seventy."

"You make it past seventy," I told her. "You outlive your mother."

This seemed to calm her. She believed me, even though I could be full of shit. I had written down the first year that popped into my head: 2015. I was so bad at math that I didn't know the number of years between 1998 and 2015 without using a calculator, and even then I'd have to think about exactly how to set about figuring this out. Frequently, I counted on my fingers. For all I knew, she would have to live to be 126 to make it to the distant date of 2015.

It was the summer of 2015 when she died. She was eighty.

Not a thirty-minute drive from this house is a witchcraft supply shop. It's called Effigy, so you know they're serious. No tacky "new age" shop with slowly swooshing meditation music playing. It's where you go if you need a scrying mirror or a very specific herb. Almost everything is handmade: jewelry, brooms, wands, altar tools. They have beautiful candles for those who practice candle magick or divination, and excellent handmade incense.

This is a very witchy area, which is less

surprising after I learn some little-known facts from a book I bought at Effigy. I had no idea that forty-five years before the Salem witch trials of the early 1690s, Connecticut had its own persecution fest. Alse Young, from Windsor, Connecticut, was the first person in America to be executed for witchcraft. Where is the college named in her honor? I wonder. Or the highway? Or the holiday?

Salem's trials lasted for one year, ours for fifty.

In all, thirty-five cases of witchcraft were brought before the courts, resulting in the execution of eleven people, compared to the twenty killed in Salem. Surely there are still ancestors of those eleven, and maybe they're some of the many witches living and practicing their craft in the state today. Covens exist, but I know that Connecticut has many *solitary practitioners,* witches who work alone.

Witches have a way of finding each other. A recognition occurs even if a realization does not. My friend Suzanne and I have been friends now for decades and she is a witch, as is her mother. They are of Puerto Rican descent, so Suzanne does lots of spells with elements of Santería blended in.

The two women I'm closest to are both

witches, and I didn't know this until relatively late in our friendships. *We are everywhere.*

The culture of persecution continues, so the vast majority of witches remain cloaked. "Hi, I'm something toddlers dress up as at Halloween and there's not an educated, rational person on the planet who believes I am even remotely possible."

People don't understand what witchcraft is and what it is not, which makes sense, since witches themselves may disagree on these points. Most agree that witchcraft is not only natural (as opposed to supernatural) but elemental: born of the glue that shapes everything around us and connects us all.

"Thank you for letting me know," I say to Maura when she tells me about herself.

"You're welcome," Maura says with a slight smile. I love her.

The day we met, she said she knew me.

The day we moved in, she dropped off a gift: a black iron cauldron and about fifty used books on plants and herbs. I should have known then. She shouldn't have had to tell me.

Some people are born with distinct advantages, like wealth, the durable kind that has

been — and will be — around for generations. They don't know financial insecurity,
and the very best opportunities are available to them.

Is being born a witch, who is the son of a
witch, an advantage?

As a child I experienced a great deal of
anxiety, confusion, loss, fear, and pain. The
chaos became woven into the fabric of my
being, so that I would replicate many of the
familiar feelings from childhood as an adult
— living on the financial edge, the rug
always about to be pulled out from under
me, a hairs-breadth away from total self-
destruction at any given moment and yet
changing absolutely everything, all at once,
at the speed of a snapping finger.

*I am going to be a published writer,* I
decided, which took twenty-four months.
From being hungover and in my underwear,
sitting on a plastic lawn chair in my apartment, surrounded by empty beer cans
numbering into the multiple hundreds, to
holding a book I wrote — twenty-four
months. A mere two years after that, my
face was on the front page of *USA Today*
and I was prepared.

I told my therapist, "My book is going to
come out, and it's going to be huge, so I'm
in this strange limbo, this floating time." I

smiled when I said this, because it was exciting — but it was also terrifying.

He replied, "You have unrealistic expectations, and it concerns me."

His remark was almost word for word what Christopher, merely my agent at the time, had told me. In both cases it made me laugh. I knew how delusional I sounded, and I could imagine the pity I would feel for me if I were sitting there listening to me saying, "And it's going to be huge!"

I would feel skeeved out by such a person. I would advise him, "Think the *worst,* so you won't be crushed when it sells five copies."

That's what made me laugh. It wasn't that I needed the book to be successful. My first book, a paperback original novel, *had* sold five copies and was reviewed in maybe two places, one of which was online, and back then nobody was online.

This time my memoir was being published in hardcover. It was when I finished writing and it was in production with my publisher that I saw its success. I knew, in fact, the book was not going to be the low seller they were expecting — and with a small first printing, were prepared for — but rather the opposite: it was going to be so successful that it was ridiculous.

It made me laugh. And it made those around me feel kind of bad for me.

Until it happened. *Running with Scissors* was on the *New York Times* bestseller list for years. The rest of my career was based on the success of that one book.

The witchcraft advantage was when I decided, *I'm going to be a published writer.* The training I received as a child from my mother in concentration, focus, and image-forming, combined with my own spectrum-directed mind, resulted in writing a book and then getting it published. Exactly what I determined *would* happen *did* happen. It involved a great amount of work and relentless persistence, but I am intense and driven, so I accomplished my goal.

The book's success was not the result of witchcraft. But because I'm a witch, I saw in advance that it would be a surprise bestseller, the book that came out of nowhere and that everybody who does read *would* read.

Witchcraft, or at least my kind of witchcraft, cannot control the success of a book. I can't "make" people go spend their money on my book or "make" them read it. Christopher already checked on that. "Whatever you did that time? *Do it again.* Then do it for all my other clients."

I don't believe a witch can control the behavior of any other person. A witch can influence the experience of another person by perhaps "removing" something from view or creating something shiny and sparkly in a different direction, but to actively seize the strings and control the actions of another would be like taking flight: against the nature of things, therefore not within the realm of possibility.

Witchcraft works best on the micro scale, not the macro. But the micro can have enormous impact on the macro.

When we first got together, Christopher felt feverish one evening, like he was coming down with the flu. He was coughing. As he slept, his breathing seemed labored. And this frightened me. I spent the entire night wide awake — as alert as if I were taking the LSAT — breathing with him and using the tips of my electric fingers to draw the infection from his body.

On the one hand, this is patently absurd *and I get that.*

On the other hand, he was fine in the morning and has hardly been sick one day in the twenty years he has belonged to me.

The macrophage listens to the witch.

# MAIDEN'S HAIR

"I just think you'd have to be crazy to want to live there," my grandmother Carolyn said when I called her at home in Alabama from my Greenwich Village apartment.

"Oh, it's not at all like you think it is," I said. "You could come for a visit."

"Goodness gracious, I could do no such thing!" she replied, as though I'd suggested she earn some spending money by becoming a pole dancer.

Although I didn't say it to her, I thought *she* was the crazy one for leaving Atlanta, where she'd lived all her life, for Dothan, Alabama. Why would you trade your plate of lobster thermidor for a roadkill skunk?

I heard similar things anytime I left the city. "Doesn't the pace make you crazy?" people would ask. Or, "Everybody there is nuts!" And I get it. I saw a microwave oven hurled out a window, watched Uma Thurman walk barefoot down lower Fifth Avenue to get a sandwich, and witnessed a girl wearing nothing but her bra and panties playing the cello in Central Park — all on the same day.

It isn't until we move to rural Connecticut, though, that I understand that country crazy is different from New York City crazy. Country crazy is free-range. In the city you can't help but be in contact with people, and someone is bound to keep you in check. One afternoon when I was leaving my old apartment, a doorman told me to go back upstairs and shave because I looked like the Unabomber. Here in the dirt-road country you can go days — weeks, maybe — without seeing another soul. You can lose track entirely of what it means to "pull it together" when you leave the house. The liberating thing is that you can be completely yourself. The frightening part is that eventually others witness you being you.

Maura has begun taking me with her to meet some of her real estate clients. The idea freaks me out at first. "Won't they be suspicious, like, 'Who is this guy?' "

"You're my marketing consultant," she says.

Sometimes I bring my camera and photograph the houses, and these images end up in the ads to sell the properties, so I *am,* in fact, her marketing consultant.

Maura's career as a high-powered real estate agent is fascinating. "You meet people at important moments in their lives," she explains. "It's usually one of the three Ds: divorce, death, or debt. But there are happy reasons, too, and I love that, like when you have a young family just starting off and they're buying their first house."

"Yeah," I said, "I don't need to meet any of those people."

Maura is one of the worst drivers I've ever encountered. In the short time I've known her, I've been in the car with her for three accidents, all of them her fault, so there's no telling how many others happen when she's on her own, loose in the world. They're mostly fender benders — it's not like anyone's vehicle has been accordioned — and Maura's solution is to hop out with her wallet and offer cash to the other driver. To my surprise, they accept every time. "No one wants to have to deal with insurance over something tiny like this," she says.

"Tiny? Maura, you rear-ended them at a stoplight and smashed their tail light. What if they develop whiplash?"

"Whiplash is a myth," she says dismissively.

One day I am in the passenger seat, anxious, of course, but it's not Maura's lack of skill behind the wheel that is worrying me. She has just revealed something about the owner of the property we're about to see, and I tell her, "I don't want to go if she's going to shoot us."

"She probably won't. I'll call first to be sure."

The use of "probably" is alarming; phoning ahead is only vaguely reassuring.

"How did you get this client?" I ask.

"I know Billie from the gas station where I get my coffee every morning. Real local place. Billie works behind the counter, and people kind of brush her off. She's missing some teeth, and she talks like a hick in this deep smoker's voice and they think she's white trash."

I nod. "I get it."

"But Billie is anything but dumb. I had told her I was a real estate agent, and it turns out that she wants to sell the property she lives on: sixty acres of prime undeveloped land. She has no money, you know, paycheck to paycheck, like a lot of people. She lives in a tiny tear-down of a house, and behind her is this magnificent property that is worth a fortune."

Maura can be hard to follow if she's telling a long story, but she really nails it when she gives highlights. Billie is exactly as advertised, and so is her land. She walks us around and relates an amazing anecdote when we come to the crumbled remains of a former outbuilding.

"I'll never forget it. Even though it was more than fifty years ago, it feels like yesterday. That foundation right there, or what's left of it, anyways" — Billie points — "was the icebox building. You see, Daddy was a mink farmer. Oh, he sold to the best of the best — fancy stores in Chicago and New York City, they all bought Daddy's minks. Movie stars wore them, you know." She lowers her gaze and looks at me to make sure I grasp the significance of this last piece of information. "For alls we know, Marilyn Monroe herself wore one. After all, she lived not far from here 'tall, in one of the 'burys, anyways."

"Roxbury, I think," Maura offers.

"That sounds right," Billie says. "Anyways, it was a whole building kept cold with blocks of ice. When I got married to Purvis, Daddy had my wedding cake sitting on a table right in the middle of the room, and all the mink skins were nailed to the walls all around from floor to ceiling. I swear, you never saw such a sight, it was beautiful."

She is so on-brand — *my* brand. Seriously, one of her best memories is her wedding cake being surrounded by dead minks? I can envision how it must have appeared that the frosted tower was swaddled in a coat as fine as any Marilyn would wear. It is thrilling.

" 'Course these days," she continues, "everybody is anti-fur and anti-everything. I think if people actually got to meet a mink in person, they'd have no problem at all wearing a coat made outta a whole slew of them hateful things. Minks is assholes."

This woman that people write off? She isn't crazy at all. She is eccentric as hell, but she is dignified and she is private, and she is missing teeth and she lacks the polish of an education.

That doesn't make her trash. That makes her me.

A couple of days later, Maura calls again. As she frequently does, she begins almost midsentence.

"Apparently this guy is moving overseas, and he's talking a mile a minute about how he has to sell his vintage home. You should come. I'm telling you, just from speaking with him on the phone for five minutes — or, really, *listening* to him for five minutes

— I can tell he's a total nutcase. What is it about me?" she asks rhetorically. "Why do I attract them?"

"Let me know when you figure it out," I tell her, "because I have it, too."

"Come on out. I just pulled into your driveway," she says.

As I'm walking past the maple tree, it gives another loud "pop" like a fire log, and I expect to see sparks flying. It's so loud and startling that I jump, literally leaving the planet for a fraction of a second. When I climb in her car, I say, "What was that? Did you hear that?" but she's busy shoving a potted orchid in my hands. "Can you hold this for me?"

"Why do you have it?"

"It's a small gift for the homeowner," she says, "a way to introduce myself."

Maura is a giver — of presents, of time, of attention. I quickly understood that she is not out to earn points; she gives because that is the thing she does. Like some people hum or knit, she gives.

As we pull up the steep driveway, a beautiful eighteenth-century Greek Revival is on our left, with moneyed landscaping. A very tall and slender man who looks to be in his early sixties, wearing faded blue hip-hugger jeans that flare at the ankles and a soft pink shirt open midway down his chest, is trimming the boxwoods beside the door with a pair of electric hedge clippers. The clippers are loud, but out of the corner of his eye he sees us, and we see him see us. Even as we stand by the car thirty feet from him, with Maura holding a large orchid in both hands, the man refuses to turn our way.

"Oh, this one's trouble," Maura says in a low voice. "Look at him pretending not to notice us, would you? And those shoes!"

I hadn't noticed the footwear, but I certainly do now. They are some sort of carpet slipper, as in made from Persian or Turkish carpet, and they curl up at the toe, like those of a cartoon genie.

Maura calls out, "Hello! I'm Maura, the real estate agent!"

Only now does he turn to face us and act surprised. He is a dreadful actor. His eyes widen in mock startlement and a huge fake smile appears, his Pantone 11-4001 brilliant white teeth gleaming. "Why, hello! I'm sorry. I didn't hear you pull up." He turns off the cordless hedge trimmer and approaches us. Or maybe "approaches" isn't the right word. He catwalks toward us, one foot landing directly in front of the other, his jaw muscles clenched, shoulders back.

I notice the gigantic — I mean walnut-sized — South Sea pearl suspended from a thick, heavy gold chain around his neck.

He has a full head of thick white hair that is natural — no plugs, no hairpiece — but it is intensely coiffed. He possesses fine bone structure, which has allowed him to retain his handsomeness into his sixties. He is heavily moisturized and would be slippery to the touch, a thought that makes me shiver with revulsion. It's a relief that he doesn't extend his hand to shake when he proclaims, "I am Jeffrey!"

We follow him onto the covered porch that extends the length of the house. Jeffrey walks fast and talks even faster. It's like he's on the wrong speed, or maybe that he's on speed.

He takes the orchid. "Is that for me? How thoughtful," he says without a trace of gratitude in his voice, bending at the waist and setting it on a small wicker table beside a vintage hickory chair next to a Dutch door, the top of which is open. "You're here to see the house? Well, don't delay, come inside. It's a gem," he says. "The finest antique home in the Tribury area."

We step through the door and into a blindingly wallpapered and faux-finished eye-assaulting fusion of interior decorating and mania on vivid display in what I suppose is . . . a sitting room? The wallpaper is a vibrating gold and burgundy. The trim and doors leading out of the room are the same shade of burgundy. Two antique glass-front cabinets loom on two adjacent walls at right angles to each other, both packed with decorative objects. Not one oil lamp but forty; not two teacups, two hundred.

Everything is done in multiples, and the effect screws with my brain, makes me feel like I am looking at overlapping images or that I am having a stroke. A leather wing chair sits beside an antique pie crust table that is topped with a brass candlestick lamp with a large cream shade. A second wing chair is tucked into the corner by one of the cabinets, this one covered with a mink throw, not to be confused with a faux-mink throw. (Did it come from Billie's father's cake abattoir?) All the pillows have piping that picks up one of the colors in the carpet. Plaids are mixed but in different scales, so they "work," and everything is layered; the windows have shades, scrims, and two sets of drapes. Trim is painted, glazed, then sealed. No bulb is over 40 watts, but there are so many accent lamps — so many *pairs* of them — there isn't a shadow to be seen.

Jeffrey speeds us from this room into the kitchen, which hits me in the chest like an air rifle. It is so intricately decorated that it makes the previous sitting room seem like a minimalist space for doing yoga. Hand-planed and wax-finished cabinets inset with beveled trim moldings, a counter that branches into an L where stacks of cubbyholes have been built in to store pens, pencils, papers, paperclips, basically two of everything from Staples, all neatly organized at a standing desk at the end of the kitchen counter. Overhead, antique beams complete with hatchet marks have foxy little antique brass hooks — probably Dutch — screwed in, and from them hang dozens of bundles of dried herbs, each tied with spun flax twine. Multiple chile pepper ristras drape either side of the bay window, which itself is cushioned with a smorgasbord of down pillows upholstered in a red-and-gray toile. Several iron racks are suspended from the beams, and each is crammed with antique copper pans, pots, kettles, and skillets.

In front of the window seat is a very fine antique French round table surrounded by what I believe to be five or six Burr Yew Windsor armchairs that probably cost $50,000 each.

"I've got to sell this place, and fast," Jeffrey gushes breathlessly as we stand in the middle of the stupefying room. "I'm moving to Morocco, you see, immediately," only he pronounces it "imeeeeeeeeeediately." "I'm signing with Elite model management over there; it's a done deal. They're going to relaunch my career and make me a super-model again."

*Again?* I think. Then I wonder, How would he and Vivi get along? I want to lock them in a room together and see which one makes it out.

Maura smiles warmly and says, "Oh, I see, well, that's —"

He cuts her off. "There's enormous de-mand for gentlemen my age who have" — and here he turns and looks at me for the first time — "no offense" — before turning away and continuing, "all their hair. Most men my age have lost theirs, but mine is as thick as it was when I was twenty-two. And not only that, see these hands?"

He whips those hands up in the air so fast I flinch, thinking he is about to slap us both. He positions them right beside his face, manicured and buffed fingernails facing us, a pinky grazing each cheekbone. On his right pinky is a chunky and lurid gold ring with an enormous red gemstone encircled with a thick braid of gold and what look like miniature flying buttresses on the sides and a Greek key cut-out design. The ring is

302

a conglomeration of different design motifs, each in conflict with the other.

As much as I covet jewelry, this ring makes me feel like a straight guy looking at Chris Christie naked in the locker room.

He sees me staring at it but misreads my fascination for envious admiration. "What, this?" he says coyly, expertly repositioning his fingers, bending them slightly at the knuckles in such a way that the overhead pinprick halogen lights capture the gemstone's facets and make the stone glow with fire. "I have my own line of exclusive luxury jewelry." He speaks so rapidly that every sentence sounds like he's listing the side effects on a commercial for medication. "This is a nine-carat tourmaline from Mozambique surrounded by nonirradiated green diamonds from Australia, all set into three different colors of solid eighteen-karat gold: yellow, white, and rose. Did you know the melting point of platinum is 3,215 degrees Fahrenheit? It requires a special kind of torch to work with. But I prefer gold, anyway — it's more classic. *Nothing else feels like real gold,* do you remember *those* commercials? I auditioned to be the voice-over, but I think they ended up going with Kevin Bacon, who looks like a lesbian and you can hear it in his voice."

He turns his attention back to the more important issue at hand: his hands. "No cuticles," he announces. "It's genetic. That's why I was one of the top hand models for years. American Express, Marlboro cigarettes, Bic lighters, wines, liquors — you name it, I've held it, believe me."

Poor Maura. I can see her looking around the kitchen and wanting to ask him real estate questions, but she smiles and says, "That is so impressi—"

"But I prefer runway work," he continues. "Perry Ellis *always* had me model his furs. Not just any male model can carry off a fur. You can't prance down the runway or you'll look like a sissy; you have to walk like a real man." And here he demonstrates, sashaying from one end of his kitchen to the other, nose elevated at a forty-five-degree angle to the floor. He looks like a real man, all right. If real men sneeze glitter and are coated with a quarter inch of cocoa butter.

"Here, come with me, right now, hurry." It's a command: he clap-clap-clap-clap-claps his hands and begins striding so quickly we have to jog to keep up with him.

I notice something fascinating during our sprint.

As he moves through the labyrinthine house, small halogen spotlights hidden in nooks and corners suddenly illuminate him. He has them everywhere: tucked on a shelf between volumes of leather-bound books organized by spine color, atop a Chippendale display case filled with lead crystal goblets, balanced on the edges of heavily ornate gilded picture frames. All of them are motion-activated, so he is personally illuminated in flattering lighting as he walks through his home.

Whether anyone is there to see it or not.

We follow him up a rear stairway, and the lights go on one at a time, like we are on the set of a 1930s Busby Berkeley musical where each stair illuminates as Fred Astaire steps on it.

Once we reach the landing, he makes a quick right. "This is a guest room, but I use it for working out," he says. There is a large blue rubber fitness ball in the middle of the room and several colorful elastic bands, like you'd find in a gym.

He opens the closet door and it is packed with fur coats — white fox, mink, sable, coyote, chinchilla, and ermine. It's like a zoo where everything is dead.

He brushes his fingertips across their sleeves like he is playing a harp. "Perry Ellis 1980 collection, 1982, 1983, 1984. He loved me in this," Jeffrey says, pulling out a silver floor-length coyote coat and trying it on for us. He buttons the bottom button, raises the collar as if snow might suddenly fall from the ceiling, and then he rotates, unbuttoning the coat when his back is turned so that when he faces us again, the coat is open and one hand is in his pocket, the other clutching the lapel, folding it back to expose the silk lining. "Still fits like a dream."

He places it back on its padded black velvet hanger and says, "See these shoes?" Extending his right foot, he motions down with both hands. "Carpet slippers. I have dozens of pairs, see?"

He directs our attention to the floor of the closet. Indeed, at least forty virtually identical pairs of his curly-toe Aladdin shoes are lined up beneath the furs. "They're my personal signature statement shoe. Nobody else is wearing carpet slippers. But once they see them, of course, everybody wants them. Nobody else knows where to get them. However," he adds with a smug smile, "I have sources for things all over the world. From gemstones to slippers. Even my personal signature fragrance is custom-blended just for me. It wouldn't smell right on anybody else, because it was designed for my particular body chemistry. Four thousand dollars for half an ounce. The base note is orris, Bulgarian rose, oud resin from the agar tree, and of course ambergris — lots and lots of ambergris — and from sperm whales, not the synthetic garbage they use in *parfum* today." I don't speak French, but he *couldn't* have pronounced that correctly.

He slams the closet door with such force that Maura and I bump into each other and say "sorry" simultaneously. Our eyes meet: she's as shell-shocked and unnerved as I am. She shakes it off, her Kathleen Turner hair swinging against her shoulders.

"Wow, Jeffrey," she says, "you have an amazing collection. May I ask you a few things about the property?"

He looks at her like she spilled a full glass of cranberry juice on the cream carpet. "If you would allow me to give you a proper tour, you shall have these 'questions' of yours answered." He pivots away from her like a model at the end of the runway and exits the room. "I'll show you the master bedroom next," he says over his shoulder, expecting us to follow, which we do, across the hall and into a large bedroom with a centrally positioned four-poster king-sized bed draped with multiple mink blankets, beneath which is a deep red velvet bedspread, beneath which are deep red silk sheets. Perhaps a dozen — probably more — pillows are positioned at the head of the bed, each "dented" perfectly in the center with one decisive karate chop of the hand.

On the wall opposite the bed is a collection of framed photographs — Jeffrey in Paris! Jeffrey in the snow wearing a fur and laughing, his teeth one shade whiter than the snow itself! Jeffrey in a white tuxedo, arms crossed and smiling! Jeffrey in a powdered wig and waxed mustache! And in the center of these photographs is a gigantic oil painting of his face set like a rare blue diamond into a gilt rococo frame. His own face would be the first, second, third, fourth, fifth, sixth, seventh, eighth, and ninth thing he'd see each morning.

At the foot of the bed is a small love seat, or at least I think that's what it is; it could be a demure table with a ruffled chintz tablecloth. There are fur pillows on nearly every surface. Like the rest of the house, this room is so overdecorated that one simply cannot absorb it all.

Many of the individual objects are beautiful — that chair, this case, that lamp over there — but there is so much of everything, the effect is a neutralization, a castration of style.

We follow him back downstairs and into the ballroom-sized formal living room with its enormous fireplace and floor-to-ceiling windows. Each window appears to be draped with an exact replica of Lady Diana Spencer's 1981 wedding dress, with its 25-foot train and 153-yard veil of tulle. "I designed all the draperies in the house, every pair. And I sewed them all myself."

Chairs, both upholstered and not, are positioned all around the circumference of the room. Are there fifty of them? A hundred? They are of various scales; some are normal, human-sized chairs, but others are clearly intended for dolls, and then there are even smaller ones for tiny mice-people. The room has been staged for a parallel-universe AA meeting.

"See this chair?" Jeffrey says, striding over to a relatively unadorned, almost primitive wooden chair opposite the fireplace, beside a highly polished Queen Anne table topped with at least ten sterling silver framed portraits of dogs, along with what appear to be an equal number of cremation urns.

"I created this chair when I was fifteen. I was the youngest certified chair craftsman in America, and that's a fact," he says.

I had no idea there was such a thing as a certified chair craftsman.

"I'm positively in love with chairs, as you can see." He makes a grand sweeping gesture of the room. "But I've also made tables, bookcases, desks, coffers, nightstands, and three small coffins." He lowers his head when he says this, and I think, *Coffins for . . . children?*

Really fast, to take advantage of the odd silence, Maura points across the room and inserts a question. "Jeffrey, does that door lead to the exterior of the house?"

Jeffrey looks up, momentarily stunned by the question, by the fact that Maura has spoken in the first place, or that she is even standing beside him. And then his expression changes to one of contempt, as though she is a rag-clad simpleton begging on the streets of London in the 1800s and ought to know better than to speak to him. *"Well, of course it does,"* he replies, as if this is universal knowledge possessed by all of mankind. Undaunted, Maura presses on: "Do you know if the house has its original knob-and-tube wiring, or has it been updated?"

"Everything has been updated to be the best. The wiring is perfect, and there are plenty of outlets."

"Do you know what condition the plumbing is in?"

He actually rolls his eyes. This is torture for him. *"Everything is in the best possible condition imaginable, as I said."* Suddenly, he adopts a tone of acquiescence.

"Mary, or was it Marie? I know it was Mmmmmm-*something.*"

"Maura," she says, smiling.

"Yes, that's it. *Maura,* all the plumbing in the house is copper, my dear, and *flawless.* I personally polish it once a year. Go downstairs and see for yourself, it absolutely gleams. My basement looks like a jeweler's case."

"I'm sure it does," Maura says.

Jeffrey continues. Of course. "There's never been so much as a backed-up toilet. I don't even own a toilet plunger. Why on earth would I? No need. Which reminds me." He pivots and exits the living room, turning left and out of sight.

Maura looks at me, her eyes wide in mortification and disbelief and delight as she mouths "Oh my God."

We chase after him and find him standing beside the opened door to a powder room in a narrow hallway somewhere in the rear of the house. He has been waiting for us. I step inside. The walls are highly polished mahogany. "See those walls? Looks like a train coach, right?"

311

It does, in fact, look like a compartment aboard the Orient Express. Or at least what I imagine one would look like.

"It's *paint,*" he says. "Not wood. I'm one of the best professional faux finishers on the East Coast, you can ask anyone. I've done celebrities' ceilings, added columns to living rooms, made plain old nothing drywall look like sodalite, alabaster, Emperador marble — and that one's tricky, because it can end up looking like worn-out leather if you're not careful. Of course, I've also created leather walls and crocodile, lizard, and even ostrich."

I zoom my face in really close to the wall and stare at one tiny spot and I am like, Holy guacamole. What are there, thirty, *fifty* tiny brushstrokes per inch, more? And I can see at least six shades of brown. Instead of feeling impressed by his obvious talent and skill, I feel like I swam out too far and the undertow is dragging me down.

When was the last time I'd felt overpowered by another person? When I was eleven? Clearly he is some kind of sorcerer. He's not normal. He's not fully mortal.

Suddenly a dog barks from somewhere deep within the house, but at the same time it sounds as if it is coming from everywhere, as if the dog lives inside the walls. Jeffrey stomps angrily down the hallway in his carpet genie slippers until he reaches the kitchen. Maura and I chase after him. There is a door in the rear of the kitchen we hadn't seen before because it's painted to blend in with the walls. He scolds the door. "You hush in there."

Maura and I look at each other.

Jeffrey turns in our direction, though he doesn't actually look at either one of us. "Don't mind her, she's a bitch. I had two but the good one died, so she's in there."

We don't ask where "there" is. He opens the door a crack. "Shhhhhhhh, be a *good* girl. I know you miss him, *I miss him, too!*" Then he slams the door shut. He sighs dramatically. "Only the good die young, isn't that what they always say? Leaving behind the simply tedious."

There is a moment of silence as Jeffrey exhales and runs his fingers through his glossy white hair.

Maura wedges another question into the moment. "Jeffrey, how many bedrooms does the house have in total?"

Jeffrey lifts his nose into the air as if he has detected a faintly unpleasant aroma. "Well, Marilyn, I'm afraid that's *quite* impossible to say. I mean, there's my bedroom, of course, and the room where I use my exercise ball and my elastics. Down the hall from there and up a very narrow set of stairs is a small pied-à-terre with what I suppose you could call a bedroom, but it's really a combination sitting room and kitchen. There's a little stove up there and a refrigerator. That's if you have a guest who's planning to stay a while. There's another room down the hall from the master bath and then a room after that you could call a bedroom, though I use it for gift wrapping and sewing. And didn't you see the silo when you drove up?" he asks in an accusatory fashion.

"As a matter of fact we did," Maura says. "I was planning on asking you about it, because it's very interesting and highly unusual."

"Of course it is," he says, "I designed it myself. There's nothing else like it in the state. I hired an architect to do the blueprints because I've never liked to sketch, but I designed every inch of that space. I was just never able to finish it," he says. A forlorn look shades his blue eyes. "It's a pity, really. It would have been such a beautiful space. You climb the stairs and enter this magnificent great room. It was designed to have two bedrooms, and I'm including the plans with the house in the selling price so the new owners can complete it, though it will require them to bring over craftsmen from Europe to do the masonry and wood-work properly and according to my design. Let's see, there's another room or two that one could use as bedrooms but which I have used for other things. Put it this way: this house has more bedrooms than any person could reasonably want or need. You aren't the first real estate agent to represent me, you know."

Maura says, "Oh, yes, I know, and I am honored that you're now giving me the opportunity to sell this lovely property. And I'm sorry to keep pestering you with all these questions, but these are the technical details I need to know so that I can do my job and market your property effectively so that exactly the right buyer sees it."

Suddenly Jeffrey begins walking in the other direction, back toward the main living room with the chairs. He stops when he reaches the curious long, rectangular room next to the living room. "Perry Ellis also loved to use Beverly Johnson," he says, entirely out of the blue. "And do you know, that woman's arms are *literally* twice the length of a normal woman's arms. I mean, it's the most bizarre and remarkable thing. You can't really tell in pictures. It's not something anybody would want to emphasize, but they are the longest arms you've ever seen on a human being. I did love working with her, though. Unlike Kim Alexis." He smiles a huge fake smile; his teeth are so gleaming white they look like bleached elephant tusk. As he speaks he maintains the forced smile but adds a cartoonish Southern accent. "Hi, y'all! My name is Kim Alexis an' I speak with a Southern accent, even though I'm from Buffalo. Smile, smile, smile, that's the only thing I know how to do!" He snaps out of character. "That girl fell out of the stupid tree and hit every branch on the way down, let me tell you."

Jeffrey takes a step forward but then stops and turns back around. "I can also do a British accent, by the way." He launches into the worst, most un-British accent (faux Cockney, of course) I have ever heard. "Why 'ello there, bloody old chap, I say, which way is it to the Big Ben?"

Our slack jaws must register as rapt fascination to him, because he continues. "I-uh can-uh be-uh Italian-uh too-uh."

Maura gives me a desperate *We need to get the hell out of here* look. I feel physically restrained. Some sort of force field surrounds him that prevents us from escaping.

I have been out-witched by a snow-headed lunatic in genie slippers.

"Oh, I can do them all. I studied acting for years. I've done tons of commercials. Directors adore me because my face, my bone structure? You can shoot me from *any* angle, any angle at all." He suddenly drops to the floor, squatting and framing his hands like a director, angled upward. "You can shoot me from below, no problem at all. Just you try shooting Liza Minnelli from that angle and you'll be in for a very rude awakening. She and Judy both had to be shot from above." He stands, then leaps onto one of the upholstered dining chairs that sit around the large oval table, for we have somehow been herded into a blue-and-white-striped dining room where the drapes are gathered into gigantic ruffles of fabric on the floor.

From his position on the chair he again frames his hands, this time angled downward. "You had to shoot them both from this direction. They had to have their heads back so their necks would be taut. Thyroid eyes, you know. They bulge out, so you need to flatten them back into the face by getting the camera angle just right. Susan Sarandon has those big, bulging thyroid eyes, too, but nobody seems to mind them on her for

317

some reason, although I can't watch her, her face is too disturbing to me. Now, Meryl Streep? You can shoot her from any angle, too. But not because she's some great beauty. She's such a brilliant actress that she makes you *think* she's beautiful."

He steps down from the chair. He places both hands over his heart. "I'm extremely fortunate. And I understand that. I can't exactly say it's an accomplishment. It's genetic. Or a gift from the universe, if you want to be all spiritual about it. But I am grateful." He closes his eyes and goes blessedly silent.

Maura leaps at the opportunity, but no sooner has she opened her mouth than Jeffrey announces, "I have a new photographer in Hartford I'm working with. Ben something or other. He's just starting out so I thought I'd help him along. He does nice work, I think. Here, have a look." He removes his iPhone from his hip pocket, unlocks it, and begins scrolling quickly through hundreds — literally hundreds — of images of himself. "Well, his shots are on here somewhere. I'll send you a link."

We end up once more in the kitchen, where I notice a box of Wheat Thins on the counter. This stuns me more than anything else in the house. How did he get them?

Did this person leave his house and go to an actual store and exchange money for the box of crackers? I cannot imagine him being in any way capable of doing that. Somebody must have brought them to him, but who? He is too far removed from reality to buy Wheat Thins.

I lean over to Maura and whisper, "I am dead."

She nods. She tells him we need to leave and he cries, "No! You haven't seen the garage!"

We wind back through the delirium-inducing madhouse to a room we haven't been in before, though I don't know how that's possible. The walls are lined with shelves all the way around, and each shelf is packed with those small porcelain villages some people put out during the holidays, with buildings that have windows that light up. He has hundreds and hundreds of them: small churches with porcelain thatched roofs, houses, shops, each window illuminated. "I painted all the figures myself," he remarks proudly as we breeze through the room. I stop and look closely at a little church. Sure enough, there are tiny dolls inside it, wearing little sweaters, slacks, vests. It's the same in every single building, each inhabitant wearing a different hand-painted outfit. It would take a factory of skilled Chinese workers months to do all this handiwork. Why do I think Jeffrey did it in a day?

The buildings are arranged on sparkly polyester fluff-snow, and there are illuminated streetlights. The only furniture in this room is a leather sectional sofa beneath the shelves and a TV, along with a coffee table and a floor rack for magazines. A fresh copy of the *New York Times* is folded up and tucked into the rack with the magazines. That he can read also surprises me. This feels like the most "lived-in" room, the one where he spends most of his time. I can see him in in here with his carpet slippers, curled up on the sofa beneath a mink blanket, the TV on, his idyllic wintertime village lit up above his glossy white head like the stars in a Montana sky.

Just before we reach the garage, he stops and pivots. "Popped collar on a polo shirt? That was me," he says, stabbing at the center of his own chest with his index finger. "I start trends, I don't follow them."

He swings back and continues walking. Maura and I follow, overwhelmed and feeling trapped and drunk.

In the garage he has four cars: two identical Volvo station wagons, two identical

BMW convertibles. Sets of everything or, at the very least, pairs. He'd had a pair of dogs and when one of them died, the survivor had to be removed from sight.

"We really have to go, Jeffrey, we're due at another showing in seven minutes. I'll be in touch, thank you so much for your time and for showing us your beautiful house."

He says nothing. He opens his mouth to speak but then closes it into a firm, artificial smile and waves from the elbow, like a British royal on the balcony or from inside the golden carriage.

The entire drive back to my house we speak not a single word. It is like we have been muted by PTSD. When Maura lets me off in my driveway, we exchange a weary look. Still we say nothing. I open the door and climb out, not even able to muster my usual "I hate you" as I pass the maple tree. In the kitchen I find Christopher preparing a pasta dish. He smiles and the dogs come up, tails wagging. "Hey, how was it? You were gone a long time!"

Three hours. We'd been trapped in his house for three hours. It seems impossible, both that it was such a long time yet so short. Weeks seem to have passed. Jeffrey has somehow managed to remove a chunk of time from the continuum and — crafty as he is — sew it neatly back together so that nobody else will notice.

I reply, "Just you try shooting Liza Minnelli from that angle and you'll be in for a very rude awakening."

"What?" he says.

"That woman's arms are literally twice the length of a normal woman's arms," I shriek.

I can't stop. I am spewing back everything Jeffrey'd drenched us with. I am manic, like him, prancing around. "See these hands? No cuticles. It's genetic. That's why I was one of the top hand models for years. American Express, Marlboro cigarettes, you name it, I've held it."

It takes me an hour before I can explain what has happened. When I'm done, Christopher has a brilliant thought. "Let's see if he has a YouTube channel."

And he does!

His videos are beyond spectacular. In most of them he's clearly shot himself on his phone while he is in the car driving into the city for an audition, talking about how he's not nervous, his voice cracking with nerves. He's alone in all the videos (except for the two or three in which he plays a small role in a low-budget local commercial). There are videos of him working out with his exercise ball, wearing nothing but a thong bathing suit, his body oiled. The videos are as fascinating as they are depressing. They are pathetic yet mesmerizing. Repellent and captivating. He *is* performance art.

Originally, each video had two or three views. It's not like they go viral, but within several days each video has fifty, a hundred, two hundred views. Christopher has shared the links with several close friends and they — like us — cannot stop watching. Jeffrey in his fox coat, his snow-white hair, his feline face. Jeffrey doing every conceivable racist accent. It is a treasure trove.

Several months later Maura calls. "Oh my God," she said. "Jeffrey is dead."

"What? How?"

"That's all I know. He was fifty-nine —"

I snort. The nine is always a giveaway to the lie.

"I know," she says, "except he had a brother who died at fifty-nine from a heart defect, I think. I'm trying to find out more, like how? Was he sick when we saw him? He sure didn't seem sick. But was he?"

"Maura, I can't believe this. He has created a void in the world by leaving it."

"I know," she says. "It's awful."

We don't talk about it anymore. I tell Christopher.

"We did it," he said. "We killed him by watching his videos, like *The Ring* but reversed."

We had done the same thing to Bea Arthur in 2009. We spiraled down an intense Google wormhole about her, and two days later she was dead. And in late November of 2013, Christopher and I were in bed and he started talking about an actor I'd never heard of. He was reading his IMDb page, and then he shut off his phone and went to sleep. In the morning, the top trending news story was the death of Paul Walker, the actor I'd learned about the previous night, mere hours before his car crash.

"We were too interested in Jeffrey, and we caused some sort of aneurysm in the universe that took him out," I say.

"Damn," he says.

"I know." We are silent for a moment and then I look at him, lift my chin, raise my left eyebrow independently from my right, and say, "Popped collar on a polo shirt? That was me."

# Priest's Crown

When a "situation" arises, some witches invoke pagan deities to assist them in their craft. For strength, a witch might call upon Odin, the father god in Norse mythology, also known by the name Woden, which is the origin of the word "Wednesday." One might call upon Apollo, the Greek god of the sun, music, healing, prophecy, and beauty. Or Fortuna, the goddess of fate and destiny, and the only ancient Roman goddess to have a game show named after her. She would spin her wheel — Rota Fortunae — and alter lives and destinies with every turn. The wheel could bring great fortune and luck, but it could also create destruction and ruin. (Just ask Vanna White, whose hope of any non-letter-turning career was dashed after she portrayed Venus in an '80s TV movie called *Goddess of Love*.)

I do not call upon deities.

I call upon Arborist Dude.

Arborist Dude is a native of Connecticut, but his disposition is much more Southern Californian. He's friendly, laid-back. If he says he'll be there on Tuesday at three, he'll show up . . . just not always on the *next* Tuesday, or the one after that. It takes a lot of pestering texts, but eventually he pulls up in his pickup.

Moments later he is examining the foul, oozing gash running up the trunk of the evil century-and-a-half-year-old maple. "Slime flux," he says.

"What did you call me?" Christopher asks, one of his favorite corny jokes.

I stare at the black tar, teeming with insects. What a horribly perfect name. I had noticed the crack before, but that's what it looked like: a crack. Old trees have them. Cracks are part of their charm. But this is no longer merely a crack. It is alive. Or dead. Or somewhere in between, the Schrödinger's cat of landscaping.

It is a giant crone's vagina, like something out of *Game of Thrones* that, if you step too close, can flutter its wooden labia and inhale you into the slime-flux underworld.

I've been right to hate it all along.

Arborist Dude shrugs. "I mean, we can see if it clears up on its own. It's a bacterial infection, but there's nothing we can really do."

"Slime flux fixes itself?" I ask in wonderment.

"Sometimes." He shrugs.

"So . . . we do nothing?" I say with a trace of sarcasm.

"Pretty much," he says with his arborist cool.

I envy people who are so easygoing, but I also don't understand them at all.

I want action, solutions, salvation, a remedy. I need the gaping wound closed, the rent sealed, the black festering rot vanished. I think how easily Samantha on *Bewitched* could replace this tree with an easy twitch of the nose. *If you can't do that,* I inwardly steam, *what's the point?*

Knowing the limitations of witchcraft and not being frustrated by them are two very different things, especially for witches like me with advanced degrees in frustration.

Arborist Dude climbs back into his Silverado 2500 pickup and starts the engine. "Text me if it gets worse."

*Right,* I think. *I'll make sure I have my phone with me when I get impaled by a branch.*

I only met Christopher's doctor in Manhattan once in passing, but he spoke of the man as he would a dear friend, one who had literally saved his life. Twice. They had gone through a lot together; Christopher had been diagnosed with HIV in the mid-eighties, when pretty much everyone died from it, like most of his friends. But he lived.

Then there was the lymphoma. "But it was the good kind, Hodgkin's. I mean, not that there's a *good* cancer, but at least it's better than non-Hodgkin's. The 'non' part is usually *your life.*"

Christopher has survived two significant, potentially deadly diseases, and he is as upbeat, funny, and himself as he has always been. It is like he had a set of wisdom teeth pulled. He fills me with my favorite emotion: awe.

Then the doctor vanished. Apparently he was done saving lives. Treatment had progressed to the point where patients were stable, so it was no longer an office where people were dying on a daily basis. With a month's warning he simply closed his practice, offering barely an explanation or a good-bye. His own staff learned of this drastic turn only when the office manager opened a letter from the landlord, confirming that they'd be vacating by the end of the year and not renewing the lease. Happy holidays!

Not one to get emotionally rattled, Christopher was still disturbed by the loss. "He is a genius and kind of a freak and definitely the best doctor I have ever had — I've been seeing him for twenty years. One of my longest relationships ever just dumped me. And it's not only me, it's a loss for the world. He was a pioneer in HIV treatment, with a vast amount of knowledge and experience that can't be replicated. And he *took it away.*"

This struck me as morally and ethically repugnant. The contempt that I felt for this ex-doctor was instant, and so intense I felt my face flush. Christopher calmed down and forgave him but I retained anger for two.

His next physician gifted him with a curious new diagnosis: hemochromatosis. It's the opposite of anemia, so there's too much iron in the blood. Christopher was delighted by the treatment: "Phlebotomy! It's literal bloodletting, like it's the nineteenth century. Bring on the leeches!"

Soon after this diagnosis we move to Connecticut, and he finds a doctor at Yale. I feel a gigantic *yes* unfold within me: the two-word combination "Yale Medicine" carries significant prestige.

He is impressed with the team of physicians. His personal doctor is smart and engaged, if alarmingly young ("maybe a newborn when I got my HIV diagnosis"). The department is run by a husband and wife, whom I dub "the Infectious Disease Power Couple." Tests are performed, Christopher's medical history examined, and two developments are presented:

He does not have, nor has he ever had, *hemochromatosis.*

What he has is previously undiagnosed *hepatitis,* which has decimated his liver.

He comes home one afternoon following a long day of blood work and meetings. Standing in the middle of the kitchen, he says, "I have stage four cirrhosis."

I can see it on his face: *this is what's going to do me in.*

I wouldn't say it's resignation, but his expression is a fatigued sort of acceptance. *I've been living on borrowed time, and the debt is coming due.*

When magick engages, when it works, you feel it and you know it; there isn't any doubt at all.

I find instead that I am suspended within acrylic, like one of those scorpion paperweights they sell at every gift shop in the Southwest. I am frozen in place, waiting for that feeling of magick to engage, listening for it. No matter how hard I keep looking in the direction the train will be coming, there is no light, no magickal engagement.

I hear the news: he has stage four cirrhosis. And? And? *And?* That's what's missing. I usually have a *sense,* even an odd one that I might not understand until later. When there is an absence, a blackness, an inability to visualize, to see anything? That's historically been a bad sign. I'm not experiencing *that,* which is good. Instead what I see is: white. Like I am standing in front of a 100-foot-wide by 100-foot-tall evenly lit white wall. It's like I didn't pay my monthly dues to the Oracle Society for Witches and they have suspended my soothsaying abilities.

Christopher is waiting for me to speak.

He expects me to behave as I normally would: knowing what to do.

I don't know what to do. I am useless. Part of me has gone missing, the most important part. His news, my bounce against the white wall of nothing, has made me feel unsettled and alarmed.

I say, "We'll get through this. I'll read about some healthy liver diets online, and we'll start there."

The look on his face — the one that says

acceptance, the one that says *this is how it ends* — terrifies me, because what if he knows what I can't see? What if *he* can sense the outcome, and the outcome is death?

It is like trying to imagine the sun imploding. I can say the words, but I can't actually visualize it happening.

Magick should just flow, it should just be there inside you. It's not something you have to hunt around inside yourself to find. It's certainly not something that should one day suddenly go missing. On the day you happen to need it the most.

I change our diets. No salt, no sugar. All junk food is gone now. This is not a gradual change. It's a "box of plastic trash bags carried out to the garage followed by a trip to the health food store" change.

We are mostly vegan. He eats foods he doesn't like because I disguise them. I have to make everything myself, because salt is like a virus; it's everywhere, in everything. The recipe calls for pesto? A container of pesto at the supermarket is basically a green sodium bomb. I'm spending more time rinsing grit off basil than I'd imagined I would in midlife.

This is not a complaint. It gives me a feeling (an illusion, really) of control. Plus, I'm learning interesting things, like: there is no need for salt when there is a spice called "sumac." It's at a disadvantage, since most people imagine the word "poison" before it, but it's a taste revelation.

I've added two medicinal mushrooms to our morning coffee; studies in Japan and China indicate benefits to the liver.

It's not enough. I feel like I am driving at night with my eyes closed. I can practically hear the mailboxes being smacked down flat as I pass. This is not good at all. How do people who aren't witches even survive in this world?

Stage four cirrhosis — "without the upside of being a hopeless alcoholic," he says. What I don't like at all is that it only *has* four stages. When you reach the fifth stage, you arrive in a coffin.

Today Christopher puts on his rubberized waders and walks across the stone dam of the brook to remove branches and debris so the water will flow more freely.

I am in the kitchen rinsing kale and apples in the sink and watch him out the kitchen window as he bends over to pull clumps of umber, yellow, and red maple leaves that have gathered against the stones.

He stands commandingly on a rock older

than his great-grandparents, carrying a walking stick both for balance on the slippery dam and to poke at things. A good walking stick is essential if you live in the country. When I was very small my father taught me how to carve a proper one from a sturdy wood — hammer a nail into the bottom so the wood doesn't wear as fast, and wrap a rawhide cord around the top for grip. This is the single useful thing my father ever taught me.

Christopher rises very early, and he is in his office before eight every day. When he is finished, after the publishing houses have closed for the day, he changes into his "outdoor clothes" and does yard work or carries firewood inside. One day I see him weeding between the bluestone steps of our front walkway. As I watch him pull the weeds and throw them in a wheelbarrow, I remember how I had envisioned exactly this scene in my mind's eye.

Without pushing or exerting any effort, I focus my mind on that sense memory. I see it again, imprinted over the real Christopher — then it all goes white, the vast expanse of bright white on all sides, like when he gave me the news. Something won't . . . engage.

He is protected here by the land, the dogs,

the thick plaster walls, the foot-thick wood frame of the house.

I just need to get my magick back before he needs a liver transplant.

# White Man's Foot

Three of the four stovetop burners are going, the oven is on, and I am improvising a sauce for the stir-fry: ginger, garlic, white pepper, chopped scallions, and Lapsang souchong tea. This is a Chinese tea from the Wuyi Mountains that gets its distinctive flavor from being smoked over pinewood. I catch my reflection in the dark kitchen window — we always eat late — and I think of the lyric to that annoying Talking Heads song: "How did I get here?"

How did I become this person who has recipe ideas and tries them and they work?

For all my adult life, I was certain I was not a kitchen person, and I was wrong. In fact, I am the kind of kitchen person who likes to peel potatoes and then make one thing from the potatoes and another thing from the peels.

I've become Samantha Stephens, a witch fixing dinner for my husband. Except right now, I'm not a witch. I am still facing a white wall of static where there should be visions, knowledge, information. I know I'm not "blocked" by Christopher's upsetting news; my entire life has been upsetting news. This has never happened before, and there's something curious about it. It feels like I am experiencing electrical interference. Until this passes or I figure out what's going on, I'm this person I don't know.

I do midcentury housewife things for Christopher that improve the quality of his life. I make a sugar-free chocolate cream pie that is nutrient dense and filled with antioxidants, yet it tastes like chocolate cream pie. He has no idea that the exotic ingredients keep him healthy.

I wax the floors. I clean the windows with apple cider vinegar and newspapers, I make sure the shower is always spotless and dry and smells fresh. I change the bedding frequently and iron the sheets.

Harold and Elinor's washer and dryer finally shook, trembled, and died on us. The new washer is okay, but our less environmentally harmful "high-efficiency" dryer has turned out to be so earth-friendly that it barely draws enough current to warm a sock. Towels and sheets have to be run for hours, which wouldn't seem to support any claim of efficiency.

In the summer there is nothing like sleeping on sheets that have been dried in the sun, fresh air blowing through them all day. Plus I could give our electric bill the equivalent of a gastric bypass.

At the hardware store I buy the cotton line, wooden clothespins, two metal pulleys, and a clever little line tightener. I attach it from the rear post of the tall garden fence down to a tree, a span of about thirty feet in length, eight feet off the ground. It must be high enough that Gunther won't grab every item I hang and carry it out to the field, like he did with all my car-washing sponges that I kept on a shelf in the barn.

The clothesline horrifies Christopher. "It's hillbilly," he says, thoroughly aghast, as if I'd hung a Confederate flag beside the front door.

"Oh my God, no it's not," I tell him. "You only think that because you grew up in suburban Ohio. I can assure you, a clothesline is not tacky in New England. I'm sure Katharine Hepburn had one."

He begins texting me pictures of disgusting homes featuring sloppy clotheslines hung with garish, brightly colored bro shorts and sports bras.

I text him back a tasteful picture of Martha Stewart pinning sheets to her own line.

"You've gone from eccentric country gentleman to Swamp Yankee," he tells me. Maura taught us that phrase for "New England hillbilly."

I take a picture of towels drying on the clothesline and post it to Instagram, where it gets almost two thousand likes right away. That, my friends, is a twenty-first-century acquittal.

We have this heavy velvet bedspread that I love because it's not skimpy in its cut; it hangs well over the edges of the bed and it's as heavy as a lead dental cape, which I have always wanted. But the thing takes forever to dry, a minimum of three ninety-minute cycles on high heat, and even then there's likely to be a damp spot or two remaining. The other day, I washed it and hung it outside on the line. By the end of the day it was completely dry and as wrinkle-free as if I'd ironed it.

Christopher will loathe the clothesline until he sees how much money we've saved.

He also didn't want a garden. He made it clear. "If this is something you really feel you have to do, go ahead and do it."

Eddie and one of his meat-headed ape freelance helpers clear a pile of rocks and dirt next to the barn and create raised beds with inset bluestone aisles between the rows. The whole garden is encircled with a fifteen-foot-high fence so deer can't jump it and eat our stuff.

Exactly as I had predicted, Christopher takes over the garden. He checks the progress of each tomato and cucumber daily, texting photos of the little buds that will one day be red peppers to his college friends Martha and Lee, both of whom garden.

He's composting.

The garden is his domain, and I question whether he even remembers protesting its creation. He may never love the clothesline, but I think he'll like that his T-shirts will smell like apples from the trees that surround it.

I always serve him the prettier plate of food.

I wash his car and vacuum it and get the oil changed. He never notices when I have cleaned the car. Once, I point it out in a not-so-subtle way by saying, "So? Doesn't the interior look cleaner?" He glances around and locates the single spot I missed, the smudge on the clear plastic that covers the speedometer. "All I notice is that this mosquito I squashed a couple of weeks ago is still right here at the sixty-five-miles-per-hour mark."

"The floor was filthy," I say, looking down and admiring my own thorough vacuuming. No more dog hairs, broken rust-colored pine needles, no more of the endless, endless, endless small pebbles from the driveway that find their way absolutely everywhere.

He takes his eyes off the road for a second and looks into the well. "I don't know," he says, "I never really noticed that it was filthy. I mean, we live in the country and we have four dogs and shit gets everywhere, and a car is a car and I never really notice whether it's clean or dirty."

This is one area in which we're different. I notice; he does not.

Like when he takes the Subaru out of the garage and hits the side of the truck, crunching the rear right passenger door and giving the Subaru a slight black eye. I haven't had time to get the door replaced, and honestly, I can't imagine when I ever will. Now when I look at the truck, all I see is the crunched-in door. But I don't imagine he considers this a thing to be fixed. "Why?" I can imagine him saying. "The door still closes. Plus, it's black, you can hardly see it."

*He* can hardly see it because he's color-blind, which leads me to believe he's genetically predisposed to not noticing a lot of things.

I am doing chores because I can't cast spells.

I am in limbo. And a state of frustrating confusion. What is this wall of white? Why can I see no future? Nothing bad, nothing good, just nothing?

Am I being fucked with? That's impossible. There's only one person who could interrupt my abilities and she's dead.

# RED COCKSCOMB

As our two-year anniversary as homeowners swiftly approaches, we have fairly well transformed the place. So have the dogs. The wide ring of well-established hosta, a hard-to-kill ground cover around the base of the Crone Vagina Maple, has been killed. The dogs love to chase each other around the tree, a blur of motion with a soundtrack of nonstop barking. To guard the hosta, I had put up a chicken wire fence, which they had basically laughed at and proceeded to stampede. There are deep scrapes throughout the yard where grass once was; these are now wrestling patches and running tracks. The landscape is marred but it's also invigorated. A host of new wildflowers appeared this year, and foxgloves sprouted their tall stalks of beautiful poison all over the lawn.

One of the best things about the property is the little artist cottage from the 1920s that sits at the edge of the brook. It is most charming, however, when one looks at it from the outside and *imagines* being inside sipping coffee or taking a nap by the water. The reality of being in the cottage is a dream-crusher. It is like the grossest camp cabin you ever had to endure as a kid, with a more revolting toilet situation.

The first time we step inside, we utter "Ugh" at the same moment. A wall divides the interior into a super-low-ceilinged front half and a what's-behind-that-wall? half. The answer is: a twelve-year collection of spiderwebs, plus the remnants of a bathroom. There is a hole where a toilet once sat, a cool old porcelain-covered iron sink, and an equally cool oval mirror above it with etched glass. A shower stall with Masonite walls has folded in on itself. Masonite is kind of like a dense cardboard, not exactly a suitable material to withstand a constant spray of water. And the rusty showerhead could give you tetanus if you look at it for too long.

Back outside, the front porch is sagging, and the whole structure is so neglected I imagine it will survive only a few more years without a little attention. There is already a hole in the rear of the cottage large enough for a fox to step through. Or a beaver. Or a worse.

Fat Fuck Eddie to the rescue, in his rusty blue shitmobile with the coat-hanger door handle and no brakes!

He takes one look at the bathroom and says, "Rip this fucker out. First of all, there's no septic system attached to the cottage. Maybe there was a tank at one time underneath, because I can see some pipes that have been capped. I bet the tank got full so they closed it and rerouted the pipes so that everything drains right into the river."

"That's vile," I say.

He proposes knocking out the wall, ripping out the bathroom, and tearing down the low ceiling. "Open it up in here, expose the rafters. Rebuild the front porch so that it's stable, and screen it in."

"How long will it take you?" I ask.

"Coupla weeks," he says, pulling a lady cigarette out of his front pocket and lighting it.

"Coupla weeks" in Eddie time is roughly three months, but I know it will be fantastic.

As Eddie works on the cottage, we hire a painter to begin the exterior transformation — or correction, as we see it — of the house itself. Black. And not some chicken-out shade of "eggplant" or "berry." It is called

Midnight Dream and it is *black* black. The trim is the same color except slightly glossy; the doors, oxblood red. The barn is the reverse, red walls and black doors.

Some houses hate the color their owners have given them. There's a midcentury home nearby that looks like Philip Johnson designed it, except he wouldn't have painted it salmon. And the house *knows* this. Instead of sitting proudly, iconically, on its lawn among the whimsical junipers, it seems to be cringing, hiding behind them.

Our yellow house is elegant. Yellow is not a shameful color, like salmon, or fearful, like beige, but it's so *welcoming.* And really, that is our primary issue. We aren't "Welcome!" people. We're more "Don't worry, it's not usually contagious" people.

When the painters finish, the difference is shocking. The house looks more dignified, more declaratively antique, more imposing, and far more grandly creepy than we could have imagined. Black on black with blood-stained doors is spectacular and, it turns out, unsettling for some.

On both a subconscious and a conscious level, people are unnerved by black houses, because they're rare — and the concept *sounds* drastic. Two of the most famous are

346

both in Salem: the Jonathan Corwin House, also known as the Witch House, and the House of Seven Gables. I was prepared to move into either of them after I visited as a child.

Every friend in the city asks the same question when we tell them we've painted the house black: "The . . . inside?" As life-long apartment dwellers, they all think "painting" means doing the interior walls. They can't fathom that we also own the outside of the building. The question comes up so frequently that I start answering, "Yes."

There is magickal power in a black house. It looks foreboding in the day and disappears at night, and as I say to Christopher, "Not that we are in a high-traffic area, but we only *hoped* we didn't get trick-or-treaters before. Now, we're child-repellent." You can hear the mothers saying, "Not there, honey, let's move on to the next one."

Yes, excellent idea.

We admit that it is slightly macabre, especially behind a ten-foot-high black fence and tall stone pillar gates, each door as heavy as a loaded hearse.

Two years? I still can't believe it. Those years flew by on a broom.

The paint on the old wood wainscoting in the living room is dirty and chipped, so I need to make touch-ups. The color is great, a peculiar green that is so out of style I suspect it's been this exact shade for the last sixty years. Luckily, Harold kept records, which he left on a shelf in the basement with approximately one million gallons of paint and stain. Once I locate the can for the living room and pry off the lid, I am stunned to see it is creamy and seemingly fresh, not a solid block of uselessness like several of these remnants have been.

First I put the dogs outside, despite their making it clear that they really, *really* want to help. Then I turn on the TV, which I never do in the afternoon, and TCM is playing a silent movie. There's a difference between watching old films on mute and silent movies with the cheesy plunking piano music and scenes that look like they're lit with candles. They are relics I can't bear so I flick a few channels back to Lifetime.

Much to my own mortification, I become caught up in some of the best bad acting I have ever encountered. The lighting is perhaps *worse* than a silent, and the plot is so absurd it must be a parody of a domestic thriller. The title is I'M GONNA CUT YOUR BABY RIGHT OUT OF YOU AND RAISE IT AS MY OWN EVEN THOUGH I'M YOUR SISTER BECAUSE I WAS ADOPTED AND THEREFORE AM NOT REALLY YOUR SISTER, YOU BITCH, WHO GOT EVERYTHING WHILE I GOT NOTHING! or something close to that.

Painting with my neck craned to watch the screen is fun. It is satisfying work, because the color matches perfectly and dries instantly, so it's more like a retouch app on my phone than real life. The actual dabs only take about fifteen minutes but I remain glued to the TV for ninety more.

Now it is getting dark. I bring the paint and the brush back downstairs to the basement and wash the brush out in the utility sink. Upstairs again, I look around the room, and it doesn't appear that I missed any spots. I'll check again in the daylight tomorrow, but I'm sure they'll be fine in the House of Shadows and Low-Watt Bulbs.

I step out on the porch and holler for the dogs. "Hey! Otis! Gunther! Radar!" (Wiley is upstairs in bed buried beneath the covers, as he is all day, every day.)

No dogs come.

I walk down the steps, knowing they are in the field behind the barn. On the driveway I stop and yell again. "Otis! Gunther! Radar!"

When I was a kid and I called for the dogs, I did it at the top of my lungs. Here, even though we have only two neighbors and they're not terribly close, I'm self-conscious every time.

They still don't come. I'm sure they hear me, but whatever they are doing is far more interesting than anything I plan for them, which is getting them to lie on their sofas and be calm. How spoiled are these dogs that they need to be begged to lie on the furniture?

I call one last time, and that's when I see that my call has worked. Except instead of the dogs, it has brought Vivi. She has come all the way from the woods and down the road and is now approaching the gates to our driveway, which I knew should be closed 24/7 but which Christopher insists remain open during the day. ("For *your* deliveries," he says pointedly.)

I jog, then run, to the gates. I cannot let her in. She must stay outside, I remember this part. "Hello, Vivi," I say, fake smiling. "How are you?"

Vivi is annoying, because she sees clean through bullshit. Normally this would be a quality that would make me love a person, but in this case it gives me one less weapon with which to face her.

"I can hear you calling for your dogs from my living room," she says. "Not just today. Every time."

I feel my face flush. (Even into middle age, I am a blusher.) "I am so sorry," I say. "I will not shout so loud from now on."

"No, no, no, no, no," she replies. "I'm not complaining. I'm here to help."

Unless she has cubes of raw sirloin in her pockets, she probably can't help.

"You are calling from here," she says, patting her upper chest, right below the hollow of her throat. "It is as if you are timid, afraid. If you were at the Palais Garnier in Paris, well, my dear, your voice would not even make it off the stage, let alone up to the majestic ceiling, which was painted by Marc Chagall." She is no longer looking at me but staring wide-eyed above my head, both hands raised as if she is preparing to catch a watermelon about to be dropped from the sky.

"Everyone in the house must hear you." Now she is looking at me intently. "So you must learn to sing from your diaphragm."

She dramatically raises and claps her hand to her lower belly — though less on her stomach and closer to where a woman would *insert* a diaphragm. "Stand like this," she instructs. She straightens and shakes out her shoulders, allowing her arms to hang at her sides.

"Relax. Inhale, exhale."

I do what she says because I have no other choice.

"Call for the dogs once again, but instead of calling from your throat, call out their names *from your soul.* Do this now."

Oh my God. "Otis! Gunther! Radar!" I sing out, but I do as she instructs and it comes from deep within me, not a lower voice but a much more normal and comfortable one. It sounds and even feels like it travels a much greater distance.

The dogs appear a few instants later, wagging and panting. Then they see Vivi and they bark.

She smiles in complete self-satisfaction. "You see?" she says. "That sounded quite good. A dramatic improvement in tone and clarity. Even the animals could tell the difference."

I am trying to think of a reason *why* she cannot come inside, because now she is going to want payment for her services in the form of an invitation to coffee or tea. Instead, to my complete amazement, she turns without saying good-bye and heads back toward her own house and her surveillance equipment and footman/husband.

I am tempted to close the gates, but I restrain myself.

"Come on, boys, let's go inside and have treats," I say, emphasizing that last word to ensure they will follow me inside, which they do.

An hour later I am still stunned by the encounter. All this time that I've been self-conscious about calling for the dogs, a retired opera singer has been listening to me and diagnosing the insecurity in my voice, and now she has solved it.

She's been listening to me call for the dogs for *two years*.

My paranoid delusional fantasy, "the neighbors will hear me calling for the dogs and will judge me," turns out to be completely true. I just received notes on my vocal performance.

I also think, It's amazing. My voice, when I used to shout for them, was a lie, in a way. It wasn't my real voice. She called me out on it.

I kind of feel *put in my place.*

"Thanks, Vivi," I whisper. I am certain

she hears me, because I know she really does have a directional microphone in that third-floor room. And now she knows I know.

I want her to feel put in her place, too.

One sunny January afternoon I am in the kitchen making brownies. I have just let the dogs in, wiped the icy snow and slush from between their pads and toes, and given them each a treat of dried apple. They've been running circles around the Game of Crone's Slime Vagina Tree and are all tired, ready to claim their own sofa or chair.

They file out of the kitchen, and at the exact moment my fingers touch the edge of the mixing bowl, there is an explosion outside. My hand jolts the bowl, and batter flies onto the counter. I hastily wipe my hands with a dish towel and go to the kitchen door, but I don't even need to open it to see the source of the noise: a ginormous branch from the evil tree is now lying across our driveway. More accurately, the branch extends from the base of the tree across the *entire* driveway — wide enough for two cars — landing within inches of my truck.

It has fallen exactly where the dogs were playing not even sixty seconds earlier. What if we'd woken up and let the dogs out one minute later than we did?

All four of them would be dead, since they run in such a tight pack.

If our day had been shifted ever so slightly, everything would be terrible.

I didn't see it coming. I should have, but that damn wall of white is right there at the center of my being where witchcraft ought to be.

I have to lean against the door jamb to steady myself. I feel physically sick. It is shocking how huge the branch is. Finally, I slip into my boots, throw on my parka, and go outside, under the absurd impression that I will "move" the branch so it isn't blocking the driveway. As soon as I touch it I realize it weighs a lot more than I can lift.

Why has it just now fallen? The air is so cool and still, there isn't even the slightest breeze.

The gash splitting open the base of the tree is gleaming with black slime. The condition does not appear to be improving.

What alarms me the most, though, is how instantaneous it was. I heard the explosion and felt the impact as it hit the ground at the same time. There was no warning. The branch did not creak and crack and stretch and strain and finally break away accompanied by the sound of tearing wood. It wasn't like that at all. It was instant.

I'd said it to Christopher, half joking, but now I believed it more than ever: we really *will* be the last people to live in this house. One of the beautiful trees — perhaps the award-winning honey locust, one of the largest *in the world* — will drop a branch on the dining room roof one day and crush us while we are eating Cajun tofu in red sauce.

Or perhaps one of the old-man pine trees that line the front of the yard and shield us from the narrow old road will give up and topple over onto the bedroom while we sleep, dividing our legs from our heads without us even knowing it. If the dogs survive they'll be trapped upstairs, and eventually they'll eat our remains.

I know a guy in Chicago who adopted a collie after its owner perished, and the collie ate her. But who would adopt a Great Dane who ate both his daddies?

The falling branch seems like more than an omen. It is a direct message. This is the very tree that gave me pause the first day we saw the house. Actually, it did more than give me pause; it creeped me the hell out. I can't help it, when I look at that tree, *I see death.*

Correction: I saw death.

Now I see static.

A wall.

White.

Everybody else sees a nearly two-century-old maple — a rare and glorious tree, the crown jewel of any property. While it is all these things, it is also a serial killer.

I hadn't felt this way about any of the other trees on the property until having the realization that they are all potential predators. This is not particularly rational thinking on my part. My father, who was the head of the philosophy department at the University of Massachusetts and taught logic for decades, would have been pained by my thought process. It is intuitive. And it is how — and where — I've lived my entire life.

Just beneath the surface of this world is another world, a network of connections, a subworld not everyone can see or experience. But some people have the necessary neurological apparatus to sense this universe and operate within it — to manipulate it, even. It's not unlike the way dogs can hear high frequencies that we lack the receptors to detect. Without technology (or dogs), we would not even imagine such elusive sounds were possible.

I often wonder what else surrounds us that

we are unaware of because of our physical limitations. Or maybe we have the receptors, but they are rusty from lack of use. It makes sense that there is much more to our universe than we can experience — that we are surrounded on all sides by forces and energies of which we are completely unaware.

"We" are all unaware, that is, except witches, for this is exactly the space witches occupy.

I never get annoyed when I'm stuck in traffic. I see it as a correction to the time line. Something in my future requires this delay. Perhaps being on time would land me in the path of an oncoming trucker who is not paying attention to the road because he's staring at his phone, trying to figure out what emoji his daughter sent him: Is it an anvil? A unicorn? Roast beef?

There is also the possibility that my belief in how things work is wrong. I think the universe operates in a certain way, but that could be incorrect.

If you believe in God, maybe your level of faith should remain at or below 99 percent.

The decided mind is a closed mind. A closed mind can keep you separated from the ultimate truth.

Scientists should take special note here.

What I *am* certain of is that there's something wonky going on beneath the surface of what we call reality. Things are not as they appear. They are much, much more.

# Semen of Ares

When Samantha Stephens was feeling ill, all she had to do was walk into her living room, stand on her avocado wall-to-wall carpeting, and say, "Calling Doctor Bombay!" Mere instants later, a put-out, mustachioed, middle-aged man who was always in the middle of something like downhill skiing with two blondes in fur bikinis arrived in her living room. Whatever was wrong with Sam, Doctor Bombay would fix it.

I need my own Doctor Bombay because *something isn't right.*

Physically I am fine. In fact, physically I am in the best shape of my life because I'm doing so much work around the house and property, plus not eating sugar. Emotionally I am better than I've ever been, too. My marriage is so good that it would be sickening to even discuss.

Magickally I am off. As in turned off.

Magickally I am *gone.*

By which I mean my spells aren't working and my sixth sense is missing. If something is going wrong with Christopher's health, I can't sense it. I'm trying to focus on his being well, but it doesn't feel productive. Without anything to go on, it's like I'm dialing random phone numbers, hoping the right person will pick up.

I am . . . ordinary, a bank teller or a customer service rep.

*I can't live this way.*

I am a catastrophist, but I am also a witch. Or was.

Our first Connecticut winter had been unwintry. October through December was the warmest ever recorded in the state. It seemed we were still picking raspberries at Christmas.

Our second was a cinematic winter wonderland, with huge old evergreen branches yielding to the weight of the snow; our house and yard looked like a movie set from the Technicolor 1950s, as if Elizabeth Taylor might peek out from behind a cedar tree at any moment, laughing while she tossed a snowball at Paul Newman, who would of course catch it in midair and take a bite out of it like it was an apple while Elizabeth clapped and shouted, "Oh, bravo! Bra-*vo*!"

It is our third winter when the lighting on the wonderland set collapses and Elizabeth Taylor's hair catches fire while Paul Newman is mauled to death by the trained bear.

First, it is so cold that the copper pipes in the kitchen freeze. They do not burst, but I have to move a space heater into the crawl space beneath the kitchen, where the plumbing is positioned on an exterior wall. I leave the heater on twenty-four hours a day, and for all twenty-four of them, I worry it will burst into flames and incinerate our home. Isn't that how every headline for every winter house fire reads: SPACE HEATER CAUSES FIRE, KILLING PHILANTHROPIC MORMON FAMILY OF TWELVE. It's a literal amped-up version of getting electrocuted by putting a knife in a toaster. So I buy a fancy-ass oil-filled space heater with safety features. The area beneath the kitchen is stone and dirt, so I am able to create a sort of platform. If the heater falls over, it will land on good old nonflammable grime.

There are days when it is ten and even twenty degrees *below zero*. That's arctic cold, not Connecticut cold. This is not normal winter weather. I grew up in New England, and it wasn't this bitter back then.

362

One evening I am in the kitchen cleaning up after dinner when I hear an odd sound outside. It is almost a moaning, like an animal in pain, but I can hear what sounds like ice cracking, too. I step out the kitchen door onto the porch and listen. At first I hear nothing, but then there it is: painful moaning, ice cracking. And, wait . . . is it coming from the Crone Tree's vagina? *Ugh, not you again.*

I walk halfway to the tree and pause. Silence again and the breeze dies down. Then I watch the tops of the trees across the street begin to quiver as the wind picks up again. It is a blustery night, with strong gusts coming at us from the north. Several days ago we had a nor'easter that dumped two feet of snow — was it the fifth nor'easter? Or sixth? Maybe this is leftover wind, the tail end.

I approach the massive old tree, and as soon as I do, I can hear and feel that something is seriously wrong. The moaning is vocal, as though the tree is in the last throes of an agonizing death. It is the most haunting sound I've ever heard, nearly human, nearly animal. And what I'd thought sounded like ice cracking is very low-pitched and coming from deep inside the tree, from the center of it. It is wood fracturing. The tree is screaming as its frozen flesh is torn apart in the powerful, twisty wind.

I run inside and tell Christopher that he must come and listen to the tree. He slides into his snow boots but wears no jacket, and follows me outside. We stand beside the tree and listen. Then he says, "Yeah, it's windy, so the tree is creaking. I don't hear any 'screaming' coming from inside it. It's a big old tree that's survived hundreds of winters like this one and probably a lot worse. I'm going back inside, it's freezing out here." He trudges away, up the steps and into the kitchen.

He can't hear screams. I can. Does that mean the static is evaporating? I still "see" nothing but white, I still feel zero about the future, but I *can* hear the tree screaming. Maybe a little something has returned.

I pull my phone out of my pocket, wait for the wind to pick up, and then record a video. I play it back, and even though you can't see much because it is so dark, you can hear sounds of creaking and cracking, though no screaming.

I text the video to Arborist Dude, who's probably at home wearing fluorescent patterned boardshorts even though it's freezing. In my mind he is lounging on a futon sofa taking hits from his glass bong and flipping between football and the Cartoon Network. I imagine him glancing down at his phone when it trills with my message, rolling his eyes, and reaching for his lighter.

But no, even though it's approaching midnight, he texts me right back. "Keep the dogs inside. Sleep on the opposite side of the house. I'll be there tomorrow morning at 7 am."

Arborist Dude is the opposite of a dramatic personality type. He can be so Malibu Ken that it seems like he shouldn't even be allowed to hold a chain saw.

Therefore, I read his text as: **KEEP THE DOGS INSIDE!!!!!!! SLEEP ON THE OPPOSITE SIDE OF THE HOUSE!!!!!!! I'LL BE THERE TO-MORROW MORNING AT 7 AM!!!!!!! OMFG!!!!!!!!!!!!!**

This gigantic old tree *is* screaming inside, and it is going to kill us. You do not have to be a structural engineer to see that if this tree cracked and fell, it could slice the house clean in two. When Arborist Dude removed the branch that had fallen across the driveway, he told me it weighed at least two thousand pounds. "And it lands weighing ten times that."

Now there is no doubt: the Slime Tree equals death. Is tomorrow morning too late?

There is no "opposite end" of the house that is far enough away. The tree has to make it through the night. Splitting apart in these powerful, gusting winds and crashing into the house is not an option. I have to be proactive.

I begin composing a spell, and then I use my phone to translate it into Early Modern English, because I feel it should be in the language from the tree's childhood.

I repeat the words under my breath to learn it as I walk away from the maple toward the barn and then past it, trudging through the thick, heavy snow down the hill through the clutch of apple trees. It is dark as I cross the footbridge over the stream and walk to the rear of the field, the wind kicking up from behind and propelling me forward. The moon is waning and dark, but the stars are out — trillions of them on this crystalline night — which is enough for my eyes to adjust so I'm not wandering around in complete darkness.

I reach a white oak tree and find small branches that have fallen. I require only a tiny piece of oak: a little branch no larger than a toothpick will work fine. I snap the end of a dried limb and carry the twig back to the garage.

From my tall metal tool chest I choose

one of my leather-sheathed carving knives. A smaller one that I've recently sharpened with sapphire dust will be perfect. I carefully scrape the twig with the edge of the blade to remove the bark and burnish the grain until it's tight and shines, almost like I've waxed it.

As I do this, I repeat the spell:

As the winter winds blow through its core
    of might
the maple tree, it screams i' fright
oak, thou might not alloweth this maple
    falleth tonight
'mongst all trees thou art the king
and only royal blood can keepeth a fallen
    tree upright

Swiping the snow from a small area at the base of the tree, I stick the tip of the smooth oak twig into the frozen earth, then gently angle it so that the other end rests against the trunk of the giant old tree.

Forget *my* powers. The maple would not dare fall upon a monarch.

The wind is still blowing strong, and the maple is creaking, but I cannot hear it screaming. The instant the oak twig touched its trunk, the maple knew it had to hold itself together. Exactly like you would not fart in front of Kate Middleton. Even if your small intestine popped, you'd hold it inside.

I fall asleep instantly and am up by six.

Arborist Dude arrives promptly at seven, wearing a fleece pullover like it's early fall and not the middle of a polar deep freeze. He examines the tree and studies the thirty-foot crack that has formed, essentially dividing the trunk in two. Because the massive upper limbs of the tree have been cabled for years, if it does break, he is worried that half will pendulum-swing into the house or the barn.

In the light of day, I doubt myself. Am I crazy for even considering destroying this grand old tree? Is my hate/hate relationship with it justified? "Does it have to come down? Yes or no?" I ask.

He kicks at the ground like a kid. "That's the thing, this isn't a yes or no. I have some clients who would take it down for sure. I have other clients who would have more of a wait-and-see attitude."

I think, Wait and see what? If it's ripped from the earth and kills me?

Then he says, "Personally? If it were *my* tree, I would take it down. That's by far the safest option. This tree is over a hundred and fifty years old. Trees don't live forever — they have a limited life span. You can plant a new tree in its place."

The idea sickens the tiny part of me not ruled by panic and fear and witchcraft. You don't whip out a chain saw and cut down a magnificent force of nature like this tree. You just don't.

The other part of me — the part with the black pointy hat and the broom — thinks of the screaming I heard from deep inside it, screaming that Christopher *could not hear* but that was as clear to me as a ringing bell. Even if I've temporarily (please let it be temporarily) lost some measure of my powers, *I heard it.*

The screaming was real, but it was happening in the world *beneath* this world, down in the hidden everything, where all is connected. If I could hear it more clearly, I'm certain it foretells horror.

"Chop it down," I tell Arborist Dude. "Now."

He nods. "Will do."

I walk inside and tell Christopher that I have just ordered the destruction of the grand maple in the front yard.

"Okay," he says. "If that will make you feel safer. We don't want it falling on the house, that's for sure."

There is not a trace of hostility in his voice. There never is (Dick Voice aside, but

369

that's something else). Christopher is never passive-aggressive. He is only always honest. God, that is rare.

"You wouldn't take it down if it was just you, right?" I ask him.

He smiles at me, then he shakes his head. "No," he says, "I wouldn't. But I get it. *I get you.*"

I know I am doing the right thing, yet the stubborn, mortal side of me continues to be a pest and question, Am I being paranoid? Am I crazy?

God, how do normal people live without a direct connection to the underworld? I guess Netflix really is, like, everything for people.

Soon a full crew arrives with a massive wood chipper — which of course makes me think of the notorious wood-chipper murder of Helle Crafts by her husband that occurred one town over — and a dump truck with a cherry picker attached at the back. I retreat upstairs to my office, which faces the other direction, so I can't see anything. But when it begins, I can hear the sawing. And when a heavy branch falls, the house shakes.

I am surprised that I feel conflicted. The sound of the saw is a relief, and I feel like, *Ha! I won!* Yet doubt claws at my brain: Am I only paranoid? Is it a normal, noisy old tree and my distrust of it pure delusion?

Relief and regret. The two contrasting emotions crash against each other inside me.

I google, "What's the oldest tree?"

And the answer is five thousand years old. A pine tree in California, the land of smog, earthquakes, and rampant wildfires. Arborist Dude told me "trees don't live forever," but apparently they can come pretty damn close. Now I feel monstrous, like I am stuffing a toddler into a coffin. One hundred fifty is a baby! It was just a fetus tree.

Then I remind myself of my very first impression, when the tree seemed to say, *I am going to kill you.* I simply got to the trigger first.

It takes all day, eight full hours. That's the length of time for a complicated surgical procedure like a pancreaticoduodenectomy. When they are gone, I go into the guest bedroom that overlooks the front yard. It is shocking to see the stump, a massive scar nowhere near round; it is shaped like a splatter, a drop of ink falling through the air, landing on a piece of paper. It is a Rorschach splotch. The snow on the front yard is blanketed with sawdust.

The threat is gone.

The screaming silenced.

The days pass.

More snow falls, over a foot on the roof, the porch railings, the birdbath. We are pinned in place beneath the weight of the weather.

Over the following weeks I find myself standing in the window of the guest room looking down at the oval front lawn with the gigantic raw stump, sheared as close to the earth as they could manage. Each time I look, I see a new thing in its form: a butterfly, a dragon, two teacups with handles facing one another, a bat in flight, mid-turn.

I keep thinking about how Christopher would never have taken this tree down. This thought is accompanied by a sinking feeling that things might have worked out fine. They always do for him. Even when they don't, they do; who has HIV for thirty-five years and never even gets a cold?

Now that I no longer hear the screams coming from deep within the tree, now that my own powers have weakened, it is simple to imagine the danger away. I attempt to have a rational conversation with myself. "When you first heard screaming that you identified as coming from the tree, given the mental illness in your family, did it not occur to you to seek the counsel of a psychiatric professional? Trees lack vocal cords. They have neither feelings nor brains. Instead, you identify as a witch: a supernatural, mythical being with abilities that are incompatible with contemporary scientific knowledge."

I realize I am speaking to myself in my dead father's voice and OH MY GOD of course I should have seen a therapist. This could not be clearer to me now as I look down upon the stump, a physical symbol of my mental illness. I am Hester Prynne, and the stump is my scarlet *A*. It is a reminder that I am impulsive, destructive, prone to periods of paranoid, delusional, obsessively catastrophic thinking, that I'm afraid of the unknown and all that I cannot control and that I have chosen to live according to the supernatural belief system indoctrinated in me by my mentally ill and benzodiazepine-addicted narcissistic and bipolar mother.

I have single-handedly ruined the aesthetic appeal of a property that has been stunning since before Maine was part of America. I did this because I got into a grudge match with a piece of wood that I thought was screaming at me. I feel a grief much more potent than when my father or mother died. With both of them, first my father and then, a decade later, my mother, I felt nothing beyond *it was your time.* I suspected I would be hit with emotion at a later date, but it's now been years, and I don't think of them and certainly don't miss them.

I can't complain about cutting down a big old tree in my yard when every day there's a new school shooting or another chunk of Antarctica the size of Rhode Island breaking away and melting. It really, really doesn't matter.

Except to me it does.

When I start to bemoan the loss of the tree once again to Christopher, he puts up his hands and says, "Yes, I know, you ruined Connecticut, maybe all of New England."

The only person I can complain to who won't detest me for my privileged misery is Maura. I text her. "I'm still not over it. It will be summer in two weeks and all I can see is the stump, I can't even see the house anymore."

She texts right back. "I understand. We had to take one down at the farmhouse in Newtown and everyone says, 'It's just a tree, plant a new one!' But you can't replace history."

She has perfectly articulated why I am grieving. It mortifies me to think that if the lady bachelors who lived here in the 1940s and built the beautiful sunporch were to suddenly return, the first thing they would say is, "Where the hell is the maple tree? What kind of steward of the land are you? What's next, Modern Guy, aluminum siding? How about replacing all the original leaky old windows with brand-new ones from Pella? That'd be sweet. Asshole."

It isn't the tree itself I am mourning but rather the history of the tree — the people who planted it, the lives it saw come and go. I am mourning the children, long dead, who jumped into freshly raked piles of its brilliant autumn leaves.

We will replace the tree. We will have the roots excavated and a new tree planted in its place. And it will look beautiful. But beauty can be empty. A thing can be beautiful and be nothing more than beautiful. We can plant the prettiest tree we find, but history has been reset to 0.000.

I must remember that the witch part of me didn't care about any of this. The witch part of me needed that thing gone.

In the garage is a perfect rectangle of maple approximately the size of one of those ice coolers you stuff with beer and sandwiches and bring to the beach.

Only it weighs a couple of hundred pounds, at least.

As the crew was finishing removing the last of the trunk, I asked one of them if he could carve out a large chunk of wood from the very center, the heart of the tree.

He nodded and smiled. "Sure thing."

When they were gone, I didn't see the chunk of wood. I figured he'd forgotten and now it was too late; the tree had been turned into sawdust by the Helle Crafter.

I open the garage door and there it is, this block of wood, cut so carefully on all sides. He has tucked it squarely beneath my workbench, out of the way.

Seeing this, I feel something inside me leap forward. It is a physical sensation as I depart my grief over the tree, forgive myself for cutting it down, and realize all of history was not lost after all. There is a small piece of it right here before me.

I could carve it into a bowl — many bowls. Or a table. Or cutting boards for everyone I know.

It is like the great Parthenon atop the Acropolis of Athens. All that remains are the crumbling ruins, the bare bones. Which is *just* enough.

# SNAKE'S TONGUE

My last primary care physician in New York City was a warm, charismatic, and sociable guy. Even if I was only there for a flu shot or to check in to see if there had been a medical breakthrough in the area of hair-regrowth pharmacology, he always took the time to sit down with me and ask me how I was doing.

He was empathetic and caring, the kind portrayed on television shows depicting a bygone time in America, when you never had to worry that your doctor would sedate you and then jerk off on your face, like Manhattan physician David H. Newman did to a woman who came to the ER for a shoulder injury.

I always thought of mine as a country doctor who happened to practice in the city, though he was also a modern, up-to-date doctor engaged with the latest advances. He was both a gastroenterologist and an internist, and the wall beside his desk was shingled with framed certifications, affiliations, and assorted accomplishments. He would even make house calls if you weren't feeling up to traveling to his chic office suite on the Upper East Side.

Leaving New York meant leaving the only doctor I had ever liked. After we move to Connecticut, it takes me a year to find a doctor. Not a year of research and go-see appointments but a year of putting it off. Finally I pick a doctor at random whose practice is in a bland medical office building ten minutes away.

My new doctor is professional and courteous but not terribly warm or friendly. He is intelligent and clinical, constantly making notes on his ThinkPad. Most notably, he diagnoses a thyroid disorder that has somehow gone undetected. When I ask him why my previous doctor didn't discover this, he shrugs.

On one visit, he sees me remove an oval white pill from a small blue plastic bottle and pop it in my mouth.

"What is that?" he asks.

"Nicotine pill."

"Oh," he says. "And when did you quit smoking?"

I could see his fingers poised over his

378

laptop as he started to make a note on my medical chart.

"In 1999," I reply.

He doesn't type a word. His fingers remain suspended above the keys, only now he looks up from them and at me. "You quit smoking eighteen years ago and you're still using nicotine pills?"

Was it eighteen years? How could he have possibly performed that calculation so fast?

"Well, I don't know how many years off the top of my head, but, yeah, I stopped in 1999 and have been on the nicotine pills ever since. Well, no, that's not true. I was chewing the gum for most of that time and only switched over to the pills a few years ago."

"If you quit in 1999 and it's 2017, that's eighteen years," he explains, now showing off his skill with numbers. "How many of those do you take a day?"

"How many bottles?"

Now he is alarmed. "I meant how many pills. Do you consume more than one bottle?"

"Two, usually. Sometimes a little more."

"What's a little more?"

I pause ever so briefly. "Another bottle."

"And how many pills are in three bottles?"

Jesus, why all the math today? He is making me feel anxious, like when I was back in grade school and didn't have the faintest idea how many sevens went into ninety-four and why I would ever need to know when I could just ask somebody. Tabulating, I felt, was beneath me. "There are seventy-five pills per bottle," I tell him, and it comes out on a sigh of exasperation, which both surprises and embarrasses me, because I can hear how vapid I sound.

He types a very long notation in my chart, and then he looks at me matter-of-factly and declares, "Well, you have to stop taking those." It is not phrased as a suggestion; he speaks these words as one would a deep and inarguable fact of the solar system. "Mercury is closer to the sun. That's why it's hotter than Earth."

The nicotine mint is hidden under my tongue, where I've heard people with chronic heart failure place their nitroglycerin tablets for faster absorption. And where he can't pluck it out of my mouth.

I reply, "Come again?" as if I have been momentarily distracted.

"You need to wean yourself off the pills. You should be able to do this in three weeks."

He has caught me off guard.

My previous doctor never suggested I give

up my nicotine pills. They were so much a part of me that the *New York Times* even did a little piece about us, although back then it was gum. Surely the *New York Times* would have told me if I had to give them up; who would know better than they? And where did three weeks come from? Why was that the magic number of weeks? Why not three hundred weeks?

I feel a horrible sensation of being left behind, of standing on the dock with my ticket as the ship sails away, blaring its horn. "Wait," I say. "I thought they weren't bad for you."

He raises his eyebrows. "Why did you think that?"

I have no good answer for him. It is something I've heard or maybe assumed or maybe imagined. "I don't know, maybe I read a study out of Stanford? Or somebody told me nicotine itself wasn't so bad."

"Three hundred milligrams of nicotine a day? Believe me, that's bad."

There he goes again with the math. The worst part, of course, is that he is right — about me, not his quick multiplication skills. I've never felt like an ex-smoker, because I am still addicted to the very chemical that makes people want to smoke in the first place. Nobody smokes because they enjoy the flavor. Cigarettes taste like death, and the physical sensation of filling your lungs with smoke is horrific. That's why most people practically cough up their larynxes the first time they take a puff.

When I was growing up in the 1970s, it was a given that one day you would smoke. Everybody did. On talk shows, the celebrity guests were provided with a coffee mug (probably filled with gin or rye whiskey) and the ubiquitous Steuben crystal ashtray. My obsession with black-and-white movies led me to believe that life would be filled with clouds of smoke.

As a kid, I could not wait to start smoking. By which I mean, I literally could not wait. At eleven I was riding my bike seven miles to the tobacco shop on Main Street in Amherst, where I would perform for the clerk the role of Dutiful Child Buying Cigarettes for His Mother and Being Only Slightly Resentful.

I pulled this hackneyed routine at all the local stores. I tucked the packs into my tube socks, brought them home, and stored them in a tin canister that once held Danish butter cookies, which were about as buttery as iceberg lettuce. I had decoupaged the outside of the canister with pictures of cigarettes I'd clipped from magazine ads. I had quite the collection: everything from Lucky Strikes to Kool Super Light 100s, which combined the nicotine taste of the grave with the menthol sensation of having your lungs frozen.

Even back in the primitive '70s, everybody knew cigarettes caused cancer, but it killed *other* people. The one brand I hated was Newport, with their ghoulishly cynical ad campaign — "Alive with pleasure!" — promising that you would not just live if you smoked Newport, you would live happily.

These days, there isn't really a reason to *start* smoking in the first place. True, there are occasional news stories about vape pens exploding in people's faces, sending shards of the apparatus into the brain and killing them while burning down their house, but this is rare. Like, lightning-strike rare.

As the doctor stares at me, I realize I am out of excuses.

I'm not in my twenties anymore, though other than chronologically, I have not in any way progressed beyond them. You can really make a mess of yourself in your twenties and still self-repair. In fact, that should be a requirement of your twenties so you aren't a universally despised "I've been into high-intensity interval training my whole life!"

person by the time you reach forty. It's infinitely more interesting to have recovered from something than merely to have continued to raise the bar on your personal best.

The more fun you have, the more you'll pay for it later. And I have reached "later," that theoretical, math-free date I was certain would never arrive.

"You're right," I tell him. "I do have to stop."

He nods in encouragement. "That's good. So you can taper and —"

"No. I'm not going to taper. I'll stop."

"Well," he says, kind of moving his head from side to side, like it is loose on the stalk of his neck and might roll off and onto the table. "You don't need to be extreme about it."

I laugh at his ignorance. "Of course I do," I reply.

He backs off. "Okay, if that's how you need to do it. But if that proves too difficult, it might be easier to wean yourself off the pills gradually over time."

"The worst it can be is *uncomfortable.* It has nothing to do with *difficulty,* just discomfort. I really don't want to stretch it out. If I must stop, I will stop right now."

Three hours later, when I am home and in the hateful vise-grip of nicotine withdrawal, I realize I need something. It cannot, however, be any kind of *something* the doctor will one day make me give up. I drive to a pharmacy and buy a package of cough drops: sugar-free Green Tea with Echinacea Ricola.

Weirdly, they do the trick.

I suspect I am now the single heaviest Ricola user in North America. (Years ago, when I ordered guestroom toiletries from the trendy Manhattan Kiehl's "Since 1851" pharmacy, they told me they had *never* received such a large order online. Meaning I ordered more of that shit than Madonna. Than *Cher.*) I was successfully able to cross-addict from the harmful nicotine pills to the harmless throat lozenges. Thank God for the Swiss.

The barbed-wire-mattress discomfort of nicotine withdrawal lasts for about three weeks. A calculator (eventually) helped me discover this is 30,240 minutes, and I was aware of each of them.

Now, though, I feel something unexpected: freedom.

True, I am still stuffing something into my mouth every ten minutes, but I am no longer being held hostage by a drug.

I *am* Tina Turner, rising from the dust of the Australian Outback in my chain mail gown with seventeen-inch shoulder pads, and I don't need another hero.

At my next doctor's appointment, I am not prepared for the tone of confrontation. "What's going on with your diet?" the doctor asks. "Your glucose levels are off the charts. And these are fasting blood glucose levels. Something is seriously wrong here. We're in diabetes territory."

"I don't understand," I say. Hasn't he been taking vial after vial of my blood for months, checking my thyroid levels, adjusting and then readjusting the dose? Why now, all of a sudden, is my glucose level a problem?

"We're vegan," I said. My tone of voice implied, "Therefore, you are mistaken." We *are* vegan now, except for Fridays, which are steak nights. But other than that tiny blip of murdered animal, we are vegan.

"Tell me everything you eat," he says.

I shrug. "Last night we had a roasted chickpea kale salad, and tonight I'm doing portobello mushroom fajitas." He continues to stare at me. He doesn't blink. He waits.

Then the funniest thing happens. His penetrating gaze somehow brings to the front of my mind something I keep stuffed in the very back. I blurt it out, my dirty little secret. "Well, then, there is the candy."

His eyebrows rise in interest. "The candy?"

"Yes," I say with as much dignity as possible. "The thing is, every night after we go to bed, I eat seven Snickers bars. But they're the big double Snickers bars, so really I eat fourteen of them."

"You eat fourteen Snickers bars every night?"

"Yes."

"How long have you been doing this?"

"Oh, I don't know. I mean, the Snickers are kind of newish. It changes. For a few years it was one of those pound-sized bags of peanut M&M's. Before that, Reese's Peanut Butter Cups. I would have about ten double-packs of those."

His mouth is open and it makes me laugh. *My doctor's* jaw is dropping as I talk about my diet. Because he doesn't laugh with me or even smile but only looks at me with clinical bewilderment, I feel insane. By the expression on his face, I know he thinks I may be mentally ill, and if I told him right now, "Also, I'm a real witch. Like, I cast spells and shit goes down," I believe he would have me committed for a twenty-four-hour psychiatric evaluation that it is quite possible I would fail.

Hearing myself confess to my post-bed

eating habits is as shocking to my ears as it is to his, yet I can't stop. "For a while it was candied ginger. You know that stuff? God, I loved it. The twenty-four-hour market downstairs sold it — this was when we lived in Manhattan — and I would buy two containers a night."

He tries to talk. "This has. You can't." He stares at me and tries again. "You have to stop this right now. Why are you doing this? Why don't you have a piece of fruit?"

Now I am the one looking at him with clinical bewilderment. "Because I don't want *fruit*, I want fourteen Snickers bars."

"You don't like fruit?"

"No," I say.

"What about a handful of almonds?"

"Oh my God," I said. "You sound like *Men's Health* magazine in human form. A handful of almonds? Did you really just say that?"

"You have to stop with the candy," he says again.

Oh, I detest this horrible man.

*Again* he is right.

I have known for years I couldn't keep doing this. At my last dental exam? Eighteen cavities. I didn't even think I had eighteen *teeth*.

"I know," I admit. "You're right. I can't

keep eating candy like a kid."

He doesn't laugh, he does that thing where you kind of half guffaw in a way that means *You've got to be kidding.* Then he says, "Kids don't eat candy like you do. Kids eat fruit."

"Wait, then who eats all the candy?"

He looks at me, doesn't smile, but speaks very slowly, articulating each syllable for maximum impact.

"Old people."

I might actually gasp at this, but I pull it together fast. "Well, then. Good to know. Thanks for the heads-up. I won't ever have another grain of sugar for the rest of my life."

He nods. I am pleased by how quickly he's learned not to suggest I "limit" my sugar intake or remind me I don't have to be "extreme." No limits. All extremes. That's me.

I leave his office and drive home, where I carry the remaining *ninety-six* Snickers bars out to the barn and toss them into the trash. The doctor has won. At last, he has taken *everything* away from me. I have nothing left. I am a California hilltop after fire season. I am emptiness.

At my next appointment my blood glucose levels are normal and I have gone from a weight of one hundred ninety-two to one hundred sixty-seven, such a low number that my long-dormant vanity flickers briefly to life. *I could be a supermodel again!*

In the truck I pop a Ricola and I am back to earth.

Originally Christopher did not like and would not eat: sweet potatoes, chickpeas, coconut, lentils, kale, green tea, dates, oats, and squash, among other foods. I have found ways to disguise these things or rethink them, and now he consumes them, albeit unknowingly. He won't eat an actual coconut; that would make him puke. But he has zero problem with brownies made from dates boiled in coconut milk and green tea.

Six months have passed since his last doctor visit. This time, the results of Countdown to Liver Failure are stable — almost exactly what they were before — and I'm comforted that he's strong; he was fighting invasions of his own body long before I knew him. I'd feel better if I weren't trapped in the white walls of witchcraft purgatory, but it's not something I can change, so I'm not letting it bother me. Too much.

It turns out that Christopher's Dr. Infectious Disease Wife is alarmed about one of his results: he's lost seventeen pounds. She asks him if he has changed anything in his diet. *And he has to think about it.*

"Didn't you tell her that you are now vegan? That you eat no processed foods? And that we're off sugar?

He did remember to tell her about the no-sugar thing, but that was it. "Don't let her turn a benefit into a symptom," I tell him. "Call her back and tell her you forgot you were vegan."

"Maybe I 'forgot' because I'm not."

"You are. Except for steak on Fridays. We're like inverted Catholics. Or something."

"Except for *also* every single morning when I put butter on my toast and whole milk in my coffee. By 7:00 a.m., I am not vegan."

He's right. I need to get that crap out of the house. Also, I don't want to hear these annoying little facts. I tell him, "There's the deeper issue that you've identified as a corn-fed midwestern supercarnivore your entire life and you don't want people thinking you're a smug, on-trend vegan who probably does Bikram yoga and has anxiety attacks over the size of his carbon footprint."

"You're right. That's fifty percent of it. The other fifty percent is actually consuming the cow."

"And the third fifty percent," I say, "is that you lost seventeen pounds."

I have two remnants from my chaotic teenage years that somehow, miraculously, I have managed to hold on to through all the decades and cities and apartments: my apron from the Ground Round and my Calvin Klein jeans from 1982.

I can fit into them both.

I try on the absurdly skinny threadbare designer jeans and almost begin to sob when I can button them.

I have come full circle. Or maybe I'm the snake that perpetually eats itself, but here's what I mean: I no longer have my life stretched before me, where anything is possible. I am facing joint replacement, mental decline, the shriveling, wilting decay of old age. But I face it wearing the exact same jeans I wore when I was seventeen and felt electricity flash and slide along my skin, when I burned inside to make something of myself, something big, something loud and powerful and strong, something you couldn't look away from or ignore.

# Toe of Frog

It is difficult for me to apply the linear concepts of time and aging to myself. For instance, I am in my fifties and I think of myself as "old," but if I live for (God forbid) four more decades, I will think or more likely say out loud to nobody, "Why did I waste my *youth* being old?" It will, however, provide clarity about my being rejected by the college guy who worked the counter at the Star Market when I was thirteen. I mean, of course, how completely stupid.

I am accustomed to being *thirty.*

My professional life in advertising began before most people my age had even finished their first year of college. I had no formal education beyond elementary school, and my boss boasted about it in every client meeting. Still a teenager, I was by far the youngest person working at the ad agency and decades the junior of many people in the creative department, where I was a copywriter. I knew I was young, but I also felt like I was the same age as my colleagues. None of this was helped by my poor math skills.

I was thirty-five when my first book was published. That period was chaotic and exciting and intense, and I was so consumed with my career, I forgot I was aging. I was still thirty-five when we moved to Connecticut in 2015, when in fact I was fifty.

My forties had gone the way of my twenties; both lost to blackouts, though of different natures and causes. I remember turning thirty and thinking, Wait, this isn't right. Thirty is *old.*

Thirty-five seemed late in life, and I would actually say this. "I didn't become a writer until rather late in life." Which is absurd, because suddenly I am a half century.

Shortly after we arrived in Connecticut, and when I was still in age denial, I asked Christopher, "Is it weird to be young and move out to the country?"

This was followed by a long, weighty pause. "Are you talking about . . . *us*? Because we're . . . old."

This was a stunning new shock — I went from thirty-five to Grandpa. A chunk is missing and I am pretty sure I am owed a midlife crisis.

AARP sends us mail on an almost hourly basis. I don't even know exactly what it is, and I don't want to know. To me, it's Death with its gleaming curved sickle coming for you, Eileen Fisher full-length crepe poncho billowing behind. To have an AARP card is to be officially old, and the proof is there every time you open your wallet with your arthritic fingers.

To be fair, there *are* good things about being this age. My need to seek approval is *gone.* Maybe it helps that both my awful parents are dead. Or maybe it's no more complex than the freedom to wear Wrangler jeans.

I never realized how vain I was, how obsessed with my body, until now, as the mirror reflects a guy who looks like my father but not overweight. I took steroids in my thirties and worked out with free weights and got big. I have a couple of pictures from back then and when I look at them now I'm like, Whaaaaaaaaat?

I will never see the inside of a gym again in my life. That is a fact.

I get plenty of exercise around the house, hoisting bags of cement or mulch, hauling broken branches, throwing large and heavy rocks into the trailer of the garden tractor so I can work on a wall. No longer a gym rat, I am now a farmhand.

Is a witch something else I *used to be*?

I got my first tattoo when I was thirty and just shy of three months sober. I was living in the East Village, where I walked the same limited grid every day, like a rat learning its maze. Usually I had my camera and I thought of myself as a kind of hunter, stalking pieces of beautiful light. The endless pictures of trash cans and doorways and apple cores on the sidewalk weren't taken because I am attracted to these things. I shot the light, and whatever happened to be stained by it.

It was ever-changing, the light, and thus my small grid-within-a-grid of streets. With each season, the angle of the sunlight and its saturation and hue shifted, the colors warming and cooling. One day I noticed a smear of something in the corner of the frame. When I lowered the camera, I saw that it was a slice of light clinging to the top of a window of what appeared to be a store in the basement of a brownstone. I crossed the street. The dirty glass was papered with faded illustrations, a skinless chart of tattoos, a menu. Where the top of the paper had curled, a sliver of white light escaped. Tattoo parlors were still illegal in Manhattan, so if you didn't know the exact location — or you didn't see the smear — this place would go unnoticed.

Inside, every millimeter of the walls was covered with classic sailor and outlaw and hippie designs: hearts and anchors and mermaids and bulldogs, knives and MOTHER, R. Crumb characters and biker logos, Corvettes with flames shooting from the tailpipes, wheat-colored breasts with fire-engine red nipples, skulls with candles in the eye sockets, abstract symbols and shapes, the yin/yang circle, the fluted-edged cap from a beer bottle. It was as if somebody had opened the mind of a man born in 1942 and drawn a small cartoon of every thought, fantasy, obsession, and fear he'd had for the next thirty years.

I did not know I was going to get a tattoo until I was there, so of course I had no design or even an idea in mind. I shut my eyes and I felt very small, like I was standing in a giant bathtub as water spiraled down the drain. Because I was nearly three months sober, everything was a metaphor for alcohol and the avoidance of it. Spirals, yes, exactly. One drink and then another and an endless spiral opened beneath you to carry you down, down and around until you reached a single tiny point and the only thing that existed in the world was drink.

"I need a spiral," I told the guy at the counter. I hadn't needed a spiral until I said the words.

It surprised me that I enjoyed the pain, or rather, that I liked being able to place the pain inside a container so that I was not bothered by it. I liked the challenge, the magickal solution: observe it from a distance. I am not one of those people who likes to be spanked or whipped. I dislike pain, even in small doses. But the needle in my arm, the buzzing, the heat — this recipe was oddly soothing. The pain was steady and never sharp, a thick, low frequency, a constant sting without the bite of poison.

I did not have a true feeling of time as I sat in that chair, but I was surprised when suddenly my shoulder fell silent and throbbed. The wound was wrapped in gauze, I was told to keep it bandaged and clean, I paid three hundred dollars, and I walked home, amazed by what had happened.

My left shoulder felt hot and it was still thrumming. I had committed a minor crime and I wondered if the people I passed on the sidewalk could tell. In my apartment I peeled the bandage off immediately and studied the wet-black lines carved into my skin. "It's like a scar, from drinking," I said to myself.

In the morning, there was a copy of my tattoo on the fitted sheet, like I'd used my shoulder as a rubber stamp. Apparently that is what the "keep it bandaged and clean" instruction is for. A week later, I saw as I showered that a few of the details in the spirals on my flesh had vanished.

Maybe it was fading away, but I could feel the tattoo beneath my shirt and it made me different. I couldn't say exactly how, only that there had been a shift. Surely the tattoo would keep me sober — how could I drink with this constant reminder? — and it would provide me with a strange sort of power, perhaps one born of petty crime and pain tolerance.

At the gym, guys who had never spoken to me came up and wrapped their hands around my arm. "Nice ink." Gentle stroke of the index finger along the outer edge of the design. Slap on the back. "See ya around."

Had I known the secret power of tattoos, I would have gotten my first at age six.

It has been over twenty years since that day in the East Village basement, and now my arms are somewhat covered. I have a phrase in elegant large script on my right arm that reads, in Latin, "The Scar Remains." This is the truest thing I know. Scars are nothing to hate, they are nothing to deny. They serve as our proof of what we've survived, and there is nothing more beautiful than to have survived something.

On my other arm is a filigree design. On my shoulder, now covering my spiral, long faded and blurred, is the beginning of a universe, complete with planetary bodies and stars and different kinds of light. There will be more. I never expected to be the guy who allowed himself to be a human sketchpad. It always seemed important that I be careful and not, as they say, do something I would regret.

I do not fear regret. It is a marker, a scar of another kind. It is only my body. Any remorse I may eventually experience will be inconsequential. In thirty more years, when gravity has abandoned me, will it truly be that my arms — or whatever else — are any *more* ruined, etched with regrettable ink? Or perhaps I will look at those words and lines and curves and stars and recall, however dimly, the young man who sat at the end of a needle and endured their creation? Might they be a kind of scrapbook? All that remains of what, at the time, felt like my only life?

Could, then, my ink be the last thing of beauty left on me?

My mother didn't see her mother for the last decade of her life, just as I never saw mine, so we don't know firsthand what happens to the magick as we grow old. I wish I could ask my mother, *Is it different? Is it less?* Did she wish she had asked the same of her mother? I didn't think I had anything more to say to her, but it turns out I do.

# UNICORN'S HORN

Eddie comes over to fix some of our broken-ass stuff, and all three of our phones go off at the same time, like an Amber Alert but a different, more urgent tone. What's more dire than a kidnapped child?

"A tornado is approaching and will reach your location in five minutes. Seek immediate shelter," reads the emergency message.

Eddie is on his way up from the field and Christopher is putting his phone away and looking unconcerned. I say, "Come on, everybody, into the house, let's go."

Christopher kind of laughs. "Okay, we're coming, don't panic."

Three of the dogs are lazing in the sun and Radar is positively frolicking through a wildflower patch. "Hey!" I call. "Aren't you supposed to be the ones warning *us* about this? Get inside now!" They can read the intensity and seriousness in my voice, and they dutifully trot after me.

The sky has darkened as quickly as if someone pulled a thick curtain over it.

Eddie and Christopher are hanging back, yammering. "You two, move it. Get in the house, this is not a joke. There's an actual tornado and it's gonna be here in four minutes."

Once we are all inside, Eddie and Christopher sit on the living room sofas. "What are you doing?" I say, striding past them and opening the basement door. "Down here, right now. Both of you. Let's go."

I can't believe how casual they're being. Jesus, has neither of them even seen *The Wizard of Oz*?

I call for the dogs to come downstairs, but now my tone alarms them — or something else does — and they run down the hall.

I scream for them to come, but they won't.

"Augusten," Christopher says, "we've spent three years training them not to go down those stairs, so I don't think they're going to figure it out right now while you yell at them."

This may be true, but I am still freaked out that a tornado is almost on top of us and he is no better at seeking shelter than the dogs are. I see Wiley and run to scoop him up but he bolts into the office.

"It's okay, they'll be fine," Christopher says.

*Yeah, right,* I want to say. *Sheltered from a twister by a literary agency.* Instead I head down the basement stairs and shout, "Come down here right now!"

The lights flicker and the atmosphere shifts.

Eddie says, "Uh-oh," something I've never heard him utter, and he goes for the stairs. "When Eddie heads to the basement, you know it's bad!" he calls back to Christopher, who is right behind him.

The lights flicker once again and then go out.

Then there is just noise.

Hail like I've never heard before. It is pounding hail and rain so hard that water begins to pump through the stone foundation walls.

Halfway up the stairs is a small window, level with the driveway. I can't see a thing. It is completely whited out but kinetic, like the window is filled with a million huge insects made of light, smashing their bodies repeatedly against the glass.

The sound is like nothing identifiable but it fills the ears, packs them with a terrible roar.

One morning in 1986 I was getting

404

dressed for work in San Francisco when I heard a freight train approaching. When I say approaching, I mean it was as though my apartment were on a set of railroad tracks. A moment later the world began to shake. It felt as if the hand of a giant had clamped down on the apartment building and was fiddling with it, deciding whether to crush it in his fist or let go.

The giant let go.

Nothing fell off a shelf, and other than a few car alarms swirling their sirens around on the street below, that was the extent of it.

In a similar unholy fashion, the tornado dropped from the sky and just as swiftly it is over. The sound lifts, like a lid off a pot.

There is perfect silence.

I walk up the stairs first and open the door. *This is the part where it turns from black and white to color, right?*

At a glance, nothing has changed. The walls are still where they are supposed to be, the dogs come up to me, all tails wagging. With a jolt I see that all the windows have shattered — wait, not shattered. Plastered with wet pine needles that look like cracks.

I peer outside at the pine tree limbs covering the lawn, the driveway. I walk toward the kitchen. And I see it. "Oh, shit," I cry.

Christopher is running up behind me. "What is it?"

A massive branch has fallen from one of the trees and pierced the sunporch roof. Water is pouring into the room. I run back downstairs to get a bucket and set it under the hole. I feel dizzy, drunk, like I might actually fall over sideways. Then I see the reason why: the whole room is tilted. I walk over to the corner, where the porch is attached to the house, and I see a crack running along the wall where it has slightly pulled away from its second-story perch.

"Okay, it's not safe in here, let's get out."

I close the door, but not before glancing out the window and seeing that one of the massive old trees behind the kitchen has fallen, crushed the landscaping and . . . did it reach the cottage? I can't tell.

Once outside, I see that it is not an entire tree but only a massive branch that was ripped from one. Though it still towers over the house, the remainder has to be taken down or it will fall on its own the next time a mild breeze wafts through the yard.

On the other side of the house there is a flagstone patio. A pine tree lies on its side, crushing the ancient lilac trees, its top resting on a lattice fence we'd had installed shortly after we moved in.

In the field I find a badminton racket, definitely not ours, the netting punched out, and dozens of cans — beer, soda, seltzer. Garbage, trash from who knows where. An egg carton. The lid from a Hellmann's mayonnaise jar.

Harold left his grease-covered gas generator from Sears, back when Sears was a place people actually went for things. Eddie goes into the barn and drags the old, filthy thing out from under the stairs. "Don't worry, girls, I'll start it up so you don't have to get your hands dirty or break a fingernail."

It sounds like a twin-prop plane has landed in the driveway, but it works, albeit in a very limited fashion: it powers the refrigerator, the stove, and one quad outlet in the basement, so we have to run an extension cord up the stairs to even plug in a lamp.

Eddie says he'd better get home. "You guys are so fucking lucky," he calls out as he pulls away. "Things could have gone a lot worse."

Christopher gives me a significant glance. He looks shaken, spooked.

"What is it?" I ask, feeling panic rise.

He says, "I thought you were crazy to have that maple tree taken down, but I also thought, *You're you, you know things.* But if you hadn't? Augusten, that tree would have fallen on the house and destroyed it." He pointed to the clear path the tornado had taken across the yard. The maple would have been lifted right up out of the ground. *"You are a witch and you knew and I trusted you and you saved our lives."*

When he says this, I know something with that same old certainty that only a witch knows, deep, deep in the core of my being: *I won't always be right. But I will never doubt myself again.*

We are unharmed, yet I didn't know a tornado was descending until I got a phone alert like every other mortal. There is still something — a scrim, a shroud — that stands between me and myself. Before this shade was lowered, the day we pulled into the driveway, I did know that there would be a tornado, and that it would pick that giant old maple tree up, roots swinging and dripping dirt, and plunge it into the heart of our house, like a stake through a vampire's chest.

It is getting dark, and we need gas for the generator.

We have no idea how bad things are, but the scenario I picture of getting gas in a town without power is postapocalyptic, with streets on fire and zombies stampeding through them.

I tell Christopher, "I'm heading out. If I can't get gas in town, I'm gonna go where I have to to get it."

He says, "Okay, the dogs and I will stay here and wait for you."

He'd already pulled one of the vintage oil lanterns out from storage and lit it. In the midst of upheaval, it casts a beautiful light in the room through its library-green glass shade.

I grab my wallet, keys, and gun and head off in my truck.

The damage I see is shocking.

One section of a nineteenth-century farmhouse next to the dairy has been crushed by a tree. Roads are blocked. The sound of chain saws is everywhere, blaring from all directions. Trees are uprooted, tossed twenty, thirty feet from their holes. Cars parked in driveways have been crushed, homes punctured by branches. My perfect rural Connecticut town, so unsophisticated it doesn't even have a bookstore — even the Kmart closed last year — looks like a war zone.

After I find gas and fill up the truck and two containers, the usual twenty-minute drive home takes more than three hours.

Being plunged into the colonial era is informative. I learn that my mental health and stability are directly proportionate to the amount of charge left in my phone.

I will not survive the apocalypse.

Power is restored after three days, but not for everyone. Many parts of the town are hit much harder. I know I should feel spared — blessed, even. But I don't. I feel cursed, like the universe is saying, "Here, catch!" and throwing me a ball of flaming kerosene.

I spend every day outside, cleaning debris, sawing large branches into smaller ones I can fit into the tractor cart and haul away into the woods. It seems like I will be doing this for many years. But really it takes only about a week to clear most of it.

Meanwhile, it appears nothing has been disturbed on Vivi and Oogah's property. Flowers bloom madly, and the bright red planting next to their house (dubbed "Vivi's Burning Bush") is flourishing, unlike our landscaping, which was battered and crushed. Not only is there no massive branch sticking out of their roof, there seems to be nary a leaf blown off a tree. How could that be? Was a protective spell cast on their home? Could Madama Butterfly herself be a more powerful witch than I? Is she the one who's leached my power?

One day I catch a glimpse of her creeping slowly from her porch to her car with the aid of what appear to be two ski poles, something no self-respecting witch would do (and I already know how much Vivi respects herself), so I don't think she's working any magick down the road.

The next day I am on the sofa scrolling through photos on my phone when I let out an involuntary gasp.

"What?" Christopher says, his head snapping around to me.

"Look at this. So on the day it hit, I took some pictures. But weird, random ones. And ugly, none of them are cool. I was going through deleting things when I noticed . . . a pattern."

He leans closer so he can see.

I show him a picture of a framed print we have hanging in the guest bedroom, a gift from one of his clients. It depicts a young girl in a satin dress with a St. Bernard. She's showing the dog a small badminton racket with chewed strings and it wears a guilty expression on its face.

"Remember the racket I found in the field?"

His eyes light. "Oh right. Harold and Elinor didn't leave that behind, did they?"

"No, they did not."

411

"How weird. So you took the picture of the dog and the chewed-up racket and then a shredded racket shows up in the yard."

"Right," I say slowly. "But look at the other pictures." I went through them one by one. "Everything I took a picture of that day was destroyed in the tornado. But *only* the things I took pictures of were destroyed. Nothing else."

"Wait, what?" he says.

"Here's a shot of lilacs tumbling over the white lattice on the cedar fence in the back. And here's one from the other side of the overgrown area in front of the patio with the tall tree in the background."

"And that tree," Christopher says slowly, "fell onto those lilacs."

"And then on the fence," I add.

He takes the phone from my hands and scrolls through more pictures. "There's the tree in front of the kitchen, *there's* the garden that tree crushed, the sunporch — Jesus Christ."

Even without magic, the deepest part of me could see the damage the tornado would cause, so I took pictures of the gone things before they were gone.

*I'm still a witch.*

Christopher looks up at me, his face the color of Cream of Wheat. "Please don't ever turn me into a goat to see if I'd be a cute one. Seriously. Not even for, like, five minutes."

I look at him with my left eyebrow raised. "What makes you think I haven't already, Mr. Falls Asleep Instantly?"

# ELF LEAF

The painting in our bedroom above the fireplace falls off the wall and lands perfectly upright on the mantel. It essentially slides down the wall six inches and comes to rest unharmed. At first I don't notice, because I have been changing some of the art around the house, and rather than hanging all the pieces, I've been leaning some on tables against walls, or on shelves. It makes for a casual and surprising display, but this one is surprising in that I didn't do it. I decide not to ask Christopher, since his nonvisual way of existing would require me to start with, "Did you know there was a painting in the bedroom?"

Several days later, though, the giant canvas by the front door, so big it hangs mere inches from the floor, is sitting on the carpet, so I ask if he moved it. My answer is clear in his uncomprehending look, or perhaps the look says, *I fully comprehend*

414

*your insanity.*

Hanging art is always a pain in this thick-plaster-walled house, because the nail either bends with the first tap of the hammer or each knock brings on a cloud of tiny paint chips and dust. Both these things happen as I rehang the paintings.

About a week later, the portrait of my uncle Mercer falls off the wall in the sun-room. It didn't budge when the tornado sent a tree branch through the roof and caused the whole room to pull away from the house. Instead, it falls on an ordinary Tuesday morning after I've had my coffee. After a four-foot drop, it's remarkably un-harmed.

The following week, the two paintings hanging side by side on the wall beside the staircase both fall, and both land upright on the ledge along the stairs, exactly like the first painting that slid down the wall in our bedroom.

I find this unsettling, but Christopher is fascinated that they all landed on their frames, upright and undamaged. "It's incredible. But it makes me worry there's something wrong with the walls. Moisture or something horrible."

I shake my head. "The walls are fine."

He looks at me, eyebrows raised in anticipation of my elaboration. I raise my eyebrows back. "Did you notice anything else a wee bit unusual about the paintings that fell?" I ask.

His forehead furrows in concentration. "Um . . . I'm the one who did a shitty job hanging all of them?"

I shake my head. "Nope. All the paintings that fell were my mother's. *Only* her paintings fell. And *every* painting of hers fell, except the one of my father."

"Whoa. You're right. I can't believe I didn't see it."

I nod. "Neither can I. I mean, not you; me. I can't believe I didn't see it earlier. I've been obsessing over Doctor Bombay and how every witch should have one of him in real life."

He looks confused but gives an encouraging "And?"

I sigh. "Something hasn't been right with me. I haven't said anything because I haven't really known what to say. But something has been wrong with my witch parts." I sound like a woman speaking to her husband about "female trouble" who's afraid to say the word "vagina."

"My magickal abilities have been missing. Things aren't right inside me. I've lost certain senses. My spells aren't working. I had no idea what the problem was, and I was worried because now you have a new disease and my flow of magick has been blocked. I started to think it was a more obvious reason, like run-of-the-mill fear of loss or something boring and ordinary like that, but now I know what it is: my mother. She has always been the only person who could intercept my magick. But I thought she couldn't do that anymore — you know, being dead and all. But clearly I was wrong."

"Yeah, but dead is dead," he says.

I shake my head. "You know how client-attorney privilege extends beyond death? Well, so does a witch's magick. It remains with a little bit of the witch inside it. Think of the magick like a mist, but with a faint aroma. The mist is the magick, the aroma is the witch. Normally, the magick is absorbed by other members of the family. But I didn't visit my mother when she was dying, and my brother isn't a witch and neither is his son, so there was no place for the magick to go."

"So . . . she's trying to communicate with you? Or . . . her . . . aroma is?"

"She had something to tell me, and I didn't care to hear it. Now she's insisting."

I have known the medical term for nasal

417

hallucinations — phantosmia — since I was a kid, because I have experienced them all my life. When I begin smelling Chanel No. 5 — faintly and fleetingly at first, then in undulating ribbons traveling through the room — I am certain it is my mother blocking my ability to be me.

I long ago forgave my mother for her abuse and neglect of me as a child. She was mentally ill and was entirely unable to raise a second child. But before her mind shattered when I was twelve, she tried. She tried hard. And in these years when she taught me and cared for and about me, I felt loved and strong.

Once the psychosis gripped her mind, she became a terrible creature. After years of this, followed by her somewhat deadening stroke, I found that I did not like her as a person; she absorbed instead of radiated, took instead of gave. Her need was bottomless, and as a narcissist she was incurable. At thirty, I was done with her.

As she was dying, I received messages from both her brother and mine that she wanted to see me. I ignored them. Now, as I sense her in a way I haven't for decades, as if she were in the very next room sitting on a sofa with her legs tucked under her, writing in her black notebook, I find that I

418

am sorry she is gone.

I wish she could have remained the person I knew when I was very young and just learning about who — and what — I was. When she was teaching, giving instead of needing, taking.

We did this thing at bedtime: I was afraid of the dark and never wanted her to leave. I wanted her to tuck me in and then sit on my bed until I was asleep. Instead, she said, "If you need me, just call me from inside a dream. You can always find me in your dreams."

I wonder if this is still true.

I lie down on the green velvet Chesterfield sofa in the living room. The late afternoon light, bent and warped by the old wavy window glass, turns the sofa a glossy black. I close my eyes and after a while I fall asleep. I wake an hour later, refreshed from my dreamless nap.

Useless. If I can't even direct my dreams, my magickal abilities are truly drained.

I lose track of time reading about the American painter Charles Demuth, who was born in 1883 and died on October 23, my birthday, in 1935, the year my mother was born. His painting *I Saw the Figure 5 in Gold* was one of her favorite works of art, and she wrote a poem about it entitled "I

Dreamed I Saw the Figure 5 in Gold." The painting itself was based on a poem by William Carlos Williams called "The Great Figure."

By the time I look up from my laptop, the room is dark. And where are the dogs? Where is Christopher? It is odd, the house so silent and empty. Has he taken them somewhere?

I walk outside, to the garden beside the barn. The tomatoes betrayed us this year, emerging green and then rotting on the vine. Two scrawny strings of green beans produced, but only a handful, curled like pigs' tails. One of the new peach trees produced five peaches — exactly like the painting! But the deer ate the fruit before we could.

As I leave the garden and walk to the edge of the field, standing between the hawthorn and the apple trees, the sky expands. It's a very dark sapphire blue, almost black but not. The apple tree is old, its gnarled branches bowing under the weight of the fruit clustered on them. Why hadn't I picked these and made pies?

I recall a line from one of my mother's poems, something about how apple trees "spill their red into the night air."

Out of the corner of my left eye I see

movement on the path that leads into the woods, probably one of the deer that bed down at the edge of the field at night. I head toward it and follow the path. It is dark in the woods, but the moon will be full in two days, so there is plenty of platinum light filtering through the trees.

There is another rustle of movement ahead, but I can't tell what the creature is; it's a dark blur. It has to be a deer. A wolf would not lead me somewhere; it would challenge me.

I've never walked this far back into our own woods before.

I wonder if my mother's favorite flowers, lady's slipper orchids, grow here like they did in Shutesbury. I look down but see none.

What I see is the door. A wooden door — more of a hatch, really. Ancient wood. With iron strap hinges and an iron handle. Somebody must have tossed this door out here, but who? When? And why? And what is under it? Mushrooms, snakes?

I have to know.

I lift the handle and the door opens. It isn't lying discarded on the ground after all. It is a proper hatch door in the floor of the forest with a set of very narrow stone steps leading down. The steps are narrower than those of the Pyramid of the Moon, in Teotihuacán, Mexico. I climbed them as a child.

I can see five steps illuminated by the moon, but only darkness after that.

I take the first step, then the second, and then the third. I continue until I am pulling the hatch door closed above me. Fully in the dark, earth on either side so I can steady myself as I continue to climb down the stairs — twenty-two, twenty-three, twenty-four, twenty-five — and that is it. Twenty-five stairs and I am standing on a firm, flat surface.

I hear the sound of water, somebody doing laps in a swimming pool, the splash of the kick reverberating off the walls and ceiling I cannot see.

My mother had been a lifeguard when she was young and a swimmer all her life, until the stroke.

The smell of Chanel No. 5 is thick in the air.

The swimming stops.

"I'm sorry I had to bring you here like this."

It is my mother's voice but different. There is a gargle to it, like she has water in her throat. "I was hoping you would come before I died. I had something very important to tell you."

"You can tell me now," I say.

"I can tell you now," she repeats. I hear a soft splash, like the sound of a surface dive.

I raise my voice so she can hear me underwater. "How have you blocked me? How is that possible?"

"I have done no such thing," she replies, her voice wildly distorted, undulating and filled with bubbles. "Three years after Mother died, I lost my sight for a week. Not my eyesight, my second sight. Mother came to visit me, and she had baby Harriet in her arms. She came to me in a dream, and she said, 'Margaret, you should have been there when I crossed under. We are Blue String witches; give me your wrist now, please.'"

I wait for her to continue, but she returns to her swimming, her crawl steady, the splash of her kick disciplined.

Then she is in front of me. My mother, alive, young, beautiful.

She holds up a length of tattered blue string, old sagging loops hanging down from either end. She slips her hand through one of the loops and lets the remainder dangle from her wrist. When she speaks, it is in the mannered southern voice she had before the stroke paralyzed her right side and caused her to sound leaned-against, crushed. "Now carefully tuck your fingers

423

together and slide your own hand through the other end so that the thread connects us."

I do as she requests.

She closes her eyes. I close my eyes and then I open them and my mother is old, gaunt. She lies on a steel-frame hospital bed, an IV drip in her arm. I watch her chest rise with the labor of inhaling. In her low, stroke-damaged voice she recites, *"Because I could not stop for Death, He kindly stopped for me; The Carriage held but just Ourselves And Immortality."*

"A spell," I joke.

She grins at me, and her old eyes shine. "Perhaps."

I can see how difficult it is for her to speak. I stare at the hollow of her neck. She looks so fragile. Her life was unhappy. She wanted me in it.

"I'm sorry I wasn't a better mother. I was born into the wrong body. I was a man inside."

"I know that, Mother. You came out as a man when I was fifteen. You said that realization was what caused your psychotic episode the month before, remember?"

She shakes her head and swallows. "I didn't know you knew. I didn't know I told you back then. Well, I'm sorry I wasn't a better father."

She reaches for my wrist and grips it with surprising strength. Her whole body tenses and then relaxes as a wave of pain passes. "It's time, my boy," she says. She withdraws her hand and places it back by her side, where the fingers twitch.

A heart monitor emits an irregular electronic *bleep-lup dup, lup_____dup*.

"Wait, I don't want to watch you die. I can't."

It is as if a great weight were atop her chest, crushing her. "You have to stay beside me and make sure the string doesn't slide off your wrist."

"All right."

She takes another deep, difficult breath and closes her eyes. Her lips barely move; she is whispering. I lean forward to hear her.

It is something I've never heard before, and yet by the third time she repeats it, I am speaking the words along with her as though I know it by heart, like a song I'd known all my life but had forgotten until this moment.

From the soil to the tree
when the acorn drops
it lands on thee.

From the mother to the son
a force divided shall be one.
Whence my last breath be drawn
shall my bloodborne gift belong to thee.
And flowing through thy veins
it does contain every possibility.

She inhales sharply. She opens her eyes. "All of my magick is inside you now. I can't hold on any longer. I love you. Forgive me."

"I do. I love you."

"*Thank you.* Now close your eyes," she tells me.

I close my eyes —

— and wake up startled, my face smashed into the corner of the sofa. I feel like I've been drugged, like I've been asleep for days. I sit up. Gunther jumps down from the brown leather sofa across from me and walks over so he can step on my foot with his sharp toenails and stick his icy nose in my mouth. "Oh God, gross," I say, wiping my mouth on my sleeve.

The other dogs lie on their beds behind the sofa.

I stand up and look at my phone. A quarter after three. I'd been asleep for only twenty minutes. That is impossible.

Christopher is outside in his sky-blue gardening shirt and thick tan canvas gardening pants, kneeling in the dirt in the bed outside the kitchen, wearing headphones and pulling weeds.

I walk through the kitchen, outside, and down the steps. As I pass him, I touch the top of his head and he falls forward, stopping himself. "Wow," he says.

"What?"

He yanks out his earbuds. "You gave me a shock. Didn't you feel it?"

"No, sorry, I didn't mean to."

"Oh, that's okay, you know me, I like getting shocked." He smiles and puts his earbuds back in.

In the garage, I open the door to the first bay, climb on the John Deere tractor, and start the engine. Out the garage and down the hill, past the garden I drive, over the bridge that covers the swale and into the rear field. I veer between the hawthorn tree and the apple tree, then onto the path and into the woods.

I've never driven this path before; I've never walked it.

Fallen rotting branches crunch under the wheels, ferns sway in abundance. Finally, I reach an elevated area where the trees are skinny, younger. It must have been a clearing not that long ago.

On the ground near the center, partially

covered by leaves, is what remains of a wooden door with rusted iron strap hinges.

I smile. I turn around and back up, careful not to ram into one of the young trees, and then I steer the tractor back onto the path and I leave the woods.

It had been good to see my mother again. It had been good to say good-bye.

And it is good to be a witch again.

Two months after the tornado made landfall in our yard, it seems like the property is ruined forever. Summer has expanded, and the land itself has absorbed much of the damage. I can't even see the downed tree at the end of the field.

The Connecticut wilderness is sultry and prolific. I would expect it of a jungle, but blue-state Connecticut seems too mannered to consume whole trees in one gulp, like a reticulated python. Outdoors the abundance of green seems to throb. I expect to hear the shriek of a macaw, the cry of a monkey. I am astonished to discover that wild grape vines have found one of the fallen trees in the back field and have already begun to spiral around it, exactly as in the "Vox Sola" episode of *Star Trek: Enterprise* (a show I finally learned to appreciate in adulthood).

Some of the Swamp Yankees nearby have

chosen to just accept the tornado damage and incorporate it into their lives. A half mile down the street, a huge tree along the side of the road fell backward onto the front lawn of a 1970s raised ranch. They can't use their front door anymore because the top branches block the entrance, and four-foot-high weeds have already sprung up as the front lawn claims it. There's something equally trashy and appealing about accepting a giant oak in the middle of your life.

We plant a Purple Fountain beech tree in the front yard in the exact spot the deadly maple occupied.

I build a stone wall around it. (I'm very good at this. It must be genetic. Fat Fuck, of course, calls them "chipmunk condos," because he can't bear to offer a compliment.) The tree is about forty feet high and the color of a dark bruise. It's weird and tall and gnarly and twisty, like something Dr. Seuss would have drawn; it's perfect for us. It looks great against the black house, just as the maple looked great when the house was pale yellow.

Except I hated that thing, *and rightly so.*

The dogs will love running around this tree. I thought about that while I was doing the stonework. Most likely there will be a ring of dirt around the stone wall that encircles the tree instead of the grass I've planted and tended.

That's okay.

It didn't used to be okay.

The tornado reset something inside me, the part that used to mind things like dirt patches on the lawn. Though I retain my suspicion that the house won't outlast us, I've accepted that landscaping will always feel new for the first couple of generations. I like thinking about fictional future people who might love what we left as much as I like imagining the people who used to live here and who baked pies and bread in the beehive oven in the living room, which was then the kitchen.

We may not all share the same spot on the time line, but we are able to send messages to each other.

# DEAD MAN'S FOOT

Christopher has had five medical appointments this month: a checkup with his liver doctor, two ultrasounds, a scan, and a colonoscopy during his week off (not a vacation, since he doesn't leave and he doesn't stop working *and* he undergoes a colonoscopy). Everything, they say, looks good. "For now," he adds.

My body hums like a crystal. I can describe it no other way. The frequency with which it vibrates increases until I myself am a high-pitched sound. I look at him. "The cirrhosis is nothing. It's not going to kill you."

Every form of energy I am made of is channeled into that single sentence. It is not a wish. It is a fact. Cirrhosis will not kill him.

It will have to get by me first, and it cannot.

This knowledge comes from a very deep

431

internal place of absolute authority: the place where magick lives.

I never *hope* it works. I *see* it work.

Sometimes when I mow near the Plant Mental Hospital, I notice some green and bushy things. I sort of nod my head and think, *Well.* Two full years pass until I venture into the area to see what has become of the plantings. I am dumbfounded. Flabbergasted. Stupefied and thunderstruck.

The redbud tree? Well, it isn't a tree per se, because it lacks a single trunk. Rather it has several "trunks," but it is thriving, as tall as a basketball player now and about as wide as a Wolf six-burner professional range. I am impressed. Green leaves shaped kind of like the spade in a deck of cards but the size of my hand are complemented by new baby leaves in deep purple.

A Japanese split-leaf maple, whose coiled branches we loved, was a stick tree when I grabbed it by its skinny dead trunk and yanked. Several of the branches snapped right off, and the root ball came up easily out of the earth in its own little dust cloud. Now I stand in my threadbare Levi's 501 jeans and sweat-soaked Biffy Clyro T-shirt and stare at the thing, mystified. Its branches are still dead and bare, but there is also a single perfect green leaf sprouting from one of these dead twigs, and there are small buds of other leaves, waiting to unfold.

"That's impossible," I mutter, but clearly it is not. Almost everything we tossed into this area is thriving, unlike the things we planted closer to the house and doted on with daily water and nitrogen and whatever else they told us to use. These neglected, banished things are fully alive.

The craggy bramble that crawls up the embankment where I found the severed doll's head is now dense with plump, glistening blackberries. Could these possibly be the result of the single runty blackberry bush that failed when I planted it beside the cottage? Could it have thrived and then spread throughout the entire area without encouragement or permission?

Even the willow trees assassinated by those loathsome beavers are growing tall and healthy and will soon be about the height they were when we planted them originally.

When I stand back and look, I can see that in time the redbud tree will fill the gap that allows people to see into our yard. We will be shielded from the riffraff.

I wonder what it is about this area — the soil? the light? — that makes everything we

433

plant here grow, even resurrecting the dead things and returning them to life, one sprig at a time. It may be a supernatural spot. I've always assumed that the lack of coverage is because large trees fell, but maybe nothing had been here until now. Maybe the land was waiting for us, for what we planted in defeat.

Over time, the Plant Hospital has taught me to allow certain things to go. I plant pumpkins and forget about them until the day I see orange leaves that look like baby elephant ears lying atop a twisty vine on the ground. Oh yeah, I think, pumpkins!

But I'm letting go of other kinds of things, too. Things that don't matter — like dog hair on the bottom of my socks. This used to make me feel this, well, not *huge* but also not *insignificant* sense of failure. The second law of thermodynamics says that everything in the universe is moving toward a state of increasing disorder, and hairy socks made me feel this too acutely.

The Plant Hospital made me stop caring about it. That may sound trivial, but it was a significant symbolic breakthrough, and we need more of those in our lives. The Plant Hospital shouldn't have worked, but it did, and this reinforced my dedication to the Mysterious Forces at Play in the world. It made me see myself more clearly.

Not many years ago I never would have told anybody what I was. I didn't like to think of myself in that way, use that word. Because of what other people might think. Would think.

*Well.*

I am a witch.

I come from a long line of witches on my mother's side. The word "witch" carries a great deal of baggage. I know what I am; I know what I can do; I know what I can't do; I know I sometimes fail. And it often takes me a great deal of distance — years — to understand why something didn't succeed that at the time seemed as if it ought to work.

Failure takes distance, but certainty is instant, and I am certain that I did the right thing: I planted Christopher here.

*Wait.*

It's like I've been hit on the head with my own shovel. Why did I ever think that Miss Regina was actually talking about planting a *tree* tree? That a wise old witch was giving me gardening advice for my middle age?

*She saw Christopher in my future.* The roots were *his:* fusing him to Manhattan, to his friends, to the dead.

I had to wait until the roots were dormant

in the spring or in the fall.

We moved at the tail end of summer, and then we weren't free of our New York real estate until . . . October.

Right before the ground froze.

It is October again.

Golden leaves float down, forming an endless carpet. I rake them into a pile in the front yard and the dogs smash right through them.

# LOVE LEAVES

I am ten, and my mother and I are sitting in the living room watching *The Mary Tyler Moore Show.* She is on the sofa and I'm on a Danish rope chair. On the coffee table between us is a large bowl of popcorn and another of cranberries, which we are stringing into garlands. The Christmas tree stands right behind us, naked and green.

I love Ted Baxter.

"It's not the same thing as wanting something," my mother says.

I turn away from the small color television set that sits atop the mahogany cabinet that my mother designed herself and had made by a man who owned goats. "What's not the same thing as wanting something?"

She is looking at her hands, pushing a needle through the heart of a cranberry, and she looks up at me, her eyebrows raised ever so slightly.

Oh.

437

"Not at all?" I say. "Not like wanting something really, really, really, really badly?"

"Absolutely not. It does not matter how much — don't say badly — how much you want something. That will not cause anything to change, that will never make it happen."

"So, I won't want anything."

"No," my mother says, "don't. *Want* for nothing."

"Okay."

"Rather," she continues, "see, instead, that it *has happened.* That it *does* exist."

She goes silent, and so do I.

I string one piece of popcorn and follow it with a cranberry. The berries are so much easier, because the popcorn kernels always split and splinter. You have to be so careful with them, and then you're paying attention to that and you stab yourself with the needle and you end up with bloody popcorn.

"I don't wish there was a lady's slipper orchid in the backyard," I say. "But in the spring, I'm going to stand in the backyard and look at all the lady's slipper orchids that grow there."

"Exactly," my mother says. "But under no circumstances should you ever pick one; they are extremely rare."

In the spring, lady's slipper orchids bloom

in the woods behind the house, next to boulders, beside ferns. It is impossible to think of them as rare when they are so plentiful in our woods.

My mother is painting one of our ancestors; the mouth is dour and downturned. Her easel is angled toward the window but not facing it, so that light flows across her canvas and does not collide with it head-on. She has her brush poised above an eyebrow, one of her finest, tiniest brushes that must be made from nothing more than an eyelash or two. Her hand is steady as she leans toward the canvas then abruptly pulls back, slides the brush against her white rag, smeared with years' worth of paint, and then dips it into a jelly jar of turpentine. She begins to smile, then laughs. "It has been years since I've heard from Susan!"

The phone in the kitchen rings, but she is already halfway there.

"Susan," she says, instead of "Hello?"

I hear her laughter. "Well, of course I knew it was you! Nobody else has your ring!"

In one of the last letters my mother ever sent me she wrote, "One day after I am dead, you may feel the need to tell me something that you wished you had told me when I was alive. You may hate me later in your life for the mistakes I've made, you may not forgive me until long after I am dead. I know what it is you need to say, I can hear you. If we were never to speak again, I would not stop loving you and I know you would not stop loving me. Please, after I am dead never waste a moment on regret."

I received this note when I was twenty and living in San Francisco, starting an advertising career I would continue for the next eighteen years. Her letter made no sense to me at the time.

She saw a future I did not.

What remains of her in me?

I inherited from her something people say cannot be real, something that defies logic and science. It is something that cannot be measured in a laboratory. Yet in science, the closer one examines something, the more impossible it becomes to measure it.

The deepest particles remain confounding, the deepest truths elusive.

We live in a physical world where the mere act of observation alone is enough to alter that which is observed, to change it from one form of matter into another.

What is that if not magick?

Is it so hard to believe what a witch can do?

When no sound occupies thy ears
And but not a single thought doth grip thy
  mind and steer
Is at which hour the bell strikes noon
Though darkness still enfolds the moon
A witch can see a moment before its time
yet cannot turn a sparrow into a lime.

# SORCERER'S VIOLET

One morning Christopher is outside on the driveway when he shouts, "Goddamnit!"

I'm in the kitchen pouring coconut milk into my coffee, and I slam the carton on the counter. I open the screen door and see that he's bent over, rubbing his left ankle, the same one he fractured a few years ago at the dog run in Battery Park City. "What's the matter?" I ask as I jog down the steps.

"Look at that," he says, furious, pointing to the ground.

I look down. There's a hole. "What the — ?"

"Chipmunks," he says.

"Y'know," I say, "I have been seeing *tons* of chipmunks. Did we have this many last year?"

"I don't know, but we're infested with them now and I almost broke my ankle again because of that hole. We have to find a way to get rid of them."

He wants to go to the hardware store and buy those chipmunk bombs that you light and stick into their holes. I kind of hate that idea, because we have no idea where the other exit hole is, so what good would it do?

He starts investigating. "They carry Lyme ticks, and they're more dangerous than deer because they get closer to the house. Eddie also said you could cut holes in a shoebox and put it over a rat trap. They're curious little bastards, so they will definitely go in and get their necks snapped."

"Just . . . let me figure something out," I say. *Something that isn't like a Chip 'n' Dale cartoon or that involves a carcass with a broken spine.*

"Well, figure it out in a hurry," he snaps, kind of pissy, and stomps off to the garage.

Four days later Christopher runs into the house out of breath. "You will never believe what just happened."

I want to scream, OH MY GOD, DON'T SAY THAT, JUST TELL ME. NEVER SET IT UP SO THAT I CAN IMAGINE THE WORST!

"What?" I ask calmly.

"I was outside deadheading the roses and I looked up, and there's an owl sitting on a low branch of the apple tree right near the fence. And it's watching me. Like, totally watching me."

I smile. "Really? You know what owls eat?"

"Mice," he says.

"And *chipmunks.*"

He stops.

I look at him and smirk. "I read that."

"Oh, did you, now?" he says slowly.

"I did."

A few weeks later Otis is barking fiercely at the kitchen door. We walk into the room and the owl is sitting on the railing, looking in, about three feet away.

I wave at it. "Thank you!"

We haven't seen a single chipmunk since I cast that owl spell.

You don't have to believe in witches.

But don't ever fuck with one.

# ABOUT THE AUTHOR

**Augusten Burroughs** is the number one *New York Times* bestselling author of *This is How, A Wolf at the Table, You Better Not Cry, Possible Side Effects, Magical Thinking, Dry, Running with Scissors,* and *Sellevision*. He lives in New York City.